THE SMALL-BUSINESS GUIDE TO
GOVERNMENT
CONTRACTS

★ ★ ★ ★ ★ ★ ★ ★ ★ ★ ★ ★ ★

THE SMALL-BUSINESS GUIDE TO
GOVERNMENT
CONTRACTS

★ ★ ★ ★ ★ ★ ★ ★ ★ ★ ★ ★ ★

How to Comply with the Key Rules and Regulations . . .

and Avoid Terminated Agreements, Fines, or Worse

Steven J. Koprince

◢AMACOM

American Management Association
New York · Atlanta · Brussels · Chicago · Mexico City · San Francisco
Shanghai · Tokyo · Toronto · Washington, D.C.

This publication is designed to provide accurate and authoritative information in regard to the subject matter covered. It is sold with the understanding that the publisher is not engaged in rendering legal, accounting, or other professional service. If legal advice or other expert assistance is required, the services of a competent professional person should be sought.

Library of Congress Cataloging-in-Publication Data

Koprince, Steven J.
  The small-business guide to government contracts : how to comply with the key rules and regulations and avoid terminated agreements, fines, or worse / Steven J. Koprince.
    p.   cm.
    Includes bibliographical references and index.
    ISBN 978-0-8144-3193-1 — ISBN 0-8144-3193-3
      1. Government purchasing—Law and legislation—United States.   2. Public contracts—United States.   3. Small business—Law and legislation—United States.   I. Title.

  KF849.K67   2012
  658.1'2—dc23

                                                                                        2012001971

About AMA
American Management Association (www.amanet.org) is a world leader in talent development, advancing the skills of individuals to drive business success. Our mission is to support the goals of individuals and organizations through a complete range of products and services, including classroom and virtual seminars, webcasts, webinars, podcasts, conferences, corporate and government solutions, business books and research. AMA's approach to improving performance combines experiential learning—learning through doing—with opportunities for ongoing professional growth at every step of one's career journey.

Printing number

10   9   8   7   6   5   4   3   2   1

CONTENTS

The easiest way to access the primary rules listed at the end of each chapter of this book is to simply go to http://www.gpo.gov/fdsys/ and key the number of the document you want into the search field. Just put the title (chapter) no., the part no., and the subpart no. For example, entering 13 C.F.R. 121.402 would take you to chapter (title) 13 of the Code, part 121, subpart 402. This is the information on NAICS codes and size standards.

If you're looking for a Federal Acquisition Regulation (F.A.R.), they are in Title 48 of the Code of Federal Regulations, so search for 48 C.F.R. You will see that the F.A.R. Regulations are grouped into two volumes. Just select the volume that contains the part and subpart you need and keep clicking until you get your exact document.

An alternative for most of the rules discussed is http://ecfr.gpoaccess.gov. *Ecfr* stands for Electronic Code of Federal Regulations.

For searches of the United States Code (U.S.C.), type in your title number, then U.S.C., followed by the part number, and you will be directed to sites dealing with that rule. For example, for information on bribery rules, enter 18 U.S.C. 201.

THE SMALL-BUSINESS GUIDE TO
GOVERNMENT
CONTRACTS

★ ★ ★ ★ ★ ★ ★ ★ ★ ★ ★ ★ ★

INTRODUCTION

IMAGINE YOUR SMALL BUSINESS losing millions of dollars in lucrative contracts, paying heavy fines, or even being prohibited from selling to your largest customer—all for violating rules you didn't know existed. It sounds like a nightmare, but when it comes to doing business with the federal government, it is a reality countless small business owners face.

If Uncle Sam is one of your small business's customers, you're not alone. The federal government spends $500 billion annually to buy goods and services from contractors, and thanks to special rules requiring agencies to award contracts to small businesses, nearly a quarter of those procurement dollars go to small companies. Contracting with the government can be lucrative—but if you don't know the key rules and regulations, it can also be very risky.

When the government is your customer, you must learn a whole new rulebook, very different from the one you may be used to in the commercial marketplace. It's a big rulebook—thousands of pages of dense text, spread out over a hodgepodge of federal statutes and regulations. And, as counterintuitive as it sounds, the rules are actually *more* complex for small businesses than for large companies. Not only does your small business have to follow most of the same government contracting regulations as big players such as Boeing, Lockheed, and IBM, but you must also obey a special set of regulations that apply only to small business contractors.

Of course, behemoths like Boeing have in-house legal departments to help them navigate their way through the regulatory maze.

But chances are, your small business doesn't have a single lawyer on staff, and you may not even know a lawyer who specializes in government contracts (especially the small business rules), much less have the budget to hire one to provide daily advice on compliance.

So what do you do?

If you're like many small government contractors, you spend a little time reading pieces of the FAR, talk to others in the industry, and attend the occasional procurement conference or symposium. You try your best to learn the rules. If you do call a government contracts lawyer, it's after something has gone wrong—you end up on the wrong end of a protest, or government investigators show up to audit your compliance with the small business rules or wage and hour regulations. By then, it may be too late.

What Are the Risks?

You may be wondering whether it's really important to teach yourself all these government contracting rules. After all, if you act honestly and apologize if you happen to inadvertently violate a rule you didn't know about, won't that be good enough?

Probably not. Government contracting isn't like being pulled over for speeding, when, if you have a good driving record and are very polite to the officer, there's a chance you will get off with a warning. Don't expect the same treatment when it comes to government contracting. Breaking the rules, even unintentionally, can have dire consequences for you and your business:

• **Terminated contracts.** Every year, the government terminates countless small business contracts as the result of competitors' successful size or eligibility protests. Other contracts are terminated—or never awarded in the first place—because contractors violate ethical, conflict-of-interest, and other requirements.

• **Suspensions and debarments.** The government is increasingly *suspending* and *debarring* contractors, that is, prohibiting those contractors from selling anything to the government for a certain period of time—often six months for a suspension and three years for a debarment. Political pressure is mounting to further increase the frequency of suspensions and debarments and make debarments mandatory for certain violations (they are already mandatory for some).

- **Fines and financial penalties.** Breaking many of the government contracting rules can result in civil fines and other financial penalties. For small contractors, the risk is especially acute in the wake of a 2010 law providing that if a company incorrectly certifies itself as "small" for a federal contract, it can be forced to repay the government the total value of the contract, plus additional damages.

- **Jail time.** Egregious violations of the contracting rules can land a contractor's owners or officers in the Big House, where you may get the chance to interact with another contractor's employees—prison guards.

If you contract with the government, you owe it to yourself, your company, and your employees to know the government contracting rules. That's what this book is all about.

Where Do All These Rules Come From?

For small contractors, learning the government contracting rules can be particularly challenging because there is no single source to find them. These rules are spread out among a variety of federal statutes and regulations, most notably:

- **The Federal Acquisition Regulation, or FAR.** The FAR is the largest single set of government contracting regulations, weighing in at around 2,000 densely packed pages in hard copy. You can find the FAR at https://www.acquisition.gov/far/.

- **The U.S. Small Business Administration's regulations.** As a small government contractor, you will discover (if you haven't already) that the SBA plays a big role in your government contracting business.

Its regulations establish the framework for deciding what companies qualify as "small" businesses, as well as which companies are eligible for the SBA's special contracting programs for disadvantaged small businesses.

- **The Department of Labor's regulations.** The Department of Labor oversees the rules governing how much you must pay your workers, how much vacation time you must give them, and other rules covering your relationship with your employees.

- **Federal criminal law.** Breaking some of the government contracting rules (like the prohibition on bribery) results in criminal penalties. This is how some unscrupulous contractors have wound up in prison.

While these are the major sources of the rules we will discuss in this book, they're not the only places the rules originate. Other laws applicable to your small business are peppered throughout the Code of Federal Regulations (CFR) and United States Code (USC). Some of the rules have not been codified at all, but instead have been developed by administrative bodies such as the Government Accountability Office (GAO) and the SBA's Office of Hearings and Appeals (OHA). With so many pages of rules, coming from so many places, it's little wonder that many small government contractors simply throw up their hands in frustration at the thought of trying to learn them.

About This Book

Written in layman's terms (not "legalese") and using easy-to-understand terms and examples, this book explains the most important rules your small business must follow to remain in Uncle Sam's good graces. The book is intended for the busy small business owner who doesn't have the resources to consult a lawyer on every government contracting decision or the time to master the thousands of pages of rules on his or her own.

In addition to clear and concise discussion, each chapter includes several features to help you understand and apply the rules:

- **Examples.** Key concepts are developed in examples, so that you can see how a rule might apply in the real world. Some examples are loosely based on real-life judicial and administrative decisions; others spring from the author's fertile imagination.

- **The Primary Rules: Where to Find Them.** If you want to read the rules themselves, each chapter includes a section telling you where to look. Simply plug in the regulatory citation to your favorite Internet search engine and you should have no trouble finding the regulation.

- **Risk Questionnaires.** Chapters 2 and 3, which deal with the important question of whether your small business is considered affiliated with other companies, include end-of-chapter questionnaires allowing you to quickly assess whether your small business might have an "affiliation problem."

- **Compliance at a Glance.** Chapters 4–15 conclude with a summary of the most important rules discussed in that chapter, each with a "checkbox" next to it so you can track your company's compliance. You will sometimes see the notation ("recommended") in Compliance-at-a-Glance, meaning that the action is strongly recommended but not required by law.

This book covers the key rules you should know in order to ensure that your company remains on the straight and narrow when it does business with the government. But with thousands of pages of rules to cover, it does not discuss everything. In particular, this book does *not* address:

- **State and local rules.** This book only covers contracting with the U.S. federal government. It does not address the myriad rules for contracting with state and local governments around the country.

- **Agency-specific rules.** Many federal agencies have adopted their own FAR supplements, which only apply to procurements conducted by that particular agency (unlike the FAR and the regulations of the SBA and Department of Labor, which apply to almost all federal agencies). We do not address agency-specific rules in this book, with one exception: in Chapter 12, we cover a special contracting program for service-disabled veterans run by the U.S. Department of Veterans Affairs.

- **Accounting rules.** As a government contractor, you need to ensure that your financial house is in order and your accounting system is up to snuff. We provide a brief overview in Chapter 10, but for space reasons, do not address accounting in-depth.

- **How to win government contracts.** This book is a compliance guide, not a "how-to" manual on winning government business. Of course, we'd like to think that gaining a reputation as a knowledgeable and compliant contractor will provide a competitive edge in and of itself.

Two Brief Disclaimers

Because this book is, in fact, written by a lawyer, and because we lawyers are a cautious bunch by nature, we want to pause here for two important disclaimers.

First, this book is intended for your educational use only. It does not constitute legal advice about any specific situation you may face. Reading it (even if you read it very carefully and dog-ear your favorite pages) does not create an attorney–client relationship between you and the author or his law firm.

Second, like most things in life, the government contracting rules sometimes change. This book reflects the rules as they were when it was written, and most of those rules are probably still the same as you're reading it now. But keep an eye on trade publications and blogs and keep your ears open for news that a rule has changed.

If you're not sure whether a rule we discuss in this book has been amended, use the "The Primary Rules: Where to Find Them" citations to help you find out. In addition, bookmark the author's blog, Small-GovCon (www.smallgovcon.com), for updates about the rules discussed in this book.

Let's Get Started

All right, that's enough disclaiming for one book, don't you think? Kick off your shoes, lean back, and let's discuss what you need to know to ensure that your small business plays by the rules.

CHAPTER 1

IS YOUR SMALL BUSINESS
REALLY SMALL?

TO BE ELIGIBLE for federal small business set-aside contracts, you must certify that your company is a small business. Get the certification wrong, and you could lose a contract to a size protest—or face much harsher penalties, like suspension or debarment.

But is your small business really "small"? It's not a trick question. When it comes to government contracts, figuring out your own company's size can be more difficult than it sounds.

Your small business's size for purposes of a government contract turns on four factors:

1. The North American Industry Classification System (NAICS) code (a standard used by federal agencies in classifying businesses by industry for purposes of collecting, analyzing, and publishing statistical data about the U.S. economy), assigned to a particular solicitation you intend to bid upon

2. The date your business submits a proposal on the procurement (or, in relatively rare cases, another date later in the procurement process)

3. Either: (a) your business's average annual revenues, or (b) your business's average number of employees, depending upon the NAICS code

4. Whether your business has any affiliates

In this chapter, we will examine the first three factors. The final factor, affiliation, is the most complex and confusing. We will look at affiliation separately in the next two chapters.

NAICS Codes and Size Standards

Size-wise, the competitive playing field can vary enormously in different industries. For instance, in the dry cleaning business, where mom-and-pop operations are still commonplace, a company with $10 million in annual revenues might be a relative behemoth. At the same time, a construction company with $10 million in annual revenues might be something of a small fry.[1]

The government understands that a small business in one industry is not necessarily small in another. For this reason, whether your business qualifies as "small" for government contracting purposes depends, in part, on the type of products or services the government seeks to acquire.

Every solicitation the government issues is designated with one (and only one) NAICS code, based on the primary purpose of the contract. Each NAICS code, in turn, carries a corresponding *size standard*, which is the threshold a company must fall below to be considered small on any contract carrying that NAICS code.

The Air Force issues a small business set-aside solicitation and designates it with NAICS code 561421 (Telephone Answering Services), with a corresponding $7 million size standard. Answering the Call, Inc., an administrative services provider, has earned an average of $10 million in revenues over the past three years.

Result: Answering the Call is not a small business under this NAICS code, and cannot bid on the solicitation.

The Army Corps of Engineers issues a small business set-aside solicitation and designates it with NAICS code 236116 (New Multifamily Housing Construction), with a corresponding $33.5 million size standard. XPert Constructors, Inc., has earned an average of $10 million in revenues over the past three years.

Result: XPert is a small business under this NAICS code, and may bid on the solicitation.

Your business may qualify as small for some types of work, but not others. It is important, then, to known which of the NAICS codes are typically assigned to set-aside solicitations in your line of work, and ensure that your business falls beneath the corresponding size standards.

If you do not know the size standards applicable to the types of work your company performs, spend a few minutes looking them up on the size standards table, which is available on the SBA's website.

By the way, did you notice that each example referred to the company's *three-year average* receipts? Determining your size for a revenue-based procurement requires you to use your company's revenues over a three-year period and do a little addition and division (your fifth grade teacher would be proud). We will discuss exactly how to calculate your receipts a little later in this chapter.

When Is Small Business Size Status Determined?

Figuring out a procurement's size standard is only the first step in determining small business eligibility. The question of *when* your business must be small is also important—after all, businesses grow and shrink all the time.

Think about a mom-and-pop dry cleaner—let's call it QuickDri, LLC. Let's say that QuickDri submits an offer on a $5 million dry cleaning procurement in November. The day before it submits its offer, QuickDri runs its numbers and determines that it is a $4.5 million business, qualifying as small under NAICS code 812320 (Dry Cleaning and Laundry Services), which carries a $5 million size standard.

Then, the holiday season arrives, and QuickDri is flooded with new commercial business. Customers bring in party dresses, winter jackets, and even a Santa suit or two. By the time the agency awards the contract in late January, QuickDri is a $5.2 million company. Is QuickDri eligible to receive the contract?

Probably. In the vast majority of cases, the so-called *initial offer rule* determines when size is determined. Under this rule, if a business qualifies as small on the date it submits its self-certification of size together with its first priced offer, it is an eligible small business for that procurement, even if it outgrows the size standard before the agency makes award.

Exceptions to the Initial Offer Rule

Like many rules, the initial offer rule has its exceptions. In a few cases, a company's size for a federal procurement is determined at some later time in the process:

- **Some task order solicitations.** When an agency issues a task order solicitation restricted to the awardees of a multiple-award Indefinite Delivery/Indefinite Quantity (IDIQ) base contract, the agency may request that offerors recertify their sizes. If the agency requests recertification, size for the task order is determined as of the date of the initial offer on the task order. However, if the agency does not request recertification, size is determined as of the date of the initial offer on the underlying IDIQ contract.

• **Design-build procurements.** Design-build procurements using the special procedures of FAR 36.3 have distinct request for proposal (RFP) and submittal phases. For these contracts, size is determined as of the date an offeror submits its Phase II proposal, not its initial (Phase I) proposal. The rationale is that price is not submitted until Phase II, so Phase II actually constitutes the initial *priced* offer, consistent with the initial offer rule.

> The Army Corps of Engineers issues a design-build solicitation using FAR 36.3 procedures and designates it with NAICS code 236116 (New Multifamily Housing Construction), with a corresponding $33.5 million size standard. When South Border Builders, Inc., submits its Phase I technical proposal in July, it is a $29 million business. However, the procurement process drags on, and South Border Builders is not able to submit its Phase II price proposal until the following March. By then, South Border Builders is a $36 million business.
>
> **Result:** South Border Builders' size is determined as of the date of its Phase II proposal in March. South Border Builders does not qualify as a small business.

• **Ostensible subcontractor affiliation/non-manufacturer rule.** For purposes of determining whether a prime contractor is affiliated with its subcontractor under the so-called *ostensible subcontractor rule*, under which the SBA will consider whether a prime contractor is unduly reliant upon its subcontractor, the government will evaluate size as of the date of the final proposal revision (for negotiated procurements) or final bid (for sealed bid procurements). We will discuss ostensible subcontractor affiliation at length in Chapter 3. Size is also determined as of the date of the final proposal revision for purposes of determining compliance with the *non-manufacturer rule*, which determines when a small business can offer the government products the small business did not manufacture itself.

Recertification After Award

If a business was small at the time of its initial priced offer, it typically remains small throughout the life of the contract, including any option years.

> The Marine Corps issues a small business set-aside solicitation and designates it with NAICS code 811111 (General Automotive Repair), with a corresponding $7 million size standard. When CarFixers, Inc., submits its initial priced offer, it is a $6.5 million business. CarFixers completes the base year of its contract, and the agency wants to exercise an option year. However, CarFixers has grown, and is now a $7.5 million company.
>
> **Result:** Unless an exception applies, CarFixers is eligible for award of the option.

Again, there are exceptions to the general rule. In four cases, a company will be required to recertify its size status during the course of performing a contract:

1. **Novations.** A *novation* is a transfer of a government contract from one contractor to another; it can only occur with the government's approval. Within 30 days after an approved contract novation, the contractor must recertify that it is small or inform the agency that it is not a small business. We will discuss Novations at greater length in Chapter 10.

2. **Mergers and acquisitions.** If a contractor merges with or is acquired by another entity, that contractor must recertify its small business size status to the agency within 30 days after the transaction becomes final or inform the agency that it is no longer small.

3. **Long-term contracts.** If a contract extends beyond five years (including options), the contractor must recertify its size status no more than 120 days prior to the end of the contract's

fifth year. From then on, the contractor must recertify no more than 120 days prior to the exercise of each additional option.

4. **Task or delivery orders.** If an agency issues a solicitation for a task or delivery order under an existing contract, the agency may (but need not) request recertification in connection with the order.

If a contractor informs the procuring agency that it has exceeded the size standard, the agency is not required to terminate the contractor. The agency can *even* continue awarding the contractor options.

The only downside, from the agency's perspective, is that it can no longer count the award toward its small business goals—the requirement that procuring agencies attempt to award at least 23 percent of prime contract dollars to small businesses each year. As a result, some agencies may decline to award options or task orders if the contractor is unable to recertify as small. However, a contractor with a strong performance record and good working relationship with the agency may be able to persuade the agency to continue the relationship.

Calculating Average Annual Receipts

We know the first two pieces of the small business size formula: the *what* (the NAICS code and size standard) and the *when* (in most cases, the date of the initial offer). Now, it's time to break out a calculator and determine whether your small business qualifies as small for a particular size standard.

Size standards come in two flavors: *revenue-based*, for which size is calculated on the basis of a firm's receipts, and *employee-based*, which requires a head count of a company's personnel. Most small businesses operate, at least in part, in revenue-based NAICS codes, so we'll discuss those calculations first. If your business only works in employee-based NAICS codes, feel free to skip to the next section (unless, of course, you are eager to do a little math with your tax returns).

The Annual Receipts Baseline

The SBA defines annual receipts as *total income* (or *gross income* for a sole proprietorship), plus *cost of goods sold*, as the terms appear on Internal Revenue Service (IRS) tax forms. So, for instance, a limited liability company (LLC) reporting its taxes on Form 1065 would add line 8 (total income) to line 2 (cost of goods sold) to produce its initial annual receipts number. A corporation reporting on Form 1120 would add lines 11 and 2.

We now have the baseline of the annual receipts formula. Let's call it **TI + CGS**.

Deductions from the Annual Receipts Baseline

When it comes to deductions, the SBA is not as generous as the IRS. The SBA recognizes four—and only four—deductions from the **TI + CGS** baseline:

1. Net capital gains and losses.
2. Taxes collected for and remitted to a taxing authority, but only if included in gross or total income (such as sales taxes collected from customers).
3. Proceeds from transactions between a business and its affiliates. According to the SBA, exclusion is intended to prevent improper "double counting" of revenues, since a business's revenues and those of its affiliates are aggregated for size purposes. However, the exclusion does not cover the costs of the acquisition of a subsidiary or the one-way reassignment of assets from a subsidiary to the books of its parent.
4. Amounts collected for another by a travel agent, real estate agent, advertising agent, conference management service provider, freight forwarder, or customs broker.

The SBA does not recognize any other potential deductions. For instance, in one case, a business changed its accounting methods, resulting in adjustments to its reported income under the Internal Revenue Code. The SBA's Office of Hearings and Appeals refused to allow the firm to make deductions based on the accounting adjustments.[2]

Let's update the annual receipts formula to account for the four permissible deductions: **(TI + CGS) – D**.

Which Annual Receipts Count?

The next piece of the puzzle is the question of *which* annual receipts to use. After all, most businesses have their ups and downs—higher receipts one year, lower another.

To calculate your size under a revenue-based standard, you must determine your business's average annual receipts over its last three completed fiscal years prior to your initial offer (or another date on which size is determined).

> In November 2012, Mess Halls-R-Us, Inc., a food service provider, submits a proposal on a solicitation designated with NAICS code 722310 (Food Service Contractors), which carries a $35.5 million size standard. Mess Halls-R-Us's fiscal year runs concurrently with the calendar year.
>
> **Result:** Mess Halls-R-Us's annual receipts will be calculated based on the average of its receipts for 2009, 2010, and 2011. Its receipts to date in 2012 are not included.

Because the formula is based upon *completed* fiscal years, it allows a small business to get away with short-term growth before it exceeds the size standard. In the case of our fictional contractor, its 2012 receipts are irrelevant for purposes of the procurement. Even if Mess Halls-R-Us hauled in $100 million between January and November 2012, it would still be eligible for award if its 2009, 2010, and 2011 average annual receipts fell below $35.5 million. Of course, come January 2013, Mess Halls-R-Us would have to stop certifying itself as small.

Now we have the remainder of our average annual receipts formula. If your business has been in operation for three completed fiscal years, it is:

$$([[(TI_1 + \mathbf{CGS_1}) - D_1] + [(\mathbf{TI_2} + CGS_2) - \mathbf{D_2}] + [(TI_3 + \mathbf{CGS_3}) - D_3]) / 3.$$

What If My Business Hasn't Completed Its Tax Returns?

If a company has yet to file a tax return for one of its completed fiscal years, the SBA will determine size using "any other available information," such as the firm's books, audited financial statements, or even information contained in a sworn affidavit.

> In March 2013, Mess Halls-R-Us submits a proposal on another food service solicitation carrying a $35.5 million size standard. Mess Halls-R-Us's three-year average annual receipts are $38 million. However, Mess Halls-R-Us has not yet filed its 2012 tax return.
>
> **Result:** Mess Halls-R-Us's annual receipts will be calculated on the average of its receipts for 2010, 2011, and 2012. The SBA will use the company's financial statements or other information to determine its 2012 receipts.

If you do not have a completed tax return for your last completed fiscal year, you should follow the SBA's example and use other information, like your financial statements, to verify that your business is still small prior to submitting an offer on a set-aside procurement.

What If My Company Is Less Than Three Years Old?

If your company has not been in existence for three complete fiscal years, you might think that you can plug a bunch of zeroes into the standard formula—likely resulting in your firm qualifying as a small business. Unfortunately, it's not that easy.

For any company that has not been in business for three years, the SBA uses a different formula: the total receipts for the period the business has been in operation, divided by the number of weeks in business, multiplied by 52, or **(TI/WIB) x 52**.

In November 2012, Kid-nergarten, Inc., a youth services company, submits a proposal on a set-aside contract carrying a $7 million size standard. As of that date, Kid-nergarten has been in operation for 30 weeks and has earned $1 million.

Result: Kid-nergarten's annual receipts are calculated by first dividing $1 million by 30, to obtain the company's weekly receipts (approximately $33,333). Then, multiply the result by 52, arriving at an "annual receipts" figure of $1,733,333.

If Kid-nergarten used the standard formula, it would have been able to claim zero receipts, since it has yet to complete a single fiscal year. Using the alternate formula, however, Kid-nergarten is a $1.7 million business, which is more than it has actually earned in its brief existence. Fortunately for our upstart youth services provider, it qualifies as a small business for this procurement anyway.

What If My Company Has a Short Year?

If your company has been in existence for three or more complete fiscal years, but has a short year as one of its tax years within that period, you must also forgo the standard annual receipts formula. Instead, you should use another alternate formula to figure out your annual receipts.

First, add the total receipts for the short year and the total receipts for the two full fiscal years. Then, divide by the total number of weeks in the short year and the two full fiscal years. Finally, multiply the result by 52. The formula is $[(TI_{SY} + TI_{Y1} + TI_{Y2})/(W_{SY} + 52 + 52)] \times 52$.

> In September 2012, The Looth Tooth, LLC, a dental care provider, submits a proposal on a set-aside solicitation carrying a $7 million size standard. As of that date, The Looth Tooth has two full tax years, in which it earned $2 million each, and a 30-week short year in which it earned $1 million.
>
> **Result:** First add the total receipts, arriving at $5 million. Then, divide by the total number of weeks, 134 (30+52+52). Multiply the result, $37,313.43, by 52, to arrive at an annual receipts figure of approximately $1.94 million.

Give yourself a pat on the back—you've made it to the end of our trek through the SBA's annual receipts formulas. Find the formula that fits your business, plug in your financial numbers, and you will be well on your way to determining if your company qualifies as small.

Calculating Average Number of Employees

Compared to average annual receipts, calculating size under an employee-based NAICS code is easy. The baseline formula is simply the number of employees on your payroll for each pay period for the 12 months preceding your certification, divided by the number of pay periods.

> Draper's Papers, a printing company, submits a proposal on a small business set-aside solicitation carrying a 100 employee size standard. Over the preceding 12 months, Draper's had 24 pay periods. For the first 12 of those periods, it had 97

employees, at which point it hired an additional four employees. For the remaining 12 pay periods, it had 101 employees.

Result: Draper's average employees are calculated by adding the number of employees for each pay period (97+97+97 . . . +101+101+101. . . .), resulting in a figure of 2,376. Divide by the number of pay periods, 24, to arrive at Draper's average number of employees, 99. Draper's qualifies for the contract—barely.

In real life, of course, employees are rarely as loyal as the hardworking printers at Draper's Papers. Employees come and go, and your small business may have a different number of employees for each pay period over 12 months. If you are close to an employee-based size standard ceiling, keep a close eye on your payroll-by-payroll employee count.

If your small business has been in operation fewer than 12 months, simply calculate the average number of employees for the time you have been in business.

In September 2012, Pete's Paint Pros, a paint wholesaler, submits a proposal on a small business set-aside contract carrying a 100 employee size standard. At the time it submits its offer, Pete's has been in business for three pay periods. During the first two pay periods, Pete's had 99 employees. As of the third pay period, Pete's had 106 employees.

Result: Pete's average employees are calculated by adding its numbers for the three pay periods together (99+99+106), then dividing the result, 304, by the number of pay periods, 3. Pete's average annual employee count is 101.3. Pete's does not qualify for the contract.

Small businesses are responsible for determining their own pay periods, but don't rush to adopt a once-a-month system just to make it easier to calculate your employee count for size purposes. As we will discuss in Chapter 7, federal law may require you to pay certain employees no less than every two weeks, or even weekly for some employees in the construction industry.

Who Is an Employee?

Counting employees isn't that difficult, as long as your business keeps good payroll records. But who counts as an employee?

The SBA broadly defines an *employee* as an individual who works for your business on a "full-time, part-time, or other basis."[3] Part-timers must be counted no matter how few hours they work, and the SBA has held that employees obtained from a professional employee organization or employee leasing company count, as well.

Unpaid volunteers, such as part-time college interns, are not considered employees. You need not count bona fide independent contractors, either. Be careful, though: Just because you don't issue a W-2 to an individual doesn't mean that the individual isn't an employee as far as the IRS is concerned (and the SBA adopts the IRS's views on the matter).

The IRS and the SBA will examine the totality of your relationship with the individual to determine whether the individual is a bona fide independent contractor, including whether your business:

- Has the right to control and direct the individual in his or her work
- Has the right to terminate or discipline the individual
- Furnishes the individual with tools and a place to work

When in doubt, it is wisest to err on the side of caution and include an independent contractor in your business's employee count.

What About Affiliates?

Now you know how to calculate your company's size as a stand-alone entity for federal government contracts. Don't certify as a small business yet, though. In the words of the late, great television pitchman Billy Mays, "But wait! There's more!"

Your business's own receipts and employees are only part of the size equation: you must also add the receipts or employees of your company's affiliates to your own total. The next two chapters will help you learn whether you have an affiliation problem—and how to solve it.

The Primary Rules: Where to Find Them

Here's where to find the primary rules discussed in this chapter:

- 13 C.F.R. § 121.402 (NAICS codes and size standards)
- 13 C.F.R. § 121.404 (when size is determined)
- 13 C.F.R. § 121.104 (calculating annual receipts)
- 13 C.F.R. § 121.106 (calculating number of employees)

CHAPTER 2

THE AFFILIATION PROBLEM

YOUR SMALL BUSINESS doesn't exist in a bubble. It needs strong relationships with other companies—investors, suppliers, customers, landlords, and so on—in order to survive and grow. But as a small government contractor, your business must carefully manage its relationships with other companies, because the same close relationships that allow your company to succeed may cross the fuzzy line into *affiliation*, a relationship in which one company controls or has the power to control the other, or a third party controls or has the power to control both.

Affiliation will cause the SBA to treat your business and its affiliates as one and the same when it evaluates whether your business is "small." This may turn your small business into a large one (at least as far as the SBA is concerned), and this means that you can wave goodbye to those small business set-aside government contracts.

An Introduction to Affiliation

When you think about affiliated companies, you may envision businesses like Wal-Mart and Sam's Club, which make no secret of the fact that they are related. In the SBA's eyes, Wal-Mart and Sam's Club would undoubtedly be deemed affiliates, but SBA-style affiliation goes far beyond acknowledged parent, subsidiary, and sister companies.

The SBA may find that a small business is affiliated with another company when the two businesses are too close, so that they share or appear to share common control, for any of several reasons. Shared ownership, like the relationship between Wal-Mart and Sam's Club, is a basis of affiliation, but the SBA can also deem two businesses affiliated because they share management, common investments, familial relationships, or other ties.

Given the SBA's broad definition of affiliation, it is not always easy for a small business to determine if it is affiliated with another company. The SBA often finds small businesses affiliated with other firms even where the small businesses in question had no idea that they had an affiliation problem.

Why Is Affiliation Important?

Despite a common misconception, small government contractors are *not* prohibited from having affiliates. However, when a small business has an affiliate, it must add the affiliate's revenues or employee count to its own when it calculates its size for a particular procurement. As long as the combined revenues or employee count falls beneath the applicable size standard for a set-aside government contract, the small business is still eligible for award of that contract.

> Draper's Papers is purchased by another printing company, Paper Pushers, Inc. After the acquisition, Draper's Papers submits a proposal on a set-aside commercial printing solicitation carrying a 500 employee-based size standard. Draper's average employee count over the past 12 months is 99. Paper Pushers' average employee count for the same period is 250.
>
> **Result:** Draper's Papers and Paper Pushers are affiliated by virtue of common ownership. Draper's Papers must add Paper Pushers'

employee count to its own when it calculates its size standard. The total, 349, is still well below the applicable size standard. Draper's Papers is eligible for award.

As a general matter, affiliation is perfectly acceptable, so long as the combined sizes of the affiliates do not exceed an applicable size standard. The problem arises when the affiliation causes the small business to break through its size ceiling. When that happens, the small business is no longer considered "small" for the size standard.

Big Time Construction, Inc., submits a proposal on a set-aside construction solicitation carrying a $33.5 million revenue-based size standard. Big Time's average annual receipts for the prior three years are $29 million. Big Time has a parent company, Behemoth Building Co. Behemoth's average annual receipts for the prior three years are $125 million.

Result: Big Time must add Behemoth's average annual receipts to its own when it calculates its size standard. Although Big Time qualifies as "small" as a stand-alone business, the total of its revenues and Behemoth's, $154 million, is well above the $33.5 million size standard. Big Time is not eligible for award.

As Big Time's example shows, affiliation can cause a small business to lose a set-aside contract. Many SBA size protests by competitors are based upon affiliation allegations. Over the years, countless small businesses have won contracts, only to see their awards disappear when the SBA sustained size protests on the basis of affiliation.

In today's regulatory climate, with its strong emphasis on enforcement, losing a set-aside contract might be the tip of the iceberg. For example, for procurements set aside for service-disabled veteran-owned small businesses by the Department of Veterans' Affairs, a regulation adopted in 2009 calls for *mandatory* debarment for a misrepresentation of eligibility—including size ineligibility. As the government continues to crack down on noncompliant contractors, your small business could face tough penalties if the government determines that you self-certified as small when you knew (or should have known) about an affiliation problem.

Affiliation and Program Eligibility

If your small business is a participant in the 8(a) Business Development Program, Service-Disabled Veteran-Owned Small Business Program (SDVOSB), or Women-Owned Small Business Program (WOSB), you should be especially careful when it comes to affiliation, even with another small business. These programs require a particular individual, such as a service-disabled veteran or a socially and economically disadvantaged individual under the 8(a) Program's criteria, to control your business's day-to-day management and strategic decision making. If the SBA decides that your company's ties to an affiliate are so strong that it impedes the individual's control, your company could lose its program eligibility. The 8(a), SDVOSB, and WOSB programs are discussed at length in Chapters 11, 12, and 14.

The Two Kinds of Affiliation

Like size standards, affiliation comes in two flavors: *general affiliation* and *ostensible subcontractor* (or *contract-specific*) affiliation. It is important to understand the differences between the two.

Companies engaged in a close, ongoing relationship—like Wal-Mart and Sam's Club—are considered "general" affiliates. General affiliation is typically based upon relationships that exist independent of any particular federal procurement, such as shared ownership and management. Importantly, when the SBA issues a *size determination*, a formal ruling on a firm's size, and finds that two firms are general affiliates, the firms are considered affiliates for *all* federal procurements going forward, unless they fix their affiliation problem and receive a formal size recertification from the SBA.

Big Time Construction submits a proposal on a set-aside construction solicitation carrying a $33.5 million revenue-based size standard. A competitor files a size protest, alleging that Big Time is generally affiliated with Behemoth Building Co., and that the two companies' revenues, combined, exceed $33.5 million. The SBA issues a size determination finding the two firms generally affiliated. Six months later, a different federal agency issues a new construction solicitation, with a $33.5 million size standard. Big Time would like to submit a bid on the new procurement, but is concerned about the prior size determination.

Result: Because Big Time has been found *generally* affiliated with Behemoth, and because the companies' revenues, combined, have been found to exceed $33.5 million, the affiliation carries forward to future procurements. Big Time does not qualify as small for the new procurement unless the SBA first recertifies it as a small business (and should not have attempted to bid on the first procurement, either). If it attempts to bid on the procurement without a recertification, it runs a significant risk of stiff penalties for a false certification.

Sometimes, even when two companies share few (or no) general ties such as common ownership or management, the SBA deems the firms affiliated for purposes of a single federal contract. So-called "ostensible subcontractor" affiliation occurs when the SBA believes that a small business's subcontractor has too much power and influence over a particular prime contract award—to the point where the two firms should be deemed, in practice, joint venturers. When the SBA finds a small business affiliated with another firm under the ostensible subcontractor rule, the affiliation finding does *not* carry forward to future procurements.

QuickDri submits a proposal on a set-aside dry cleaning solicitation carrying a $5 million revenue-based size standard. QuickDri subcontracts much of the work to Clean-o-Rama, Inc., a company with which QuickDri has never done business before. The SBA sustains a competitor's size protest, holding that Clean-o-Rama is QuickDri's ostensible subcontractor, and that the sizes of the two businesses, combined, exceed the size standard. Six months later, a different federal agency issues a dry cleaning solicitation, with a $5 million size standard. QuickDri would like to bid on the new solicitation, but is concerned about the prior size determination.

Result: Because QuickDri and Clean-o-Rama were found affiliated under the ostensible subcontractor rule, the affiliation does *not* carry forward. QuickDri is eligible to self-certify as small on the new solicitation, provided it falls beneath the size standard as a stand-alone business.

While both types of affiliation can harm your small business, general affiliation has the potential to be more devastating, given the long-term effects of an adverse size determination. Avoiding general affiliation requires proactive, big picture business planning about key matters such as your small business's ownership, management, and ongoing contractual relations. Ostensible subcontractor affiliation, on the other hand, requires careful attention to the details of a relationship formed for a particular procurement. That is not to say, though, that ostensible subcontractor affiliation should be taken lightly. In fact, many of the government's recent enforcement actions, such as its high-profile suspension of GTSI Corporation from all federal contracting in October 2010, involved allegations of ostensible subcontractor affiliation.[1]

Because affiliation is a particularly important and complex topic, we have divided our coverage of it into two chapters. The remainder of this chapter focuses on general affiliation. Ostensible subcontractor affiliation is discussed in the following chapter.

General Affiliation

The question of whether two businesses are generally affiliated turns on the notion of *control*. As noted previously in this chapter, the SBA considers businesses generally affiliated if:

- One business controls or has the power to control the other, or
- A third party controls or has the power to control both businesses

That sounds simple enough, but controlling or having the power to control a company, in the SBA's eyes, extends far beyond owning a majority share or pulling strings on the firm's board of directors. The SBA also looks at arrangements that create *de facto* or soft control.

Consider, for instance, our favorite fictional dry cleaner, Quick-Dri. Assume that an individual—let's call him Bob—is QuickDri's sole owner and highest officer. Bob went to high school with Jane, who currently serves as the president and sole owner of a large dry cleaning company, Dry Dry Again. Jane does not own any interest in QuickDri, nor does she play any management role. But Bob and Jane are close friends, and Jane occasionally gives Bob advice on running his business.

Wait—don't hit the panic button yet. Mere friendship between two companies' owners and officers, alone, does not create affiliation, even if the friends swap business tips. If Bob and Jane have weekly dinners or golf outings to talk shop, they have nothing to worry about.

But let's say that Jane steers several large subcontracts to Quick-Dri. Over the course of the last five years, 85 percent of QuickDri's revenues have come from those subcontracts.

Now Bob has an affiliation problem.

According to the SBA, because QuickDri relies so heavily upon the subcontracts, Dry Dry Again has the power to control Bob's business. If Dry Dry Again terminates the relationship, QuickDri might fold entirely. To prevent such an outcome, Bob will likely agree to whatever demands (perhaps phrased as polite requests) that Jane might make, so long as they are remotely reasonable.

As Bob's plight demonstrates, the SBA can find firms generally affiliated for a number of reasons. In a few instances, the SBA considers a single circumstance so indicative of affiliation that it finds the firms automatically affiliated, without regard to any other evidence. Wal-Mart and Sam's Club share a corporate owner, for example. That's enough to cause affiliation, even if there are no other ties.

In many cases, though, the SBA evaluates general affiliation on a case-by-case basis, under a variety of tests described in the SBA's regulations. Underneath the dry regulatory language lies a principle much like the old saying about an animal that looks like a duck and quacks like a duck. If two businesses look like they are affiliates and act as though they are affiliates, the SBA may deem them affiliates, even without formal ownership or management ties.

Bases of General Affiliation

Does your company have an affiliation problem? It might if one or more of the bases of affiliation described below exist.

Common Ownership. Two companies are considered affiliated if the same person or entity owns more than 50 percent of each business. When companies share majority ownership, affiliation is *automatic*, regardless of whether there are any other indicia of affiliation.

> Erik owns 100 percent of XPert Constructors. Erik also owns a 51 percent share in Tooty Frooty, Inc., a fruit stand he runs with a friend.
>
> **Result:** Erik controls XPert Constructors and Tooty Frooty by virtue of his majority ownership in each. The companies are affiliated.

If two companies each have the same, single majority owner, the affiliation analysis is easy: The businesses are automatically affiliates. But what about a company that has no majority owner?

According to the SBA, a minority owner controls a company if his or her share[2] is large compared to other ownership shares. In other words, if you are the largest minority owner in a company and your share is significantly larger than the shares of your co-owners, you will be found to control that company.

> Bob owns 100 percent of QuickDri. Bob also owns a 49 percent minority share in Dry-Athalon, Inc. The next largest minority owner owns a 36 percent share.
>
> **Result:** Bob controls Dry-Athalon because his minority share is significantly larger than the next largest minority share. QuickDri and Dry-Athalon are affiliated.

Unfortunately, the regulations do not explain how *much* larger a minority share must be than the next largest share in order for a minority owner to "control" the company. However, if your share is only slightly larger than the next-largest share, the SBA may find that you do not control the company. For instance, in one case, OHA held that a 49 percent owner did *not* control a company when the next-largest shareholder owned a 41 percent share.[3]

To make ownership-based affiliation even more confusing, the SBA may find that a minority owner controls a company even if the minority owner does not hold the largest share. Under the *aggregation rule*, a minority owner is presumed to control the company when three factors are present:

1. Two or more individuals or entities each owns or has the power to control a minority share.
2. The minority shares are equal or approximately equal in size.
3. The aggregate of the minority shares is large as compared with any other ownership in the company.

Monica owns 100 percent of Don't Pass This Gas, Inc., a gasoline and convenience store. Monica also owns a 25 percent share in See The World, LLC, a travel agency. Three of Monica's high school friends each own 25 percent of shares in See The World.

Result: Monica controls Don't Pass This Gas and is presumed to control See The World under the aggregation rule. Don't Pass This Gas and See The World are presumed affiliated on the basis of common ownership.

Notice that when affiliation is based on the aggregation rule, it is *presumed*, not *automatic*. In the example above, Monica is "guilty until proven innocent" of controlling See The World, but has the opportunity to rebut the presumption. If Monica can present compelling evidence that she does not enjoy actual control over See The World, the SBA will find that the companies are not affiliated.

What if Monica owns a 25 percent interest in See The World, but Emily purchases the remaining 75 percent from the other three owners? Can the SBA still find that Monica controls See The World, even though Emily is the majority owner?

When a firm has a majority owner, the SBA will not find affiliation *solely* on the basis of the minority owner's interest, even if that interest is 49 percent. But the minority share can be one piece of a "looks like a duck, quacks like a duck" analysis, if other indicia of affiliation exist. For instance, assume that, in addition to her minority share, Monica serves as See The World's vice president and sits on its board, and that Emily and Monica are sisters. With so many close ties between Monica and See The World, the SBA would likely find that See The World and Don't Pass This Gas are affiliated.

The Present Effect Rule

When the SBA evaluates a firm's ownership, it applies what it calls the *present effect* rule. Under the rule, stock options, convertible securities, and agreements to merge are treated as though the rights have *already* been exercised, even if the ownership transfer will not happen until sometime in the future.

> Bob owns 100 percent of QuickDri. In order to convince Jane to invest in QuickDri, Bob grants Jane, as sole owner of Dry Dry Again, the right to purchase his entire ownership interest at a specific price, if and when Jane chooses to exercise the option. On the date QuickDri submits a proposal on a set-aside procurement, Jane has not exercised her option.
>
> **Result:** Under the present effect rule, Jane's option is deemed exercised. Jane controls QuickDri, and QuickDri is affiliated with Dry Dry Again.

The SBA does not apply the present effect rule to discussions or negotiations, so long as the parties do not reach an agreement. If Bob and Jane sit down to dinner and toss around the idea of an investment in exchange for an option, but never come to an agreement, Jane does not control QuickDri.

Common Management

Two businesses are considered affiliated if one or more officers, directors, managing members, or partners who control the board of directors (or whatever management apparatus the firm has in place) of one business also control the board of directors or management of the second business.

> Brett is the 100 percent owner, sole officer, and managing member of BrettWorks, LLC, a small administrative services company. To help pay the bills while BrettWorks develops, Brett accepts Jane's offer to become the sole officer and managing member of Dry Dry Again. Jane owns 100 percent of Dry Dry Again.

Result: By virtue of his managerial position, Brett now controls Dry Dry Again, even though he does not own any interest in the company. BrettWorks and Dry Dry Again are affiliated on the basis of common management.

As with common ownership, control is the touchstone of common management affiliation. If the same individual or group of individuals has the power to control the day-to-day decisions of both companies, the companies are affiliated. But merely having the highest officer title in two companies does not, in and of itself, create affiliation unless the individual also possesses *actual* management control over both businesses.

Mary is the sole officer and managing member of MaryIT, an information technology company. To help pay the bills while MaryIT develops, Mary accepts an offer to serve as the chair of the board of Hello Electronics, an electronics wholesaler. Hello Electronics has five other directors, and each director's vote counts equally.

Result: Mary does not control Hello Electronics because she cannot make managerial decisions without the concurrence of other board members. The two companies are not affiliated on the basis of common management.

Just because common control may not exist does not mean that it is a good idea for the owner or manager of a small government contractor to accept a high-level position in another company. Even if the overlapping managerial roles alone do not create affiliation, the dual roles can be one piece of a "looks like a duck, quacks like a duck" totality of the circumstances analysis. The best practice is to avoid having any of your small business's owners or managers serve in a management role with another company if affiliation with that company would create size standard problems.

Economic Dependence

Remember our example a few pages ago, when a well-meaning Jane steered subcontracts to her friend Bob's company, ultimately amounting to 85 percent of QuickDri's revenues? The SBA has a name for this type of "soft" affiliation: *economic dependence*. In recent years, the SBA has adopted an unwritten rule: if a small business is dependent upon another firm for 70 percent or more of its revenue over a significant period, the two businesses are automatically affiliated, even if there are no other ties between the firms.

The 70 percent rule does not mean that your small business is safe from an adverse affiliation determination if it receives less than 70 percent of its revenue from one source. As with other indicia of affiliation, even if two companies are not automatically affiliated, a lesser degree of economic dependence can still be one piece of the overall affiliation puzzle.

If your small business receives a substantial portion of its revenues (though less than 70 percent) from one source, the best practice is to steer clear of any other ties with the source of those revenues, if affiliation with the source would cause a size standard problem.

Familial Relationships

The SBA presumes that if two businesses are owned or controlled by close family members, the businesses are affiliated on the basis of the family relationship alone.

Bob is the majority owner of QuickDri. His father, Bob Sr., is the majority owner of SlowDri, Inc., a long-standing family business where Bob learned the cleaning trade as a boy.

Result: QuickDri and SlowDri are presumed affiliated.

Like the aggregation test for common ownership, family members are "guilty until proven innocent," but can rebut the presumption of affiliation. Occasionally, a small business rebuts the presumption by showing that the family members are estranged. If Bob and Bob Sr. have not spoken in years, their blood relationship will not cause their companies to be affiliated.

Close family members can also rebut the presumption by showing that they have little or no present involvement in one another's business affairs. Some small level of involvement might pass muster with the SBA, but the best practice is to conduct no business whatsoever with companies owned by close family members if affiliation would cause a size standard problem.

So who counts as a close family member for affiliation purposes? Unfortunately, the SBA has yet to definitively answer this important question. However, based on SBA case law, you should assume that your small business is presumed affiliated with any company owned or controlled by your spouse, parent, sibling, or child. The presumption of affiliation may also apply to a cousin, at least when the cousins are heavily involved in one another's business affairs. On the other hand, a business owned by an uncle, aunt, nephew, or niece might not be presumed affiliated with your small business.

Economic Identity of Interest

Affiliation can be found between two businesses if the individuals who own or control the businesses have common economic interests, such as common investments in more than one other firm. According to the SBA, common business interests cause the parties to act in unison for their common benefit, giving rise to affiliation.

Cindy, who is the 100 percent owner of Cin City Operations, Inc., a Las Vegas-based warehousing company, also owns large minority interests in Acme Cleaners, Inc., and Wash-a-Ton, Inc. Jane, who owns 100 percent of Dry Dry Again, is a large shareholder of Acme Cleaners and Wash-a-Ton.

Result: Because Cindy and Jane have common investments in more than one other company, Cin City Operations and Dry Dry Again are affiliated by virtue of common economic interests. (And, depending on the relationships, Cin City Operations might also be affiliated with Acme Cleaners and Wash-a-Ton.)

The SBA's Office of Hearings and Appeals has held that to create affiliation, the common investments in question must be of the type where a reasonable person might significantly alter his or her business behavior as a result of the investments. For instance, if Cindy and Jane both have Microsoft shares in their respective retirement portfolios, it may be a common investment, but should not create affiliation (or even be indicative of it), because Jane and Cindy will not act in concert in business matters merely because of their mutual love of Windows.

Like other indicia of affiliation, common investments may be one piece of an overall affiliation puzzle, even if they do not rise to the level where the SBA deems the firms affiliated solely on the basis of common investments.

Newly Organized Businesses

When a large business wants to bid on a small business set-aside government contract, it may attempt to "spin off" a new small company to meet the size standard. Although establishing a new company, if done right, can help solve a size standard problem, a new spin-off is often affiliated with the old business by virtue of the *newly organized concern* rule. That rule provides that two companies are presumed affiliated where:

1. One or more former officers, directors, principal stockholders, managing members, or key employees of the old business organize a new business.

2. The new business is in the same or a related field or industry as the old business.

3. The former officers, directors, etc., serve as the new business's officers, directors, principal stockholders, managing members, or key employees.

4. The old business furnishes the new business with contracts, financial or technical assistance, bonding indemnification, or other facilities.

> Harry, the longtime vice president of Yes Sir Chauffeur, a limousine service, resigns and establishes his own limousine company, Harr-Ball Limos, Inc. In appreciation for Harry's many years of work, Yes Sir Chauffeur agrees to provide Harr-Ball with free office space and administrative support for the first year of the company's existence.
>
> **Result:** Harr-Ball and Yes Sir Chauffeur are presumed affiliated on the basis of the newly organized concern rule.

The newly organized concern rule does *not* prohibit spin-offs—it just means that when a company's principal or officer leaves to form a new company, the relationship must be handled carefully. Importantly, all four factors listed above must exist for the newly organized concern rule to apply. With a little advance planning, a former principal or officer can successfully avoid affiliation with his or her old company.

The fourth factor—assistance—is often the easiest to control. Simply put, if the other three factors are arguably present, the new business should not accept any type of assistance, contractual or otherwise, from the old business. Not only will this policy prevent newly organized concern affiliation, but it will also help reduce the likelihood of affiliation based upon economic dependence or the totality of the circumstances.

A riskier approach might involve avoiding the first factor, such as by purchasing an existing business formed by someone else. Although this might succeed, be careful—the SBA has held that, when it comes to the newly organized concern rule, purchasing a dormant business may be no different than starting a new business.[4]

Joint Ventures

When your small business forms a joint venture with another company, the two businesses are automatically considered affiliates for purposes of the particular procurement in question, except in a few limited cases that we will discuss in Chapters 11–14. However, in some cases, the SBA will find that the partners to a joint venture are *generally* affiliated.

One way in which joint venturers may be deemed affiliates is if the joint venture performs too many contracts. Under the so-called *three in two rule*, a joint venture can receive up to three federal contract awards over a two-year period. If the joint venture bids on additional contracts after it has already received three awards, the SBA may deem the joint venture partners generally affiliated.

After Cindy sells her shares in Acme Cleaners and Wash-a-Ton, breaking Cin City Operations' affiliation with Dry Dry Again, Cin City Operations forms a joint venture with another small business, Handle With Care, Inc., to compete for a marine cargo handling contract with a $25.5 million size standard. The joint venture, named Handle With Cin JV, LLC, wins the contract, and goes on to win four more federal contracts that year. The following year, Cin City Operations submits a proposal on a solicitation carrying a $7 million size standard.

Result: Because Handle With Cin JV violated the three in two rule, the SBA will likely find that Cin City Operations is generally affiliated with Handle With Care.

Joint venturers can avoid the three in two rule simply by terminating their joint venture after it receives three contract awards and setting up a new one. The next time you check the FedBizOpps website, pay attention to the winning joint ventures, which sometimes read like a list of big-budget summer movie sequels: lots of "IIs" and "IIIs" in the names of the awardees. If Cin City Operations and Handle With Care had set up a new joint venture, Handle With Cin JV, LLC II, to bid on the fourth contract, they would have complied with the rule, although the end result (a joint venture between the companies) would have been the same.

That isn't to say, though, that two companies can establish an unlimited number of new joint ventures and remain affiliation-free. At some point—although the regulations are vague about when—too much joint venturing will cause general affiliation. Just as moviegoers eventually tire of copycat sequels, the SBA grows weary of seeing the same two companies working together over and over without an "affiliate" label attached to the relationship. If you are thinking about establishing a joint venture with " IV" or "V" in its name, it might be time to look for a new joint venture partner.

Totality of the Circumstances

The SBA regulations do not refer to waterfowl, but the SBA has a name for its "looks like a duck, quacks like a duck" test: *totality of the circumstances*. Think of totality of the circumstances as a "sniff" test: If the overall relationship between your company and another business doesn't smell right to the SBA, it may find the businesses affiliated, even if it can't pinpoint a definitive reason for affiliation.

In addition to the factors discussed above, a totality of the circumstances analysis may take into account other relationships between the companies, such as:

- **Common facilities.** Do the two firms share office space, telephone or facsimile lines, copiers, administrative support staff, and the like?

- **Bonding assistance.** Does the large business provide your small business with assistance to obtain payment and/or performance bonds?
- **Common employees.** Does the large business lease your small business employees, or do any of your employees also work for the large business?

If you are concerned that your small business might be affiliated with another company under the totality of the circumstances, ask yourself: could a reasonable person conclude that the two businesses have a very close relationship? If the answer is yes, you might have an affiliation problem.

Exceptions to General Affiliation

Most rules have exceptions, and the rules governing general affiliation are no different. The SBA recognizes a few limited exceptions to general affiliation, described below.

Approved Mentor-Protégé Relationships. Two firms participating in a mentor-protégé relationship, under a federal mentor-protégé program that has been sanctioned by Congress or the SBA, are not affiliated merely because the protégé firm receives assistance from the mentor. A mentor and protégé can be found affiliated on the basis of relationships outside the provisions of their mentor-protégé agreement, but as a general rule, the SBA broadly exempts mentors and protégé firms from affiliation with one another.

> The Department of Defense approves a mentor-protégé relationship between Bob's small business, QuickDri, and InLaws R Us, Inc., a large company owned by Bob's sister-in-law, Julie. After the agreement is in place, InLaws R Us provides QuickDri with

two loans and a "sweetheart" office lease at below-market rates. In addition, QuickDri subcontracts some of its federal dry cleaning work to InLaws R Us.

Result: The loans and lease are assistance provided pursuant to an approved mentor-protégé agreement and cannot be used to find affiliation. The remaining factors are insufficient on their own to find affiliation. QuickDri and InLaws R Us are not affiliated.

At last count, more than a dozen federal agencies had established mentor-protégé programs and, for many years, small government contractors assumed that the affiliation exemption applied to them all. But in 2011, the SBA changed its regulations to state that only programs approved by the SBA or created by Congress (as opposed to those created internally by a procuring agency) qualified for the exemption. At this writing, only *two* agencies' mentor-protégé programs satisfied this requirement: the SBA's own mentor-protégé programs, and the Department of Defense's (DOD) program.

Under current law, participating in mentor-protégé programs run by other agencies, such as the National Aeronautics and Space Administration and the Department of Homeland Security, might actually *increase* your odds of affiliation, as there will be a demonstrated close relationship between your small business and a large company. Hopefully, procuring agencies and the SBA will agree in the future to apply the exemption to other agencies' programs, or Congress will step in and broaden the affiliation exemption. In the meantime, although this is an evolving area of the law, you should be wary about entering any mentor-protégé program other than the SBA's or DOD's.

Employee Leasing Companies

A small government contractor is not considered affiliated with a business that is primarily engaged in leasing employees to other businesses solely by virtue of the lease agreement, nor is a small business considered affiliated with a professional employer organization (PEO) solely on the basis of a co-employer arrangement. The word "solely" indicates that the exemption is limited. The SBA may find affiliation between your small business and an employee leasing company or PEO if other ties between the companies exist.

You might wonder if the employee leasing exemption allows you to lease employees from your large business subcontractors without risk of affiliation. Although the SBA does not appear to have directly addressed the issue, the most likely answer is no: If a subcontractor is performing part of the prime contract work on a government contract, it almost certainly will not qualify as a business primarily engaged in leasing employees.

Franchise and License Agreements

Many small businesses operate as franchises or licensees of much larger enterprises—think of your neighborhood McDonald's or Subway, for instance. A franchise relationship does not necessarily create affiliation, depending on the type of control exerted by the franchisor. The SBA will not deem your franchise affiliated with its franchisor solely because of restraints placed upon your franchise relating to standardized quality, advertising, accounting format, or other similar provisions, so long as your franchise has the right to profit from its efforts and bears the risk of loss commensurate with ownership.

Herman starts a new exterminating business under a franchise agreement with the McExterminate Franchise Network. The agreement prohibits Herman from selling his franchise without the Network's consent, but the Network cannot unreasonably withhold consent. Herman has the right to profit from his franchise, and the risk of loss if the business fails.

Result: The franchise agreement does not create affiliation. Herman's business is not deemed affiliated with the McExterminate Franchise Network.

Despite the exemption, a franchise may be affiliated with its franchisor for other reasons, such as common ownership, management, or other indicia of undue control. For example, if the Network appointed the vice president of Herman's company, and insisted that the vice president have the ability to block Herman's business decisions, Herman's company might be affiliated with the Network.

Tribally Owned Entities

Companies owned and controlled by Indian tribes, Alaska Native Corporations (ANCs), or Native Hawaiian Organizations (NHOs) are not considered affiliated with the tribe, ANC, or NHO. In addition, businesses owned and controlled by a tribal entity, ANC, or NHO are not considered affiliated with other businesses owned by the same tribe, ANC, or NHO based upon common ownership, common management, or the performance of common administrative services, such as bookkeeping and payroll, so long as adequate payment is provided for these services.

The special rules applicable to tribes, ANCs, and NHOs are discussed at length in Chapter 15.

From Affiliate to Former Affiliate

Unlike diamonds, affiliation does not necessarily last forever. If your company corrects an affiliation problem, your affiliate becomes a *former* affiliate. The distinction is critical because once a company is a former affiliate, your small business may exclude the former affiliate's annual receipts and employees from its own count for the *entire period of measurement*, including times when the affiliation was ongoing. The retroactive exclusions may allow your business to quickly regain its "small" status when it dissolves a relationship with an affiliate.

Jane, Dry Dry Again's owner and president, purchases a majority interest in QuickDri. QuickDri would be small on its own under a

$5 million standard, but combined with Dry Dry Again, the two companies are large. After realizing that Jane's purchase has created an affiliation problem, QuickDri's minority owner, Bob, takes action. He buys out Jane's interest in the company and becomes QuickDri's sole owner once again. Four months later, QuickDri bids on a contract carrying the $5 million standard.

Result: Bob's purchase of Jane's interest eliminates the prior affiliation between the two companies, causing Dry Dry Again to be a former affiliate. When Bob calculates QuickDri's annual receipts, he is entitled to exclude Dry Dry Again's receipts, including for the period when Jane owned a majority share in both companies. Because QuickDri falls below the $5 million size standard in its own right, it is eligible for award.

Small businesses sometimes try to correct an affiliation problem by dissolving or liquidating an unprofitable subsidiary. While dissolution can effectively shift a business from the affiliate camp to the former affiliate camp, the affiliate must be *legally* dissolved before it becomes a former affiliate. Typically, that means that a company is not a former affiliate until it has received appropriate termination papers from whatever state agency established the company in the first place. Merely transferring a company's assets, without a legal dissolution, will not suffice.

If the SBA has issued a size determination finding your small company large due to affiliation with another business, correcting the affiliation problem isn't enough to make you eligible for set-aside contracts as a stand-alone business. Instead, you must apply to the SBA for recertification as a small business. Only after the SBA agrees that the other company is now a former affiliate may you begin bidding on set-aside contracts as a stand-alone business.

However, if you noticed the affiliation problem on your own, without an SBA finding of affiliation, you need not apply for recertification. Once you have corrected the affiliation problem, you can immediately resume bidding on set-aside contracts as a stand-alone business.

The Primary Rules: Where to Find Them

Here's where to find the primary rules discussed in this chapter:

- 13 C.F.R. § 121.103(a) (general principles of affiliation)
- 13 C.F.R. § 121.103(c) (common ownership)
- 13 C.F.R. § 121.103(d) (present effect rule)
- 13 C.F.R. § 121.103(e) (common management)
- 13 C.F.R. § 121.103(c) (economic dependence, common investments, and familial relationships)
- 13 C.F.R. § 121.103(g) (newly organized businesses)
- 13 C.F.R. § 121.103(h) (joint ventures)
- 13 C.F.R. § 121.103(c) (franchise and license agreements)
- 13 C.F.R. § 121.103(b) (other exceptions to affiliation)
- 13 C.F.R. § 121.104(d) & 13 C.F.R. § 121.106(b) (former affiliates)

"General" Affiliation Risk Questionnaire

Does your small business have affiliates? The questionnaire below will help you find out. Each question addresses a risk factor for affiliation—some more severe than others. If your small business has an affiliation problem, and could be at risk within an important size standard, the time to address it is now—before the SBA comes knocking on the door.

	Risk Factor	Response	Comments
1	Does the majority owner (more than 50 percent) of your business own or control the majority of the other business?	☐ Yes ☐ No	If yes, the two businesses are affiliated.
2	Does the majority owner of the other business have the right—even though unexercised—to purchase the majority of your business?	☐ Yes ☐ No	If yes, the two businesses are affiliated.
3	Do the owners, managers, officers, or directors of your business play an ownership or management role in the other business?	☐ Yes ☐ No	
4	Does the highest officer in your business (usually president or CEO) serve as the highest officer of the other business?	☐ Yes ☐ No	
5	Does your business receive 70 percent or more of its income from the other business (such as through subcontracts)?	☐ Yes ☐ No	If yes, the two businesses are likely affiliated.
6	Is the majority owner of your business a former owner, officer, director, or key employee of the other business?	☐ Yes ☐ No	
7	Do any of your business's minority owners, officers, directors, or key employees currently serve as owners, officers, directors, or key employees of the other business?	☐ Yes ☐ No	
8	Does your business share office space with the other business?	☐ Yes ☐ No	
9	Does your business lease office space from the other business?	☐ Yes ☐ No	
10	Has the other business ever provided your business with any loans or other financial support (such as bonding assistance)?	☐ Yes ☐ No	
11	Is the majority owner of your business related to the majority owner of the other business?	☐ Yes ☐ No	If yes, a rebuttable presumption of affiliation.
12	Does your business share any facilities (such as telephones, facsimile machines, office furniture, or administrative services) with the other business?	☐ Yes ☐ No	

	Risk Factor	*Response*	*Comments*
13	Would you consider your business a "spin-off" of the other business?	☐ Yes ☐ No	
14	Does your business derive more than 30 percent of its revenues from the other business?	☐ Yes ☐ No	The greater the percentage, the more indicative of affiliation.
15	Does your business share any employees in common with the other business?	☐ Yes ☐ No	
16	Is the other business in the same or a similar line of work as your business?	☐ Yes ☐ No	
17	Are any of your business's minority owners, officer, directors, or key employees former owners, officers, directors, or employees of the other business?	☐ Yes ☐ No	
18	Have your business and the other business ever formed a joint venture?	☐ Yes ☐ No	
19	Has any joint venture between you and the other business ever bid on more than three federal prime contracts over a two-year period?	☐ Yes ☐ No	
20	Do your business and the other business have any ongoing or prior contractual relationships?	☐ Yes ☐ No	
21	Have your business and the other business agreed to a merger?	☐ Yes ☐ No	The two businesses are affiliated.
22	Do your CCR and Small Business Profiles indicate a relationship with the other business, such as a shared address or point of contact?	☐ Yes ☐ No	This type of information may be used by competitors to protest your business.
23	Does your website name the other business as a "teammate" or otherwise indicate a relationship with the other business or its owners or officers?	☐ Yes ☐ No	This type of information may be used by competitors to protest your business.
24	Does your business owe any debts to the other business?	☐ Yes ☐ No	The greater the debt, the more indicative of affiliation.

	Risk Factor	Response	Comments
25	Do any relatives of your business's owners, officers, or directors have an ownership interest in the other business?	☐ Yes ☐ No	
26	Has the other business ever assisted your business in obtaining subcontracts for work on a government prime contract?	☐ Yes ☐ No	
27	Has the other business ever performed 25 percent or more of the value of the work on any of your business's prime contracts?	☐ Yes ☐ No	If the percent exceeded performance of work requirements, you might be automatically affiliated (and potentially face other penalties).
28	If your business were to be terminated for default from any federal prime contract, would there be a negative financial impact on the other business?	☐ Yes ☐ No	
29	Did the other business, or any of its owners, officers, or directors provide any owner of your business with the funds used to purchase that owner's share?	☐ Yes ☐ No	

WEIGHING YOUR "YES" ANSWERS. If you answered "yes" to questions 1, 2, 5, or 21, your businesses are almost certain to be considered affiliated. "Yes" answers to questions 3, 4, and 19 are also highly indicative of affiliation, even if you answered "no" everywhere else. A "yes" to question 11 (regarding relatives) establishes a rebuttable presumption of affiliation, requiring you to prove that the two businesses are not affiliates. While "yes" answers to the other questions are not necessarily weighed equally in the SBA's analysis, a good rule of thumb is that the more "yes" answers, the more likely your business has an affiliate.

CHAPTER 3

SUBCONTRACTOR
OR OSTENSIBLE
SUBCONTRACTOR?

AS IF AVOIDING general affiliation wasn't enough, small government contractors must also avoid *ostensible subcontractor affiliation* (also known as *contract-specific affiliation*), a special type of affiliation under which your small business can be found affiliated with its subcontractor for purposes of a single contract—even if you have no pre-existing relationship with the subcontractor.

The government has focused on ostensible subcontractor affiliation in recent enforcement actions. In perhaps the most high-profile example, in late 2010, the SBA suspended GTSI Corporation—a computer technology company and top-100 federal contractor in revenues—from all government contracting for allegedly serving as an ostensible subcontractor to two small businesses. The SBA alleged that GTSI and the small companies were ineligible to receive set-aside contracts because GTSI, as a large subcontractor, was too heavily involved in the contract work (the SBA also suspended the small businesses in question). The federal courts have gotten into the act, as well: One district court struck down a subcontract agreement as "il-

Subcontractor's Percentage of Work

In general, the greater the percentage of the prime contract work the subcontractor will perform, the more likely the SBA will find that there is an ostensible subcontractor relationship.

> MaryIT submits a proposal on a computer services set-aside, with Macro Chips, Inc., a large IT company, as its proposed major subcontractor. The proposal indicates that Macro Chips will perform 49 percent of the work. The contract includes a clause requiring MaryIT to subcontract no more than 50 percent of the cost of the contract incurred for personnel to its subcontractors.
>
> **Result:** MaryIT's subcontract to Macro Chips may not violate the subcontracting limit (Mary would have to run a separate calculation on the cost of performance incurred by personnel to make sure). Nevertheless, the high percentage of work to be performed by Macro Chips is evidence of an ostensible subcontractor relationship.

You may be familiar with the Federal Acquisition Regulation's (FAR's) subcontracting limits, which prohibit small businesses from subcontracting more than a defined percentage of work on set-aside contracts. (If you don't know about the subcontracting limits, don't worry; we will discuss them in the next chapter.) However, merely because your subcontractor squeaks under the limits does not mean that you are safe from ostensible subcontractor affiliation. Anytime a subcontractor will perform a large portion of the work, the risk of affiliation exists.

Although less subcontract work typically equates to a lower likelihood of contract-specific affiliation, there is no "magic number." In one case, the SBA found that an ostensible subcontractor relationship existed when the subcontractor was to perform a mere 23 percent of the work, but numerous other indicia of affiliation existed.[2] For example, the subcontractor's employees were to play important managerial roles on the project and perform vital portions of the contract, the small business prime contractor lacked relevant experience in the industry, and the proposal highlighted the subcontractor's involvement—all risk factors we will discuss in this chapter.

The best practice, of course, is to perform the entire contract yourself, or subcontract only small portions of the prime contract work. In real life, though, it is not always feasible to self-perform the lion's share of the work. If your small business must subcontract a large portion of the work, you may wish to consider breaking the work up between two or more subcontractors, which could decrease the odds that one of the subcontractors will be found to be an ostensible subcontractor.

If you must subcontract a large percentage of the work to a single subcontractor, draft your contract documents carefully to minimize your affiliation risk. Your *teaming agreement*, the document establishing your agreement to pursue the contract opportunity, should identify what work the subcontractor will (and will not) perform and give you the right to reduce the subcontractor's work share if necessary to maintain compliance with the subcontracting limit. Once you enter into a formal subcontract, you should include similar provisions.

Division of Work

When you form a subcontracting relationship, ask yourself: Which company will perform the work requiring the greatest technical expertise? If the answer is "the subcontractor," it is indicative of ostensible subcontractor affiliation—especially if your small business's work will be limited primarily to administrative or clerical tasks. In the SBA's eyes, dividing the contract work in this manner indicates that the subcontractor will perform the "primary and vital" portions of the contract, while the prime contractor brings little to the relationship but its small business status.

QuickDri submits a proposal on a dry cleaning contract, with Wash-a-Ton as its subcontractor. The proposal indicates that Wash-a-Ton will perform the actual dry cleaning work at its ultramodern, eco-friendly facilities, while QuickDri will perform administrative tasks such as accounting, clerical work, and payment processing.

Result: The division of labor indicates that Wash-a-Ton, not QuickDri, is performing the primary and vital portions of the contract, and is indicative of ostensible subcontractor affiliation.

In order to avoid ostensible subcontractor affiliation, your teaming agreement and proposal should demonstrate that your small business will perform some of the more complex and "primary" portions of the work, as opposed to purely administrative or support functions. You cannot escape a finding of affiliation by simply failing to provide a "who does what" breakdown in the teaming agreement and proposal. OHA has held failing to include this information is, itself, indicative of ostensible subcontractor affiliation, because it suggests that the companies have joined their workforces and will work as joint venturers.[3]

Project Management

It should come as no surprise that the risks of ostensible subcontractor affiliation increase if the subcontractor's employees are heavily involved in managing the contract, especially at the highest levels. After all, if your employees are taking their orders from the subcontractor's managerial personnel, it is hard to argue (at least with a straight face) that your company is really in charge of the operation.

BrettWorks submits a proposal on a set-aside contract for administrative services with NationStaff, Inc., a large administrative services provider, as its proposed subcontractor. The proposal identifies one of NationStaff's employees as a key project manager. BrettWorks and NationStaff agree that, if BrettWorks wins the contract, a second managerial employee will transfer from NationStaff's payroll to BrettWorks'.

Result: BrettWorks' reliance upon NationStaff's employees for project management is indicative of ostensible subcontractor affiliation.

Did you notice that NationStaff agreed to transfer one of its managerial employees to BrettWorks' payroll? This sort of personnel shifting is a common ploy to avoid ostensible subcontractor affiliation. Sometimes, the transfer occurs before the parties submit the proposal; in other cases, the transfer is contingent upon a contract award. Here's the problem: It's not very effective.

The SBA wasn't born yesterday (it was created in 1953, as a matter of fact). So the SBA knows exactly what is happening when managerial personnel suddenly transfer from an ineligible subcontractor to the small business prime contractor, and it views such transfers as indicative of ostensible subcontractor affiliation.

Is a personnel transfer better than having the subcontractor's current employees manage the contract? Probably. But better still, manage the contract through your own existing employees or bring in outsiders with no connection to the subcontractor.

Relative Experience

Remember the example a few pages ago, where our fictional dry cleaner, QuickDri, decided to branch out and bid on a construction contract? The SBA tends to be suspicious of such sudden shifts in focus, wondering what, exactly, a dry cleaner brings to a construction project, other than its small business status. If your small business lacks experience performing the type of work the government requires, it may suggest that your company is unduly reliant upon its subcontractor—particularly if the subcontractor is highly experienced in that type of work.

A lack of experience can also be a problem if your small business has never completed a contract anywhere near the size and scope required by the government.

> Buck's Trucking, Inc., a transportation company, submits a proposal on a large hauling contract, with American Semis, Inc., as its proposed major subcontractor. Under the proposal, Buck's Trucking plans to manage a workforce nine times its current size. The contract amount is 50 times greater, on an annual basis, than Buck's Trucking's total revenues. American Semis, a much larger business, has substantial experience performing large contracts.
>
> **Result:** Buck's Trucking's lack of experience with contracts of a similar size and scope, coupled with American Semis' substantial experience, is indicative of unusual reliance on American Semis.

Don't panic if your subcontractor has more experience than your small business. After all, most large subcontractors got big for a reason—years of successful contract performance. By the same token, don't bite off more than you can chew. If a contract is far outside your capabilities, you are asking for trouble by serving as a "figurehead" to an experienced subcontractor.

To reduce experience problems, carefully review your proposal to make sure that it highlights both companies' experience, not just the subcontractor's. For example, if the proposal asks you to identify five representative past performance projects, consider submitting at least three projects performed by your small business, even if the subcontractor has performed more impressive projects—and list your own projects first, not your subcontractor's.

Also, the experience of key personnel can make a difference. In our example from a few pages ago, if Bob worked as a construction manager for 25 years before getting into the dry cleaning business, it might not be as big a stretch for QuickDri to bid on a construction contract, particularly if several of QuickDri's other key personnel have similar experience. Be sure to highlight the relevant experience of your key personnel in your proposal. But, as we will discuss a little later in this chapter, hiring experienced personnel *from the subcontractor* can be problematic.

Proposal Preparation

Large subcontractors have plenty of experience preparing government proposals, and some even boast dedicated "war rooms" where the proposal-writing magic happens. As a small prime contractor, it can be very tempting to agree to the subcontractor's offer to lead the proposal effort. But—you guessed it—the subcontractor's involvement in preparation of the proposal can be indicative of ostensible sub-contractor affiliation, particularly if the subcontractor plays the lead proposal-writing role.

No, you do not need to shut the subcontractor out of the proposal-writing effort altogether. As a general matter, there is nothing wrong with the subcontractor *assisting* you in preparing the proposal. If the subcontractor will help with proposal writing, the best practice is to ensure that your teaming agreement clearly spells out which company will do what in relation to the proposal, such as stating that:

- Your small business is in charge of the proposal effort, and the subcontractor merely provides assistance.
- Your small business, not the subcontractor, decides what goes "in" and stays "out" of the final proposal.
- The subcontractor's work on the proposal will be performed under your small business's direction and supervision.
- Your small business will be the government's sole contact with respect to questions or negotiations related to the proposal.

A strong teaming agreement is essential because, if a competitor files a size protest, the teaming agreement will be "Exhibit A" in the SBA's review of your case.

What about that war room? Again, there is nothing inherently wrong with taking advantage of these types of resources, but using them can unnecessarily suggest undue reliance on the subcontractor. If possible, prepare the proposal at your own offices and with your own personnel (or third-party consultants).

Proposal Terminology

If the teaming agreement is Exhibit A in an ostensible subcontractor size protest, your proposal is undoubtedly Exhibit B. The words and graphics used in your proposal matter. For example, if the proposal repeatedly refers to your small business and the subcontractor as a "team," includes the subcontractor's logo on every page, or calls the subcontractor a "partner," the SBA may consider it suggestive of ostensible subcontractor affiliation. Though OHA has not been consistent in recent years in its evaluation of what role terminology plays, some OHA cases suggest that even seemingly innocuous words or phrases, like "our experience" instead of "QuickDri's experience," could come back to haunt you if you overuse them.

Nova Healthcare, Inc., a small healthcare staffing company, submits a proposal on a set-aside contract with Top Docs, Inc., the successful (but now ineligible) incumbent as its proposed subcontractor. To remind the agency that the incumbent will be its subcontractor, Nova refers throughout the proposal to "Team Nova Docs" rather than "Nova Healthcare."

Result: The proposal's pervasive references to Nova Healthcare and Top Docs as a team are likely indicative of ostensible subcontractor affiliation.

Like QuickDri, you might be tempted to pepper your proposal with constant references to an experienced subcontractor, believing it will increase the likelihood of award. But is this really the case?

The agency will recognize the benefits an experienced subcontractor brings to your proposal without being beaten over the head with the subcontractor's name and logo on every page. At the same time, too much discussion of the subcontractor could present ostensible subcontractor affiliation problems. When it comes to references to the subcontractor in your proposal, the old Brylcreem jingle has it right: "a little dab'll do ya."

"Chasing" the Contract

Most often, government contracting follows a "top-down" process: A prime contractor identifies an opportunity, then goes out and rounds up subcontractors to help it perform the work. When it comes to small business set-asides, though, sometimes the opposite occurs: A large or otherwise ineligible subcontractor discovers an opportunity, then seeks out a prime contractor with the appropriate small business status or other bona fides (like an 8(a) Program certification) to pursue it. This "bottom-up" approach to putting together a team is a risk factor for ostensible subcontractor affiliation.

> Jane wants to pursue a small business set-aside dry cleaning contract, but Dry Dry Again is too large to qualify. Jane takes Bob out to dinner and, after several glasses of wine, convinces Bob to enter a bid, with Dry Dry Again as QuickDri's subcontractor.
>
> **Result:** The fact that Dry Dry Again sought out and convinced QuickDri to be its prime contractor, rather than vice versa, is indicative of ostensible subcontractor affiliation.

Why does the SBA care which company initiates the relationship? Like the father of a wealthy heiress, worried that suitors are after his daughter's fortune, the SBA wonders whether a contract-chasing sub-contractor is really interested in anything other than your company's "small" status. Remember, to avoid ostensible subcontractor affilia-tion, your small business must bring something useful to the rela-tionship other than its contract eligibility.

Location of the Parties and Project

If your offices are located far from the project site, but the subcon-tractor's offices are nearby, it may suggest that the subcontractor is the real party in interest—particularly if the work requires physical presence at a job site.

> XPert Constructors submits a proposal on a small business set-aside procurement for construction services, with Big Time Con-struction Co. as its subcontractor. XPert is located more than 900 miles from the job site and has little experience outside its home state. Big Time's office is located in the same city as the job site.
>
> **Result:** XPert's distance from the project site, coupled with Big Time's proximity, is indicative of unusual reliance on Big Time—especially because construction contracts require day-to-day work and supervision at the job site, which XPert cannot effectively pro-vide from several states away.

Location might not play a major role in the SBA's affiliation analysis if the agency does not require that the work be performed at a particular location. For instance, if the solicitation called for the contractor to develop computer programs at the contractor's own fa-cilities, it shouldn't make much difference where those facilities are located. But anytime work must be performed at a particular location, the SBA may be skeptical of your small company's ability to effectively manage the project from afar.

Financing and Bonding

Your large subcontractor probably has a lot more money than your small business does. You may be tempted to accept financial assistance from your subcontractor to help you win the contract. Unfortunately, if your small business relies on the subcontractor to provide financing or bonding necessary to complete the project, it is indicative of ostensible subcontractor affiliation.

> XPert Constructors submits a proposal for a set-aside construction procurement, with Big Time Construction as its subcontractor. In order to enable XPert to obtain necessary payment and performance bonds, Big Time executes an indemnification agreement with the surety.
>
> **Result:** XPert's reliance upon Big Time to secure necessary bonding is indicative of contract-specific affiliation.

As the example suggests, this aspect of the ostensible subcontractor analysis is often especially difficult for small construction contractors, which can have trouble obtaining the payment and performance bonds required under the Miller Act, a federal statute calling for surety bonds on most government construction and renovation contracts, on their own. Before turning to a subcontractor for bonding assistance, investigate whether you might qualify for a bond guarantee, affiliation-risk-free, through the SBA's Surety Bond Guarantee Program, or obtain bonding through a third party.

Hiring Incumbent Employees

If the proposed subcontractor is an ineligible incumbent, the prime contractor's hiring of a large number of the subcontractor's employees may be evidence of ostensible subcontractor affiliation.

MaryIT submits a proposal with Dakota Tech, Inc., as its proposed major subcontractor. Dakota Tech is the current incumbent, but has grown too large to qualify for the new contract. The companies agree that if MaryIT wins, it will hire all of Dakota Tech's key contract employees and many of its other employees.

Result: MaryIT's hiring of an extensive number of Dakota Tech's employees may be indicative of ostensible subcontractor affiliation.

Did you notice the slight change of wording in the example above? Unlike our previous examples, hiring incumbent employees *may* be evidence of affiliation, but is not *always* evidence of affiliation, at least under the law in effect as of this writing.

For many years, the SBA unequivocally held that hiring a large number of an incumbent subcontractor's employees was strong evidence of affiliation. However, in January 2009, just days after taking office, President Obama issued Executive Order (EO) 13495, titled "Nondisplacement of Qualified Workers Under Service Contracts." EO 13495 requires service contractors to give an incumbent's non-managerial employees a "right of first refusal" to retain their positions before hiring non-incumbent employees, unless certain exceptions exist. We will discuss compliance with EO 13495 in Chapter 5.

Not surprisingly, EO 13495 has forced the SBA to change its thinking about whether the hiring of incumbent personnel constitutes grounds for affiliation. In 2011, OHA wrote that when a prime contractor is required to make offers to incumbent personnel under EO 13495, "the hiring of incumbent employees can no longer be considered a meaningful indicia of unusual reliance" for ostensible subcontractor affiliation purposes.[4]

However, EO 13495 does not mean that you can simply hire all of your incumbent subcontractor's personnel without worry. EO 13495 applies only to service contracts, not construction, supply, or manufacturing contracts, and does not cover managerial employees. If you bring on the subcontractor's managerial staff, or its team of construction workers, the SBA will still deem it strong evidence of affiliation.

In addition, EO 13495 is very unlikely to be a permanent piece of the contracting landscape. When the Republican Party regains control of the White House, EO 13495 will probably go the way of the dinosaurs (President Clinton previously issued a similar order, which President George W. Bush repealed soon after taking office). If there is a power shift in Washington, be sure to do your due diligence before relying on EO 13495 to hire an incumbent subcontractor's employees.

Profit Sharing

How will you pay your subcontractor? If the answer includes profit sharing it might be time to rethink your plans. In the SBA's eyes, profit sharing is a hallmark of a joint venture, not a prime/subcontractor relationship.

XPert Constructors submits a bid on a set-aside construction contract, with Big Time Construction as its proposed subcontractor. The companies' teaming agreement calls for XPert and Big Time to split profits on a 60 percent/40 percent basis.

Result: The profit-sharing arrangement is indicative of ostensible subcontractor affiliation.

Sometimes, contractors try to avoid blatant profit splitting by agreeing to "success fees" and other incentive payment mechanisms. The SBA isn't fooled so easily. In most cases, the best practice is to price your subcontract on a firm-fixed price basis or on a fixed price formula basis (such as fixed hourly rates) to avoid the perception of profit sharing.

Unnecessary Publicity

"Loose lips sink ships," went the old World War II saying. In the modern era, loose lips can sink your contract award. If you publicize your own potential ostensible subcontractor problems, expect your competitors to take notice and file size protests.

> Buck's Trucking submits a proposal with American Semis as its proposed major subcontractor. American Semis is the current incumbent, but has grown much too large to qualify for the new contract. After the agency notifies Buck's Trucking that it has won, Buck's Trucking issues a press release describing the award. The press release states that American Semis will be a major subcontractor and that Buck's Trucking will hire all of American Semis' contract managers and many of its other employees.
>
> **Result:** Buck's Truckings' competitors come across the press release, show it to their attorneys, and Buck's Trucking soon finds itself defending a size protest.

Of course, you should do your best to minimize the risk factors of ostensible subcontractor affiliation we have discussed in this chapter. However, if toeing the affiliation line is necessary, the last thing you want to do is alert your competitors that you might have a problem and provide them with ammunition for a size protest.

Tell your employees that they are free to publicize the fact that the award occurred, and the total dollar amount of the award (that information is publicly available on the FedBizOpps website anyway) but that the details of the teaming arrangement—including the name of your subcontractor—should not be publicly released. And consider inserting a provision in your teaming agreement and subcontract prohibiting the subcontractor from disclosing details about the arrangement, too.

The Primary Rules: Where to Find Them

Here's where to find the primary rules discussed in this chapter:

- 13 C.F.R. § 121.103(h)(4) (ostensible subcontractor affiliation)

Ostensible Subcontractor Affiliation Risk Questionnaire

If you are planning to subcontract work on a small business set-aside contract to another company, you should do your best to minimize the risks of ostensible subcontractor affiliation. This questionnaire will help you identify potential problem areas.

	Risk Factor	*Response*	*Comments*
1	Is the subcontractor an ineligible incumbent?	☐ Yes ☐ No	If so, it is strong evidence of affiliation (though not conclusive).
2	Did an ineligible incumbent subcontractor "recruit" your small business to become the new prime contractor?	☐ Yes ☐ No	
3	Do the proposal, subcontract, and teaming agreement clearly indicate that your business will comply with the applicable limitations on subcontracting?	☐ Yes ☐ No	See Chapter 4 for specific requirements.
4	Does your small business have expertise in the main type(s) of work to be performed on the contract?	☐ Yes ☐ No	
5	Does your small business have prior experience with contracts of a similar size?	☐ Yes ☐ No	

	Risk Factor	Response	Comments
6	Will the subcontractor provide assistance in obtaining bonds for the project?	☐ Yes ☐ No	If so, reduce affiliation risks by using arms-length agreement with indemnification provision.
7	Will the subcontractor provide other major financial support or necessary equipment for the project?	☐ Yes ☐ No	Consider the SBA Surety Bond Guarantee Program before accepting bonding assistance from a subcontractor.
8	Do the proposal, teaming agreement, and sub-contract clearly delineate the respective roles of the prime contractor and subcontractor?	☐ Yes ☐ No	If not, amend the proposal, teaming agreement, and subcontract as necessary.
9	Does the proposal refer to a prime–subcontract "team"?	☐ Yes ☐ No	If so, amend the proposal as necessary.
10	Is the highest project manager a current or former employee of the subcontractor?	☐ Yes ☐ No	
11	Are most or all employees with supervisory or managerial authority on the project the subcontractor's current employees or former employees?	☐ Yes ☐ No	
12	Was the subcontractor the primary drafter of the teaming agreement, subcontract, or proposal?	☐ Yes ☐ No	
13	Does the teaming agreement or subcontract contain one-sided terms favoring the subcon-tractor?	☐ Yes ☐ No	
14	Are there any profit-sharing arrangements in place between your small business and the subcontractor with respect to the contract work?	☐ Yes ☐ No	
15	If the subcontractor is an ineligible incumbent, does your small business intend to retain a large number of the incumbent's employees?	☐ Yes ☐ No	Your business may be required to retain incumbent employees pursuant to Executive Order 13495.

	Risk Factor	Response	Comments
16	Will your small business perform a significant portion of the contract work requiring the most expertise?	☐ Yes ☐ No	The more such work your small business will perform, the better.
17	Will your small business perform a significant portion of the contract work deemed most important by the agency?	☐ Yes ☐ No	The more such work your small business will perform, the better.
18	Is your small business's role on the contract limited entirely or primarily to administrative or support tasks?	☐ Yes ☐ No	
19	Does your small business have an office located near the project site?	☐ Yes ☐ No	Especially important for projects requiring a physical presence, like construction.

CHAPTER 4

THE WIDE WORLD OF SUBCONTRACTING

IF YOUR SMALL BUSINESS is like many government contractors, you may find it difficult to perform government contracts without subcontractors. After reading Chapter 3, you know about ostensible subcontractor affiliation and how to avoid it. But when it comes to subcontracting a portion of a government contract, avoiding affiliation is just one of many compliance challenges.

Uncle Sam restricts *to whom* you may subcontract and *how much* of the work you may subcontract. The government also demands that you *insert certain required provisions* in each of your subcontracts. To top it off, the government requires you to *disclose* your small business's subcontracting relationships and certain data about your subcontractors—some of which will be published publicly in an online database. This chapter discusses these requirements.

To Whom May I Subcontract?

Here's the good news: As a general matter, your small business may pick its own subcontractors with minimal government interference.

But—and you knew there was a "but" coming—before entering most subcontracts, you must ensure that your prospective subcontractor is eligible to perform government work.

When a contractor has been convicted of a serious crime, committed fraud against the government, made false claims, or engaged in other not-so-nice behavior (like falsely certifying to being a small business), the government may suspend or debar the contractor from all government contracting. You may not award a subcontract to a suspended or debarred contractor if the value of the subcontract will exceed $30,000, unless there is a "compelling" reason to do so and you give the government advance notice.

> Bob, the owner of QuickDri, wants to submit a proposal on a dry cleaning solicitation with an estimated value of $2 million. He would like to subcontract with Dry Dry Again, his friend Jane's company, but is concerned that the subcontract, in addition to the existing ties between the companies, could create an affiliation problem. So QuickDri executes a $900,000 subcontract agreement with Sleez-E Cleaners, Inc., a business run by its smooth-talking owner and president, Claude. After QuickDri wins the prime contract, Bob learns that Sleez-E has been debarred from all government contracting.
>
> **Result:** QuickDri has violated its prime contract by awarding a subcontract in excess of $30,000 to a debarred business. The government may terminate QuickDri's contract for default and may take additional action against QuickDri—including suspension or debarment.

What should Bob have done differently? First, he should have checked the Excluded Parties List System (EPLS), an electronic database of suspended and debarred contractors, before signing the subcontract with Sleez-E. The EPLS is located at https://www.epls.gov/. Before executing any government subcontract, you should search for the subcontractor in the EPLS, as well as the names of its owners and top officers (both companies and individuals can be suspended or debarred). If Sleez-E or Claude had been named on the EPLS, Bob would have known that he needed to find a new subcontractor, ASAP.

In addition, Bob should have required Sleez-E to certify, in writing, that it was not suspended or debarred. Under the FAR, you must require any proposed subcontractor for work of $30,000 or more to disclose to you, in writing, whether at the time of award of the subcontract, the subcontractor or its principals are debarred, suspended, or proposed for debarment. Obtaining the certification is important not only because it is required, but because the EPLS may not be up-to-date, or your EPLS search might not be perfect (for instance, Claude might be listed under his full name, Claudius).

Had Sleez-E falsely certified, QuickDri would likely have been able to terminate the subcontract for default, and might even have recovered damages from Sleez-E in a lawsuit. In addition, the government might go easy on QuickDri because Sleez-E's false certification—rather than QuickDri's failure to follow the FAR—was the primary reason an ineligible company received the subcontract work.

What If I Need to Subcontract with a Suspended or Debarred Company?

The last thing your small business needs—especially in the current climate in Washington, with its focus on compliance and weeding out unethical contractors—is a public association with a firm the government believes cannot be trusted to do federal business. As we will discuss at the end of this chapter, the government will publish the names of your subcontractors online, so all of your competitors will know the company you keep. You should think twice (or three or four times, if need be) before issuing any subcontract of $30,000 or more to a suspended or debarred contractor.

If, for some reason, you believe that subcontracting with a suspended or debarred company is truly necessary, you must provide written notice to the contracting officer prior to executing the sub-contract. The written notice must contain:

- The name of the subcontractor
- Your understanding of why the subcontractor is suspended or debarred
- The "compelling reason" for doing business with the sub-contractor
- A list of the systems and procedures you have established to ensure that the government's interests are fully protected

You need only provide prior notice, not obtain prior approval, before entering a subcontract of $30,000 or more with a suspended party. But do not be surprised if your notice results in a quick call from the agency, questioning the wisdom of the subcontract and strongly encouraging you to consider other options.

How Much Work Can I Subcontract?

Once you are satisfied that your prospective subcontractor is not excluded or debarred, it is time to get down to the nuts and bolts of preparing a subcontract agreement. One of the key considerations, of course, is how much work your small business will assign to its subcontractor or subcontractors.

For small business set-aside contracts, the FAR's *limitations on subcontracting rules* prohibit your company from subcontracting more than a certain percent of the overall work. In other words, the limitations on subcontracting establish "ceilings" on subcontracted work. Exceed the applicable ceiling, and your small business is in breach of its prime contract.

What Are the Subcontracting Limits?

The subcontracting limits vary significantly, depending upon the primary type of work called for by the prime contract: services, supplies/products, general construction, or special trade construction. If you do not know which category applies to the contract, check the NAICS code. Many NAICS codes include words such as "manufacturing" or "services" in their names. If not, look at the number itself: NAICS codes beginning in 238, for instance, cover special trade construction.

Services Contracts

For a *services* contract, your small business must perform at least *50 percent of the cost of the contract incurred for personnel* with its own employees. "Cost of contract performance incurred for personnel" is defined as direct labor costs and any overhead that has only direct labor as its base, plus your small business's general and administrative (G&A) rate, multiplied by the labor cost.

Despite a common misconception, the 50 percent limit does not apply to the total dollar value of the contract itself. Rather, the limit is based on the personnel costs incurred by your business and its subcontractors in performing the contract.

BrettWorks, Inc., wins a $5 million contract set-aside under NAICS code 541110, Office Administrative Services. Believing that he can subcontract up to 50 percent of the total contract amount, Brett signs a $2.5 million subcontract with Draper's Papers.

Result: BrettWorks may have violated the subcontracting limits by basing the subcontract award on the total dollar value of the contract. In order to determine whether the subcontract was permissible, Brett should have calculated the cost of contract performance incurred by personnel, and ensure that BrettWorks will incur at least 50 percent of those costs with its own employees.

To determine whether a particular subcontract award will comply with the subcontracting limitation for a services contract, follow these five steps:

1. Break down the total amount of the contract into the following components: materials, direct labor, overhead (further broken down by labor and non-labor), equipment, G&A, and profit.

2. Eliminate the non-labor costs.

3. Add the remaining labor costs together.

4. Add the appropriate amount of G&A expenses.

5. Divide the result in two to arrive at the required cost of contract performance incurred by your personnel.

BrettWorks wins a small business contract set-aside under NAICS code 541110. The contract is valued at $875,500. BrettWorks' costs on the contract are as follows:

- Materials: $100,000
- Direct Labor: $500,000
- Equipment: $70,000
- Labor Overhead: $20,000
- Non-Labor Overhead: $7,500
- G&A Expense (10%): $80,000
- Profit: $100,000

Result: To determine how much work he may subcontract, Brett first excludes the non-labor costs: materials, equipment, and non-labor overhead. Then, Brett adds the direct labor costs and direct labor overhead, arriving at $520,000. He then applies the 10 percent G&A rate to determine how much of the G&A results from those labor costs, and adds the result ($52,000) to arrive at a total of $572,000 in costs incurred by personnel. Dividing by two, Brett concludes that BrettWorks' personnel must incur $286,000 of the costs incurred by personnel.

To perform the calculation accurately, you must understand how your subcontractor breaks down its costs into the various components previously described. Sometimes, however, a subcontractor balks at providing its prime contractor with its cost breakdown. You may be able to assuage your subcontractor's concern by inserting a confidentiality provision in your subcontract, prohibiting you from disclosing the breakdown to third parties.

But if you cannot convince the subcontractor to share its cost breakdown (perhaps because the subcontractor does not want to share its profit margin with you), perform steps 1–4 with respect to your own costs, add the *entire value of the subcontract* to the result, and then divide by two. By assuming that the entire value of the subcontract will constitute costs incurred by personnel, you will ensure that you do not inadvertently violate the subcontracting limit.

> BrettWorks wins a small business contract set-aside under NAICS code 541110. Brett calculates BrettWorks' own total costs as $120,000 and costs incurred for personnel as $80,000. Brett wishes to award a $90,000 subcontract to Draper's Papers. Danny Draper, the owner and president of Draper's Papers, refuses to provide a breakdown of costs to Brett.
>
> **Result:** Brett adds the entire value of the subcontract, $90,000, to the costs BrettWorks will incur for personnel, $80,000, and divides the result ($170,000) by two, arriving at $85,000.

Uh-oh. The $85,000 result—the amount BrettWorks must perform—is slightly higher than the $80,000 amount the company will actually perform. To ensure that it complies with the subcontracting limit, BrettWorks should reduce the amount of its subcontract award to Draper's Papers (or try again to convince Danny Draper to disclose his cost breakdown, likely allowing some additional costs to be excluded).

Supplies or Products. In the case of a contract for *supplies or products* (other than procurement from a non-manufacturer [1] in such supplies or products), your small business must perform at least *50 percent of* *the cost of manufacturing* the supplies or products with its own employees. In calculating the costs of manufacturing, include the direct costs of fabrication, assembly, or other production activities, and indirect costs allocable to those activities. Exclude the cost of materials and profit.

General Construction. For a contract for general construction, your small business must perform at least 15 percent of the *cost of the contract* with its own employees. Cost of the contract is defined as all allowable direct and indirect costs allocable to the contract. Again, exclude the costs of materials and profit from your calculation.

Special Trade Construction. In the case of a contract for *special trade construction*, your small business must perform at least 25 percent of the cost of the contract with its own employees. Cost of the contract is calculated in the same manner as for general construction.

What If I Have Multiple Subcontractors?

The SBA calls the limitations on subcontracting provisions "prime contractor performance requirements," which may be a more apt description. As we have seen in the examples, the subcontracting limits require your small business to perform a certain percentage of the contract with your own employees. You cannot evade the limits by dividing the work among multiple subcontractors, even if no subcontractor will perform more work than your small business.

> QuickDri wins a small business set-aside solicitation for dry cleaning services. Bob decides to subcontract 30 percent of the cost of the contract incurred for personnel to Dry Dry Again and an additional 25 percent to Harr-Ball Cleaners.
>
> **Result:** The contract is a services contract, so QuickDri must perform at least 50 percent of the cost of the contract incurred for

personnel with its own employees. Even though neither subcontractor will perform more work than QuickDri, Bob's company is in violation of the subcontracting limits because it will only perform 45 percent of the cost of the contract incurred for personnel with its own forces.

What If My Subcontractor Is a Small Business?

Unlike affiliation, a subcontractor's size is irrelevant for purposes of the subcontracting limits. If you subcontract work in excess of the subcontracting limits to any other company, you are in violation of the FAR, even if the other company is small, and even if the sizes of your two companies, aggregated, fall beneath the applicable size standard.

Harr-Ball Limos wins a limousine services contract, set-aside for small businesses under a $7 million size standard. Harr-Ball subcontracts 55 percent of the cost of the contract incurred for personnel to Mediocre Transportation Services, Inc., a company Harry found in the Yellow Pages. Harr- Ball's three-year average annual receipts are $1.5 million. Mediocre's three-year average annual receipts are $5 million.

Result: Mediocre and Harr-Ball are likely affiliated under the ostensible subcontractor rule, but their affiliation will not render Harr-Ball ineligible, because the companies' combined sizes fall below $7 million. Nevertheless, Harr-Ball has violated the subcontracting limitation by subcontracting more than 50 percent of the cost of the contract incurred for personnel. The government may terminate Harr-Ball's contract for default or take other action against the company.

When Do the Subcontracting Limits Apply?

The subcontracting limits described in this chapter apply to all *small business set-aside* procurements. They do not apply to *unrestricted* procurements—that is, contracts not set-aside for small businesses. Unrestricted procurements typically have no subcontracting limits; as long as your contract doesn't prohibit it, you can subcontract as much work as you like.

> BrettWorks wins an unrestricted contract for administrative services. Brett decides to subcontract 65 percent of the cost of the contract incurred by personnel to Draper's Papers.
>
> **Result:** The contract is unrestricted, so the subcontracting limits do not apply. Unless BrettWorks' contract says otherwise, BrettWorks' subcontracting arrangement is perfectly valid.

Contracts set-aside for various subcategories of small businesses—8(a), service-disabled veteran-owned, women-owned, and HUBZone—do have subcontracting limits, but the rules vary somewhat. For example, on a HUBZone set-aside contract, your small business may satisfy the limitations on subcontracting by subcontracting to other HUBZone firms (though not to "ordinary" small businesses). We will discuss the subcontracting limits for these programs in greater detail in Chapters 11 through 14.

What Provisions Must Be Included in Subcontracts?

You've met a potential subcontractor, shook hands on a deal, and are ready to put your subcontract agreement in writing. So what now? Do you dust off your standard commercial purchase order and insert the subcontractor's name? If you do, you're not alone. When it comes to subcontracts, small government contractors often rely upon hastily drafted purchase orders or try to tweak their commercial subcontracts to fit government work.

They shouldn't.

Your government subcontracts should look very different from your commercial subcontracts and purchase orders. If you're in the mood for a little light reading, flip through the FAR sometime, and you will see why. Many of the FAR clauses that appear in your prime contract include language like, "The Contractor shall insert this clause in every subcontract or purchase order."

These required insertions are commonly called *flow downs*. Failing to flow down a mandatory FAR clause to your subcontractor is a violation of your prime contract, and can leave your small business on the hook for your subcontractor's violations.

> XPert Constructors wins a federal construction contract. XPert issues a large subcontract to Big Time Construction. However, although the contract is subject to the federal Davis-Bacon Act, which requires contractors to pay prevailing wages and fringe benefits on construction contracts, XPert does not flow down the FAR's Davis-Bacon Act clauses to Big Time. Big Time does not pay its employees the wages and benefits required by the Davis-Bacon Act. The underpayments amount to $200,000.
>
> **Result:** After an investigation, the Department of Labor requires XPert to pay Big Time's employees $200,000 in back wages. XPert cannot recoup the $200,000 from Big Time, because, due to XPert's failure to flow down the clauses, Big Time had no contractual obligation to comply with the Davis-Bacon Act. XPert is stuck paying Big Time's tab.

XPert's predicament is not a hypothetical horror story. The example is based on a real decision issued by the United States District Court for the District of Columbia a few years ago.[2] After forking over $200,000 in back wages to its subcontractor's employees, you can bet that the contractor on the losing end of the case has ironclad flow-down provisions in its subcontracts these days. (If you're worried about figuring out the wages and benefits you must pay under the

Davis-Bacon Act, take a deep breath. We're getting there. We will discuss the Davis-Bacon Act and other wage and benefit requirements in Chapter 7.)

How Do I Flow Down FAR Clauses?

Perhaps the easiest way to flow down required clauses is by using an *incorporation by reference* provision in the subcontract. This provision refers to the prime contract, and tells the subcontractor that all clauses required to be flowed down are deemed included in the subcontract. A typical incorporation by reference provision might read something like this:

> This Subcontract incorporates, to the fullest extent possible, all Federal Acquisition Regulation (FAR) and other clauses required by the Prime Contract and/or applicable law to be included in this Subcontract, as well as all provisions of the Prime Contract applicable to Subcontractor. Prime Contractor and Subcontractor will comply with all such clauses with the same force and effect as if they were given in full text herein. Where the words "Contracting Officer" and "Government" appear in the Prime Contract, or any clauses incorporated by reference into the Prime Contract, such terms shall be deemed to refer to Prime Contractor's Program Manager and Prime Contractor, respectively, as applicable. Where the word "Contractor" appears in the Prime Contract, or in any clauses incorporated by reference into the Prime Contract, such word shall be deemed to refer to Subcontractor.

Don't just copy this example out of the book, throw it into your subcontracts and consider the job done. The clause needs to fit with the remainder of your subcontract. For example, the remaining portions of your subcontract may use the companies' names instead of the terms "Prime Contractor" and "Subcontractor," or you may have a "Project Manager" instead of a "Program Manager." Adjust the clause to fit your subcontract (or the subcontract to fit the clause).

The downside of using a broad generic incorporation by reference provision, which essentially asks the subcontractor to figure out for itself what is contained in its subcontract, is that it could give the subcontractor an opening to argue that it wasn't properly notified of what was required of it. For this reason, you should always give the subcontractor a copy of the prime contract, so the subcontractor will not be able to later contend that it had no idea that a particular clause was included.

Even after providing the subcontractor with a copy of the prime contract, some government contractors are wary of using nothing more than a generic incorporation by reference provision. Many government contractors identify, by name, particular "hot button" clauses, such as the Davis-Bacon Act clause described above, in their subcontracts. Some provide a complete checklist of all flowed-down clauses, or even copies of the clauses themselves (which can run hundreds of pages). You probably do not need to go this far, but be sure to satisfy yourself that your subcontractor is on notice of its flow-down obligations, especially for critical issues like wages, benefits, conflicts of interest, and ethical requirements.

In addition, an incorporation by reference provision alone does not meet the requirements of a few FAR clauses. For example, if FAR 52.203-12, regarding improper payments to influence federal officials, is included in your prime contract, you must obtain a formal certification from every subcontractor with a subcontract of $150,000 or more stating that, to the best of the subcontractor's knowledge, "no Federal appropriated funds have been paid or will be paid to any person for influencing or attempting to influence an officer or employee of any agency, a Member of Congress, an officer or employee of Congress, or an employee of a Member of Congress on its behalf in connection with the awarding of" the subcontract.[3] Often, prime contractors include this language in their subcontracts, and the subcontractor's signature on the subcontract constitutes the certification. Check your contract for other clauses that might require you to obtain a certification, rather than merely flowing down the clause.

What If My Subcontractor Rejects a Flow-Down Clause?

Sometimes—particularly when you deal with a subcontractor new to government contracting—a prospective subcontractor may refuse to sign a subcontract containing a flow-down clause the subcontractor finds objectionable. What do you do?

Explain to the subcontractor that you are contractually obligated to flow down the clause. If you do not, you will be in breach of your prime contract, and the government could terminate your contract for default—costing the subcontractor its work, too. If the subcontractor still refuses to budge, it's time to move on and find a new teammate. After all, if the subcontractor is okay with asking you to breach your obligations to the government (and bear the attendant risks) is this really someone you want to work with for the next several years?

What Other Provisions Should I Include in My Subcontract?

Your subcontract is much more than a vehicle to comply with your FAR flow-down obligations—it is the roadmap to your relationship with your subcontractor. Your subcontract should answer questions like:

- What work will the subcontractor perform? Be specific to avoid later disputes about the scope of work. If the contract is set-aside for small businesses, remember to satisfy the subcontracting limitations.

- How and when will you pay the subcontractor? You may wish to include a *pay-when-paid* clause, stating that the subcontractor is not entitled to payment until the government pays your small business for the subcontractor's work. Without a pay-when-paid clause, the subcontractor will likely be entitled to payment even if the government drags its feet, which could cause you cash flow problems.

- How will you handle confidential information? You and your subcontractor may collaborate on the proposal, share pricing structures, and other confidential business information. You will probably want to include provisions prohibiting each company from releasing the other's confidential information.

- When does the subcontract end? The government has the ability to *terminate for convenience*, that is, end your prime contract whenever it wishes, even if you have done nothing wrong. This might occur, for example, if Congress does not appropriate necessary funds to continue the contract work or if a change in policy makes the contract unnecessary (such as if you have been producing radar for a new fighter jet, but the Pentagon decides not to buy the jet).

- How will disputes be resolved? You should consider including a *pass-through* clause, requiring the subcontractor to seek redress from the government for damages it causes the subcontractor—rather than suing you.

Generally, so long as a subcontract provision does not interfere with your obligations to the government, you can include it, even if it is not required by the FAR or other law. Give your subcontract some thought and craft a document that protects your interests. If a dispute arises later (and you'd be surprised how often this happens, even among friends), you will be very glad you did.

You may also wish to ask your subcontractor to make additional certifications about its ethics and capabilities, such as asking the subcontractor to certify that:

- It is not aware of any actual or potential organizational conflicts of interest or personal conflicts of interest with respect to its subcontract work, and will promptly report any actual or potential conflicts to you (we will discuss conflicts of interest in greater detail in Chapter 8).
- It is in good financial health and has the resources and capacity to perform the subcontract.

- All subcontract work will be performed with a high degree of professionalism and competence, and will meet current industry standards.

- It has had the opportunity to review the prime contract and applicable FAR clauses, and will comply with them.

- It will comply with any other applicable federal, state, or local laws.

None of these certifications should be troublesome for an ethical and financially sound subcontractor. If your subcontractor balks at providing one of these certifications, consider it a big, waving red flag.

Do I Need a Subcontracting Plan?

A *subcontracting plan* is a written policy statement establishing goals and procedures for ensuring that small businesses and various subcategories of small businesses (like service-disabled veteran-owned small businesses and women-owned small businesses) receive a fair share of government subcontracts. Under the FAR, companies generally must adopt written subcontracting plans whenever they receive contracts in excess of $650,000 (or $1.5 million if the contract calls for the construction of a federal facility).

Here's the good news: As long as a solicitation is set-aside for small businesses (or subcategories of small businesses), you do not need to adopt a subcontracting plan. In addition, even if the solicitation is unrestricted, you need not adopt a subcontracting plan if your company qualifies as "small" under the NAICS code designated for the procurement.

QuickDri submits a proposal on an unrestricted dry cleaning solicitation. The NAICS code for the solicitation carries a $5 million revenue-based size standard. QuickDri's three-year average annual receipts fall beneath the size standard.

> **Result:** QuickDri is a small business for purposes of the solicitation. It is not required to submit a subcontracting plan.

Remember, though, that whether your business qualifies as "small" is a moving target. If QuickDri was a $7 million company, it would have been required to submit a subcontracting plan for a procurement carrying a $5 million size standard, even though it would still qualify as "small" for many other government contracts with different NAICS codes.

Your small business probably bids primarily on set-aside contracts and other contracts for which it qualifies as small, and will not need to worry about subcontracting plans (at least not until you grow bigger). Because most small businesses do not need subcontracting plans, we do not discuss them further in this book, except for a brief discussion about special subcontracting rules for tribally owned companies in Chapter 15. However, if you find yourself in need of a subcontracting plan, look to FAR 19.7 and the clause at FAR 52.219-9 for guidance as to what to include.

Disclosing Subcontracts to the Government

Call it "transparency," "oversight," or plain old "red tape," but in recent years, the government has placed increased burdens on contractors to report certain information about their contracting practices. As of 2011, your small business must report the following information about each subcontractor holding a subcontract valued at $25,000 or more:

- Name
- Data Universal Numbering System (DUNS) number for both the subcontractor and its parent company (if any)

- Address, including city, state, ZIP code, country, and congressional district
- Primary performance location
- Amount of the subcontract award
- Date of the subcontract award
- Description of the products or services being provided under the subcontract
- Subcontract number (assigned by your small business)
- Prime contract number and order number, if applicable
- Awarding agency name and code
- Funding agency name and code
- Government contracting office code
- Treasury account symbol, as reported in the Federal Procurement Data System
- The applicable NAICS code

You should already have most of this information available (such as the subcontractor's name, the awarding agency name, and so on), but you may need your subcontractor's assistance to determine whether the subcontractor has a parent company. You can find the subcontractor's DUNS number and address with a little online research, but you may wish to ask the subcontractor to provide this information, too. Consider including a provision in your subcontract agreement requiring the subcontractor to provide you with all information reasonably necessary to satisfy your disclosure obligation.

Where Do I Report Subcontracting Information?

You must report subcontracting information online at the Federal Funding Accountability and Transparency Act website, www.fsrs.gov. Be aware that the government will not keep this information confidential—quite the opposite, in fact. Once you provide the government with your subcontracting information, the government will publish it online at www.usaspending.gov for all the world to see (if you're curious who your competitors have been subcontracting with, you might want to take a look at the *usapending.gov* website yourself).

When Must I Report Subcontracting Information?

You must initially report the subcontracting information by the end of the month following the month the subcontract was awarded. After that, you must update the information by the end of the month following the month you make any amendment or modification to the subcontract that changes previously reported data.

In May, Draper's Papers wins a government contract for printing services. That same month, it awards a $500,000 subcontract to BrettWorks for administrative assistance on the contract. In October, the government amends Draper's Papers' prime contract to add additional work (and additional funds). The following month, Draper's Papers and BrettWorks agree to a $100,000 increase in BrettWorks' subcontract.

Result: Draper's Papers must report its subcontract with BrettWorks by the end of June (the month following the award of the subcontract). It must update its subcontract report by the end of November (the month following the amendment to BrettWorks' subcontract).

If the government will identify your subcontractor on a public database, why did we suggest in our "loose lips sink ships" discussion in Chapter 2 that you avoid press releases or other public statements naming the subcontractor if you are worried about a potential ostensible subcontractor problem? Simple answer: timing.

If you win a set-aside contract, your competitors have only five business days to file a size protest. (Of course, the same short deadline applies if you want to protest a competitor's size, so act quickly if that is the case). To continue the nautical theme, by the time you report your subcontract on www.fsrs.gov and the government posts the information on www.usaspending.gov, your competitors will have missed the size protest boat.

The Primary Rules: Where to Find Them

Here's where to find the primary rules discussed in this chapter:

- FAR 9.405-2 and FAR 52.209-6 (subcontracting with suspended or debarred contractors)
- 13 C.F.R. § 125.6 and FAR 52.219-14 (limitations on subcontracting)
- FAR 19.7 and FAR 52.219-9 (subcontracting plans)
- FAR 4.1403 and FAR 52.204-10 (disclosing subcontract information)

Compliance at a Glance: The Wide World of Subcontracting

❑ Use the EPLS database at *epls.gov* to determine whether all prospective subcontractors are suspended, debarred, or proposed for debarment (recommended).

❑ Do not award any subcontract in excess of $30,000 to a company suspended, debarred, or proposed for debarment, unless there is a compelling reason to do so, and you provide prior written notification to the contracting officer.

❑ Obtain certifications from all subcontractors stating that they are not suspended, debarred, or proposed for debarment.

- ❑ For services contracts, perform more than 50 percent of the cost of the contract incurred for personnel with your own employees.

- ❑ For manufacturing and supply contracts (except contracts for procurement from a non-manufacturer in such supplies or products), perform at least 50 percent of the cost of manufacturing the supplies or products with your own employees.

- ❑ For general construction contracts, perform at least 15 percent of the cost of the contract with your own employees.

- ❑ For special trade construction contracts, perform at least 25 percent of the cost of the contract with your own employees.

- ❑ Flow down all required FAR clauses to your subcontractors.

- ❑ In addition to using an incorporation by reference provision, specifically highlight "hot-button" flow-down clauses, such as those dealing with wages, benefits, conflicts, and ethics (recommended).

- ❑ Ensure that your subcontract answers questions such as what work the subcontractor will perform, how and when you will pay the subcontractor, how you will treat confidential information, how the subcontract can be terminated, and how disputes will be resolved (recommended).

- ❑ Obtain all required certifications from your subcontractors, including the certification that federal funds have not been used to influence government employees or officials with respect to the contract award.

- ❑ Ask your subcontractor to certify that it has no conflicts, has the financial capability to perform the contract, will perform to high professional standards, and will comply with all applicable laws (recommended).

- ❑ For all subcontract awards of $25,000 or more, report the subcontract on the fsrs.gov website by the end of the month following the month of the subcontract award.

- ❑ For all subcontracts reported on the fsrs.gov website, update the report by the end of the month following the month of any amendment or modification to any of the information previously provided.

CHAPTER 5

Uncle Sam, HR Director: Hiring Restrictions and Requirements

AFTER READING the first four chapters, you know how to determine whether your business qualifies as small and how to create compliant subcontracting relationships with other companies—not always the easiest task. But in addition to imposing requirements governing the companies you work with, Uncle Sam has a lot to say about the employees you can hire.

In this chapter, we will discuss which individuals your small business cannot (or should not) hire, and how to spot employee-related red flags. And remember our discussion of the "right of first refusal" in Chapter 3? We will also discuss which incumbent contract employees you must offer to hire—even if you would rather not.

Hiring Restrictions

Broadly speaking, your small business may pick its own employees, with minimal governmental interference (although the government may evaluate some proposals more favorably if you propose highly experienced personnel in key positions). However, the government restricts your ability to hire three categories of people: so-called non-responsible individuals, individuals not authorized to work in the United States, and current and former government employees.

Non-Responsible Individuals

The government may refuse to award a contract to your small business if it finds that one or more of your company's *principals*—that is, any officer, director, owner, or partner in the business—as well as any person having primary management or supervisory authority within the business (such as a general manager, plant manager, or head of a subsidiary or division) is *non-responsible*. Your small business runs a significant risk of a non-responsibility determination if any of its principals:

- Is suspended, debarred, or proposed for debarment from federal government contracting. A *suspended* individual is one who has been prohibited from contracting with the government for a relatively short period (such as six months), while a *debarred* individual is barred from government contracting for a longer period (three years is typical).

- Has, within a three-year period preceding your offer on a government contract, been convicted of fraud or any similar criminal offense in connection with a public contract (including state and local contracts) or had a civil judgment rendered against him or her for similar reasons.

- Has, within a three-year period preceding your offer on a government contract, been convicted of embezzlement, theft, forgery, bribery, falsification or destruction of records, making false statements, tax evasion, violating federal criminal tax laws, or receiving stolen property.

- Is presently indicted for, or otherwise criminally or civilly charged by a governmental entity (including state and local governments) of any of the offenses identified in the two bullets immediately above.

- Has, within a three-year period preceding an offer, been notified of any delinquent federal taxes in an amount that exceeds $3,000, for which the liability remains unsatisfied.

> In March, Gus's Buses, a transportation company, hires a new vice president, Sammy. The following month, Gus's Buses submits a proposal on a federal solicitation for bus services. Unbeknownst to Gus, Sammy was debarred from all government contracting a year earlier, after offering gratuities to a contracting officer.
>
> **Result:** The government will likely deem Gus's Buses ineligible for award because Sammy, one of its principals, is considered a non-responsible individual.

What should Gus have done differently? First, do you remember the Excluded Parties List System, where you can discover if a company or individual has been suspended or debarred? Had Gus checked the EPLS before hiring Sammy, he probably would have discovered the debarment and moved on to another candidate. You should consult the EPLS anytime you hire someone as a "principal," but the safest course of action is to review it before hiring *anyone*—after all, that impressive young administrative assistant you hire today may make her way up the ladder to an important management position in a few years' time.

Second, even if Gus hadn't found Sammy on the EPLS, Gus's Buses should have required Sammy to certify in writing that he was not suspended or debarred—either as part of a comprehensive employment agreement or employee handbook, or as a stand-alone certification. If Sammy falsely certified that he was responsible, Gus's Buses might still have lost the contract, but would likely stand a better chance of avoiding more severe penalties. In addition, Sammy's false certification would probably give Gus all the legal cover he would need to terminate Sammy from his position, and perhaps even recover damages from Sammy in a lawsuit.

Whenever you hire employees, you should strongly consider requiring them to certify in writing that they are individually responsible. Don't limit the certification to suspensions or debarments; ask the job candidate to certify as to all four responsibility criteria described above. And of course, if you're not comfortable relying on a prospective employee's certification, you may wish to consider a formal background check to help you determine whether the individual is non-responsible. In addition, keep in mind that even a "squeaky-clean" job candidate may run into legal problems after you hire her. Consider requiring your employees to promptly report to you if they are convicted, suspended, or debarred, and so on, *after* they are hired.

Finding out whether a principal has been deemed non-responsible is especially important because, when you submit proposals for most federal procurements, you must certify that your company and its principals are responsible (or inform the procuring agency of any problems). A false certification is subject to criminal penalties, including the possibility of imprisonment. Don't rely upon your gut feeling that your principals are good people. After all, one of your top managers may spend his weekends rescuing kittens from trees and helping old ladies cross the street, but still owe $50,000 in back taxes. Do your due diligence.

A conviction or other stain on an individual's record of responsibility does not last forever. If you hire someone whose last brush with the law or other non-responsible behavior occurred more than three years prior to your offer on a federal procurement, you need not report the matter as part of your responsibility certification.

Bob's cousin, Shari, was convicted of fraud 12 years ago. Since then, she has had no legal or tax troubles—not even a parking ticket. Bob offers her a job managing one of QuickDri's government contracts, and Shari accepts. Bob does not inform the procuring agency of Shari's conviction.

Result: Because Shari's conviction occurred more than three years earlier, Bob need not report it to the procuring agency. Shari is eligible to serve as a principal of QuickDri.

Allowing someone with a documented history of criminal dishonesty to serve as a high-ranking officer in your company may not be the wisest move from a business perspective, but if the behavior occurred long ago, it won't violate the FAR.

Authorization to Work in the United States

If your small business performs a federal government contract within the United States, every employee who works on the contract must be eligible to work in the country. As a federal contractor, you will likely be required to use the *E-Verify* system to ensure that your employees are eligible.

E-Verify is an online system that compares information from an employee's Form I-9 (Employment Eligibility Verification) with data in governmental records to determine whether the employee is eligible to work in the United States. If your business is not already enrolled, it must enroll in E-Verify within 30 calendar days after being awarded a government contract over $150,000, unless the work will be performed outside the United States, will be completed in less than 120 days, or is solely to provide commercially available off-the-shelf items. You may register your business online at https://e-verify.uscis.gov/enroll/. If you are already enrolled, but have not registered as a federal contractor, you should update your status.

Verifying Your Employees Using E-Verify. Enrolling in E-Verify is just the first step. After your business enrolls, you must initiate *verification* of each employee assigned to the contract within 90 calendar days after enrollment, or within 30 days after the employee is assigned to the contract, whichever is later. Verification involves entering data about that employee into the E-Verify system (a process the system calls "creating a case" about the employee). The system confirms that the employee is authorized to work in the United States, or issues a so-called "tentative non-confirmation," of authorization. You may use E-Verify for years without ever receiving a tentative non-confirmation, but if one appears, the employee has the right to challenge it. Visit the United States Citizenship and Immigration Services (USCIS) website (www.uscis.gov) for information about how to resolve the situation.

Note that you need not verify all of your existing employees, only those assigned to the government contract (though you may choose to verify existing employees). However, 90 days after enrollment, the government presumes that you are successfully up and running with E-Verify. From then on, you must initiate verification of each new hire within three business days after the employee is hired, regardless of whether he or she is assigned to the contract.

Let's look at three examples of how the E-Verify time periods work in practice:

New Bids on the Block, Inc., an IT services company, hires Jose as its vice president. New Bids' choice proves wise, as two months later, Jose helps New Bids win its first government contract, valued at $1 million. Ten days after the award, New Bids enrolls in E-Verify. The same day, it hires Carly as an assistant project manager and assigns her to the contract. It does not assign Jose to the contract.

Result: Because New Bids is still within the initial 90-day period following enrollment, it has 70 more days in which to initiate verification of Carly. Jose was hired before the expiration of the 90-day period, and is not assigned to the contract, so New Bids need not verify Jose.

My Big Tow, Inc., a towing company, wins a $1 million government contract for towing. Ten days after award, My Big Tow enrolls in E-Verify. Seventy-five days after enrollment, My Big Tow hires Vanessa as a driver and assigns her to the contract.

Result: Because My Big Tow is still within the initial 90-day period, New Bids has 30 days in which to initiate verification of Vanessa.

My Big Tow, Inc., wins a $1 million government contract for towing services. Ten days after award, My Big Tow enrolls in E-Verify. Five months after enrollment, My Big Tow signs a separate contract to provide towing services to Ball-Mart, a commercial retailer of golf balls, tennis balls, and baseballs. Two days later, My Big Tow hires Dmitri as its project manager for the Ball-Mart contract. Dmitri is not involved in the government towing services contract.

Result: My Big Tow is now outside the initial 90-day E-Verify period. My Big Tow must initiate verification of Dmitri within three days of his hire. It makes no difference that Dmitri will not work on the government contract; after the initial 90-day period expires, My Big Tow must verify *all* of its new employees.

Employees like Jose, who are hired before the initial 90-day period ends and who are not assigned to a government contract, are essentially "grandfathered in," and need not be verified. However, you may wish to consider verifying your entire workforce, simply so that you will have the flexibility to move employees between government and non-government work without worrying about their verification statuses.

Exceptions to E-Verify Verification. There are four exceptions to the E-Verify employee verification requirement. You need not verify an employee if:

- You hired the employee on or before November 6, 1986.

- The employee holds an active security clearance for access to confidential, secret, or top secret information.

- The employee has undergone a complete background investigation and received credentials pursuant to Homeland Security Presidential Directive HSPD-12 (Policy for a Common Identification Standard for Federal Employees and Contractors).

- You previously verified the employee's eligibility through E-Verify.

> PayStubs, LLC, wins a $1 million government contract for payroll processing services. Ten days after award, PayStubs enrolls in E-Verify. Seventy-five days after enrollment, PayStubs hires Marty as a data entry clerk and assigns him to the contract. PayStubs initiates verification of Marty five days after hiring him, and the system confirms his eligibility. Eight months later, PayStubs wins a second government contract, and reassigns Marty to the new contract.
>
> **Result:** Because PayStubs verified Marty after it hired him, PayStubs does not need to verify Marty again after his reassignment.

As the example suggests, once you have verified your entire workforce (assuming you do so), your E-Verify obligations will be limited to new hires. Although E-Verify may be a bit of a hassle when you first get started, it will soon be just another item on your "to do" list whenever you hire someone new.

E-Verify Posters. Do you have a lot of empty wall space in an area of your business readily accessible to your employees, like a break room or lunchroom? If not, you might need to find a new home for those wall calendars and prints of *Starry Night* currently on display. The government requires its contractors to hang various posters for its employees' benefit, including posters related to E-Verify (we will discuss other posters in Chapters 6, 7, and 8).

Once you enroll your business in E-Verify, you must hang an E-Verify poster in a readily accessible area. You must display both English and Spanish versions of the posters. In addition, you must display a "Right to Work" poster (also in English and Spanish), notifying employees of their rights not to be denied employment due to their national origin or citizenship, unless authorized by law. (See Chapter 6 for a discussion of your non-discrimination obligations.)

The E-Verify website will prompt you to download the posters when you enroll. You can also download the posters from the USCIS website. No one will mistake the posters for Van Gogh, but at least you will be complying with the law.

What About My Subcontractors? You must flow down the E-Verify clause, FAR 52.222-54, to any subcontractor that holds a subcontract in excess of $3,000 and will perform any of its work in the United States. In addition to using a general incorporation by reference provision, you should consider specifically identifying the E-Verify clause as one of your "hot-button" flow-down clauses in your subcontract (see the discussion in Chapter 4 for more about incorporating FAR clauses into your subcontracts).

Hiring Current and Former Government Employees

Wouldn't it be wonderful if you could hire former government employees to help develop your government contracting business? After all, who better to give you insight on the government's procurement needs? To top it off, a former government employee may have a Rolodex full of friendly procuring officials who might be more inclined to make an award to your company if someone they know and trust works for you.

Contractors frequently hire former government employees for these very reasons. But if you are thinking about hiring a current or former government official, you must be very careful. To avoid favoritism or perceived favoritism, the government restricts your ability to make employment offers to current federal employees, hire certain former government employees (such as individuals involved in awarding contracts to your small business or administering your company's government contracts), and assign certain tasks to those former government employees you do hire.

Offering to Hire Current Federal Employees. A statute called the Procurement Integrity Act prohibits a federal employee from discussing non-federal employment (i.e., working for your small business) with you, if two factors exist:

1. Your small business is currently participating in a procurement exceeding $150,000.

2. The federal employee in question is participating "personally and substantially" in the procurement.

Over an eight-month period, Harr-Ball Limos submits five proposals to the Army, but loses them all. Harry grows frustrated and believes he needs a fresh approach to pursuing business with the Army. After Harr-Ball submits its sixth proposal, for a $750,000 limousine services contract, Harry approaches Megan, the contracting officer for the procurement. Harry tells her that Harr-Ball will double whatever the government is currently paying her if she will join Harr-Ball and help it win Army contracts. Megan says she is not interested, but does not disqualify herself from the procurement. The next week, Harry calls Megan and repeats the offer.

Result: Harr-Ball is currently participating in a procurement in which Megan is personally and substantially involved, and the procurement exceeds $150,000. If Harry knows that Megan has not disqualified herself from the procurement, Harr-Ball's job offer to Megan violates the Procurement Integrity Act.

From Megan's perspective, Harry's job offer is more than a minor *faux pas*. Megan must report the offer, in writing, to her supervisor and an Army ethics official. In addition, she must immediately reject the offer, or—if she is interested—disqualify herself from the procurement. If Harry knows that Megan has not taken one or more of these steps and continues to discuss employment with her, Harry and Harr-Ball will break the law and could be subjected to severe criminal and civil penalties, including fines and potential jail time.

It should be obvious why the Procurement Integrity Act restricts conduct like Harry's job offer to Megan: If Megan is interested in Harry's offer, she will have a strong incentive to skew the results of the competition in favor of her future employer. In that light, although Harry probably made an innocent mistake, Harry's "double your salary" opportunity looks like little more than a bribe.

Even if all three factors are met, the government might not penalize you for making an employment contact if you legitimately thought the government employee in question had reported the contact and disqualified herself from the procurement, but she had not done so. But given the penalties that come with violations of the Procurement Integrity Act, why take the risk? The best practice is to avoid employment contacts with current federal employees whenever the two criteria described above exist.

Procurement Integrity and the Druyun Case. The government takes Procurement Integrity Act violations very seriously. Darlene Druyun and Michael Sears, the central figures in perhaps the highest-profile Procurement Integrity Act case, learned this lesson the hard way.

In 2002, shortly after Druyun resigned her position as a high-level Air Force procurement official, Boeing hired her. A subsequent investigation revealed that Sears, Boeing's chief financial officer, had engaged in employment negotiations with Druyun while she was still with the Air Force. Instead of reporting Boeing's offers, as required by law, Druyun helped steer contracts worth hundreds of millions of dollars to her future employer.

Boeing avoided suspension and debarment—but only after agreeing to pay a whopping $615 million fine (Boeing's CEO also stepped down as a result of the scandal). Druyun and Sears went to jail, paid thousands of dollars in fines, and performed hundreds of hours of community service.

Hiring Former Government Employees. You can make all the job offers you like to *former* government employees without running afoul of the Procurement Integrity Act. However, you cannot actually *hire* a former government employee for pay within one year after a certain event occurred, if:

- The former employee served, at the time of the selection of your small business for award of a government contract, as the procuring contracting officer, the source selection authority, a member of the source selection evaluation board, or the chief of a financial or technical evaluation team, and the contract you were awarded is valued in excess of $10 million.

- The former employee served as the program manager, deputy program manager, or administrative contracting officer for a contract in excess of $10 million awarded to your small business.

- The former employee personally made, on behalf of the agency, the decision to award a contract, subcontract, modification, task order, delivery order, settlement, or other payments to your small business in excess of $10 million.

The Navy awards XPert Constructors a $15 million design/build contract. Fifteen months later, Ricardo, the Navy's program manager for the contract, resigns and embarks on a six-month backpacking trip across Europe. When Ricardo returns to the United States, XPert offers him a job at an annual salary of $105,000, paid biweekly. Ricardo accepts and begins work the following month.

Result: Because the contract was valued in excess of $10 million and Ricardo served as the government's program manager, XPert was required to wait one year after Ricardo's resignation to hire him. By hiring him sooner, XPert violated the Procurement Integrity Act.

Why does the example mention Ricardo's salary and XPert's bi-weekly pay period? You only violate the Procurement Integrity Act if you *pay compensation* to a covered former government employee within the one-year "cooling off" period. If, for some reason, Ricardo had been willing to work for free for a few months, XPert would not have violated the law (so long as it did not assign him to a prohibited task, as we will discuss below).

The one-year period does not always begin when the former government employee leaves government service. If the former government employee was involved in the award decision, but not the administration of your contract, you can hire the employee once more than a year has passed since the award.

The Navy awards Buck's Trucking a $15 million transportation contract. Sarah, a member of the source selection board responsible for the award to Buck's Trucking, is not involved in the administration of the contract. Fifteen months after the award, Sarah resigns. Buck's Trucking hires Sarah three weeks later at an annual salary of $85,000, paid biweekly.

Result: Buck's Trucking's hiring of Sarah does not violate the Procurement Integrity Act because more than a year has elapsed since Sarah served on the source selection board.

What if your company does not anticipate a $10 million contract award anytime soon? Do you have anything to worry about when it comes to hiring former government employees?

The Procurement Integrity Act should not be a problem, so long as you do not assign the former government employee to a prohibited activity (discussed below). However, you should still be wary about hiring government employees who have served in key positions on contracts you intend to bid on in the future. Even if the hiring is legally permissible, you may nevertheless run the risk of a bid protest alleging that the employee provides your company with an unfair competitive advantage. We will discuss unfair competitive advantages, and other organizational conflicts of interest, in Chapter 8.

Prohibited Activities for Former Government Employees

If you hire a former government employee, you must be careful not to assign the employee certain tasks that are prohibited under the Procurement Integrity Act. Unlike the hiring restrictions, the "improper tasks" restrictions do not carry a $10 million threshold, but apply no matter the value of your government contracts.

Switching Sides. A government employee *switches sides* when he or she:

- Makes any appearance before the government in connection with a particular matter in which the employee participated personally and substantially as a government employee, or
- Makes any written or oral communication on behalf of another person or entity to the government in connection with a particular matter in which the employee participated personally and substantially as a government employee

Draper's Papers is performing a printing contract for the Department of State. Jill, the contracting officer overseeing Draper's Papers' performance, resigns. After waiting out the one-year "cooling off" period, Draper's Papers hires Jill as a senior vice president. Jill promptly arranges a meeting with the current contracting officer

> for the contract, urging him to exercise an option to extend Draper's Papers' period of performance for another year.
>
> **Result:** Because Jill was personally and substantially involved in the contract when she worked for the government, she cannot switch sides and represent the contractor. Jill's meeting with the contracting officer violates the Procurement Integrity Act.

When it comes to switching sides, there is no cooling off period. Former government employees are banned for life from switching sides.

Matters Under a Former Government Employee's Jurisdiction. Even if a former government employee was not personally and substantially involved in a matter, the former employee is prohibited, for a period of two years after leaving the government, from representing your small business regarding a matter that was actually pending under the former government official's jurisdiction during his or her last year of government employment.

> After one of XPert Constructors' competitors wins a small business set-aside contract, XPert files a size protest with the SBA. Lisa is in charge of the SBA area office evaluating the size protest. However, she is not personally involved in evaluating the protest. Lisa resigns and, one week later, is hired by XPert. In the interim, the SBA denies XPert's size protest. When Lisa joins XPert, she promptly writes an appeal on XPert's behalf and files it with the SBA's Office of Hearings and Appeals.
>
> **Result:** Because the size protest was pending under Lisa's jurisdiction during her last year with the SBA, she cannot represent XPert with respect to the matter, despite her lack of personal involvement. By representing XPert in its appeal, Lisa has violated the Procurement Integrity Act.

Did you notice that XPert hired Lisa just a week after she left the SBA? Hiring her was not a violation of the Procurement Integrity Act, unless XPert had a contract in excess of $10 million with the SBA and Lisa was involved in that contract (in which case the one-year cooling off period would have applied). The problem arose when Lisa contacted her former employer about a matter that had been pending under her jurisdiction shortly after joining XPert's staff.

Special Restrictions for Senior Government Officials. If you hire a former *senior* government official, the restriction extends beyond matters in which the former employee was personally involved or had jurisdiction. A former senior government official may not, for a period of one year after leaving government employment, represent your small business before the agency in which the former official served during his or her last year of government employment. The former employee is not prohibited from making social contacts with former colleagues, but may not seek official action by the agency on behalf of your small business within the one-year period.

Gus's father, Bartholomew, retires after a lengthy naval career, with the rank of vice admiral. Two months later, Bartholomew (who steadfastly refuses to answer to "Bart") becomes restless and decides to help his son build up Gus's Buses' business. After Gus puts Bartholomew on Gus's Buses' payroll, Bartholomew calls a few former high-ranking Navy colleagues and suggests that they award contracts to Gus's Buses.

Result: Because Bartholomew is a former senior Navy official, he cannot contact the Navy on Gus's Buses' behalf (or anyone else's) until one year after his retirement, even on matters completely unrelated to his command. His calls to Navy officials violate the Procurement Integrity Act.

If you hire a former senior government employee, remember that the prohibition on representation applies only to contacts with officials of the agency (or agencies) in which the senior employee served during the last year of government employment. For example, Bartholomew might have met a number of Department of State employees during his Navy service. Had he contacted these employees on Gus's Buses' behalf, he would not have committed a violation.

What if Bartholomew had called up his old Navy buddies, told them that he was working at Gus's Buses, and left it at that? Again, Bartholomew would have been in the clear. The prohibition only applies if the former government employee seeks official action. In the example, Bartholomew's calls to the Navy were just fine, but his request that the Navy award contracts to Gus's Buses crossed the line.

So who is a "senior" government official, anyway? Senior government officials include active duty military officials with a pay grade of O-7 or above, certain civilian employees in higher pay grades, and employees appointed to certain high-ranking positions. If you hire a vice admiral like Bartholomew (or someone with an equally impressive title), you can be pretty confident that he is a former senior official. But if you are uncertain as to whether a former government employee was "senior," you should check with the agency's ethics office before authorizing the employee to represent your small business before the agency within the one-year period.

The Right of First Refusal

Now that you know which individuals your business cannot (or should not) hire, it's time to look at the other side of the coin: the individuals you *must attempt to hire*, at least in some circumstances. As you know from Chapter 3, in January 2009, shortly after taking office, President Obama issued Executive Order 13495, titled "Nondisplacement of Qualified Workers Under Service Contracts" and commonly known as a "right of first refusal" provision. Executive Order 13495 requires you to give certain incumbent service personnel the chance to retain their jobs.

Is Executive Order 13495 Effective?

As of this writing, the *FAR Council*, the regulatory body that drafts FAR provisions, had not yet adopted a FAR clause implementing Executive Order 13495. However, in 2011—about two and half years after President Obama signed the Executive Order—the Department of Labor adopted regulations based on the executive order. As of this writing, those regulations had not yet become effective.

By the time you read this book, Executive Order 13495 may be effective (or may have been repealed by a new president). To find out if the order affects you, check the solicitation and your contract for a "Nondisplacement of Qualified Workers" provision. If one is included, you will know that Executive Order 13495 applies to your contract.

Which Employees Must I Give a Right of First Refusal?

Even if Executive Order 13495 applies to your contract, the right of first refusal does not extend to all incumbent employees. You are not required to make job offers to:

- Managerial or supervisory employees. You are entitled to bring in your own management team, no matter how well the incumbent managers have performed.
- Non-service employees. The right of first refusal does not extend to any employee not defined as a "service employee" within the meaning of the Service Contract Act, including construction workers and certain "white-collar" employees. (See Chapter 7 for a full discussion of the Service Contract Act.)
- Poor performers. You are not required to hire any employee whom you reasonably believe, based on the particular employee's past performance, has not performed suitably on the job.

QuickDri wins a $2 million contract to perform dry cleaning services for the Army. During discussions with the contracting officer, Bob learns that one of the incumbent's employees, Joe, has repeatedly arrived late to work and has been the subject of numerous disciplinary actions by his supervisors.

Result: QuickDri has a reasonable belief that Joe has not performed suitably on the job, and need not make an employment offer to him.

As the example suggests, you should do your due diligence prior to extending employment offers to incumbent employees. Speak with the agency and the incumbent (if the incumbent is willing to talk to you). Ask the incumbent employees to provide references. The right of first refusal does not require your business to be saddled with poor performers.

In addition to the three exceptions listed above, there are two other instances in which your small business need not need not make an offer of employment to an incumbent employee. First, if you will perform the contract with fewer employees than the incumbent, you need not make offers of employment for the positions you do not wish to fill.

Second, you need not hire an incumbent employee if hiring the employee would require you to discharge an employee who has been working for your small business for three months or more. You need not fire your own employees in order to comply with the right of first refusal requirement—unless the employees in question happen to be very recent hires.

How Do I Comply with the Right of First Refusal?

Once you have determined that the right of first refusal applies to certain incumbent employees, you must make an "express offer of employment" to each covered service employee. Each offer must state how long the employee has to accept or reject it, but in no case may the acceptance period be less than ten days. The offers may be written or oral, but the best practice is to put each offer in writing to minimize the potential for a "he said, she said" dispute regarding compliance.

You do *not* have to offer the employee the same salary and benefits he or she earned with the incumbent. However, you will likely be required to offer no less than the applicable prevailing wage and benefits under the Service Contract Act (see Chapter 7). You also need not offer the incumbent employees the same jobs they held under the predecessor contract, but must offer to hire them for positions for which they are qualified.

Once you have made employment offers to incumbent employees, you cannot make offers to other individuals to fill those positions unless and until the incumbents have declined their offers or until the acceptance period expires.

What About Subcontractors?

If the incumbent contractor has any subcontractors, the subcontractor's service employees are also entitled to a right of first refusal. If your small business will perform work currently performed by the incumbent's subcontractors, you must extend employment offers to the subcontractors' qualified service personnel.

EnviroLink, Inc., wins a contract to perform environmental consulting services for the Army Corps of Engineers. The contract includes a nondisplacement of qualified workers clause. The incumbent has 24 of its own service employees working on the contract, as well as ten employees of a subcontractor. EnviroLink intends to perform 100 percent of the work itself.

Result: Unless an exception applies, EnviroLink must make employment offers to all 34 of the incumbent service employees, including the ten currently working for the subcontractor.

If you plan to subcontract part of the work, your subcontractor must give a right of first refusal to incumbent service personnel performing the work the subcontractor will perform, regardless of whether those individuals are employed by the incumbent or the incumbent's subcontractor.

The Air Force awards SkyWatch, LLC, a contract for weather observation and forecasting. The contract includes a nondisplacement of qualified workers provision. The incumbent has 24 of its own service employees working on the contract, as well as five service employees of a subcontractor, for a total of 29 service employees. SkyWatch intends to use 15 of its own service employees to perform the contract, and its subcontractor, WeatherOne, Inc., will employ 14 more service employees working on the contract. After award, SkyWatch makes offers to 15 of the incumbent's employees.

Result: Unless an exception applies, SkyWatch and Weather One, together, must make employment offers to all 29 service employees. WeatherOne should make offers to the five subcontract employees, as well as the remaining nine incumbent employees.

How do you make sure that your subcontractor follows through with its right of first refusal requirements? You guessed it—flow down the requirement to the subcontractor (see Chapter 4 for a discussion of flow downs). Consider the right of first refusal one of those "hot-button" topics to identify specifically in your subcontract, in addition to using a general incorporation by reference provision.

The Primary Rules: Where to Find Them

Here's where to find the primary rules discussed in this chapter:

- FAR 52.209-5 (non-responsible principals)
- FAR 22.1803 and FAR 52.222-54 (E-Verify)
- 41 U.S.C. § 2103 (offering to hire current federal employees)
- 41 U.S.C. § 2104 (hiring former federal employees)
- 18 U.S.C. § 207 (activities of former federal employees)
- Executive Order 13495 and 29 C.F.R. § 9.1–9.35 (right of first refusal)

Compliance at a Glance: Hiring Restrictions and Requirements

❑ Do not hire any principal (defined as owners, directors, officers, partners, or individuals holding key managerial authority in your company) who is suspended or debarred.

❑ Do not hire any principal who has been convicted of fraud or any similar criminal offense in connection with a public contract (including state and local contracts) or had a civil judgment rendered against him or her for similar reasons, in the three-year period preceding your offer.

❑ Do not hire any principal who has, within the three years preceding your offer, been notified of any delinquent federal taxes in an amount that exceeds $3,000, for which the liability remains unsatisfied.

❑ Do not hire any principal who has been indicted or criminally or civilly charged with any offense named above.

❑ Use the EPLS database at www.epls.gov to determine whether prospective principals are suspended, debarred, or proposed for debarment (recommended).

❑ Require all employees to certify, in writing, that none of the criteria described above apply to them, and to update you promptly if they are suspended, convicted of fraud, etc. (recommended).

❑ If you have not already enrolled, enroll in the E-Verify system (https://e-verify.uscis.gov/enroll/) within 30 calendar days after being awarded a contract over $150,000, unless the work will be performed outside the United States, will be completed in less than 120 days, or is solely to provide commercially available off-the-shelf items.

❑ After enrolling in E-Verify, initiate verification of each employee assigned to the contract within 90 calendar days after enrollment, or within 30 days after the employee is assigned to the government contract, whichever is later.

❑ Within 90 days after enrollment, initiate verification of each new hire within three business days after the employee is hired, regardless of whether he or she is assigned to the contract.

❑ After enrolling in E-Verify, hang E-Verify posters and Right to Work posters (available at uscis.gov) in readily accessible areas, like break rooms or lunchrooms.

❑ Flow down the E-Verify clause to any subcontractor who holds a subcontract in excess of $3,000 and will perform any of its work in the United States.

❑ Identify the E-Verify clause by name in your subcontracts, in addition to using a general incorporation by reference provision (recommended).

❑ Do not engage in employment discussions with any federal employee if your small business is currently participating in a procurement exceeding $150,00, and the federal employee in question is participating "personally and substantially" in the procurement

❏ If you have been awarded a contract in excess of $10 million, do not hire a former federal employee for pay within one year after that employee participated in the award or administration of the contract.

❏ If you hire a former senior government employee, do not permit that employee to make any appearance or oral or written communication on behalf of your company in connection with a matter in which the employee participated personally and substantially as a government employee.

❏ Do not permit a former senior government employee to represent your business before his or her former agency within one year after leaving the agency.

❏ If your contract contains a right of first refusal clause, make job offers to all incumbent service employees except managerial or supervisory employees and poor performers, unless you will not fill the position held by an incumbent or unless hiring the incumbent would require you to terminate an employee who has worked for your own company for three months or more.

❏ For offers made under a right of first refusal clause, hold the acceptance period open at least ten days and offer to hire the incumbent employees for positions for which they are qualified.

CHAPTER 6

NON-DISCRIMINATION AND AFFIRMATIVE ACTION

AS A GOVERNMENT CONTRACTOR, you must abide by a strict policy of non-discrimination—and take certain steps to show Uncle Sam that you are an equal opportunity employer. In addition, if your company grows big enough, you must adopt comprehensive affirmative action programs to ensure employment opportunities for members of groups the government considers disadvantaged. This chapter will help you make sure your human resources programs are up to snuff.

Non-Discrimination

It should come as no surprise that the government does not like its contractors to discriminate. As a contractor, your small business is prohibited from discriminating based on eight so-called *protected characteristics*:

1. Race
2. Color
3. Religion

4. Sex

5. Disability

6. Status as a veteran (including a disabled veteran)

7. Age

8. National origin

Most of the protected characteristics are self-explanatory, but "disability," for nondiscrimination purposes, is broader than you may think. It includes many major physical as well as mental diseases and conditions, such as deafness, blindness, intellectual disabilities, mobility impairments requiring the use of a wheelchair, autism, diabetes, epilepsy, HIV, multiple sclerosis, muscular dystrophy, major depressive disorder, bipolar disorder, post-traumatic stress disorder, obsessive compulsive disorder, and schizophrenia.

Unless an exception applies (which we will discuss below), you must ensure that job applicants and employees are treated without regard to any protected characteristic when it comes to all employment-related matters, such as the decision to hire, rates of pay, promotions, and so on. Failing to do so violates the law.

> While Claude, the president of Sleez-E Contractors, LLC, is away on vacation, his vice president hires a new employee, Leyla. Upon Claude's return, Leyla introduces herself and mentions that she is a U.S. citizen of Iranian origin. Claude promptly fires her, calling her a "terrorist."
>
> **Result:** National origin is a protected characteristic, and firing an employee is undoubtedly an adverse employment action. Claude's firing of Leyla violates the law.

As a general matter, so long as an individual passes his or her E-Verify check and is authorized to work in the United States, you cannot discriminate based on national origin. However, if the government requires you to provide an individual who possesses a security clearance, it is not discrimination to refuse to hire an individual who does not have one—even if the individual's national origin is the reason.

Few employers, one hopes, would be so callous as to discriminate against an employee simply because of the employee's country of origin. Claude's actions violated the law because national origin is a protected characteristic. Not all of an employee's attributes are protected, however.

> While Brett, the president of BrettWorks, Inc., is away on vacation, his vice president hires a new employee, Martin. Upon Brett's return, Martin introduces himself, and mentions that he is a lifelong fan of the Boston Red Sox. Brett, a diehard Yankees fan, promptly fires Martin, calling him a "traitor to everything this company holds dear."
>
> **Result:** Sporting allegiances are not a protected characteristic. Brett may be a first-class jerk (or a hero, depending upon one's viewpoint), but he has not violated the non-discrimination laws applicable to government contractors.

Just because a certain characteristic does not qualify as "protected" for government contracting purposes does not necessarily mean that you are free to discriminate on that basis. For instance, sexual orientation is not a protected characteristic under the contracting regulations, but at least 20 states and the District of Columbia have laws prohibiting such discrimination, as do many state and local governments. Even in the example above, Brett's decision to fire Martin for no good reason could violate a state or local law. This book only covers the government contracting rules; it is not a comprehensive employment law guide. Before taking any adverse employment action, ensure that your reasons pass muster under state, local, and other federal laws, as well as under the government contracting regulations discussed in this chapter.

Since the protected categories are similar to those covered by other federal employment laws, such as Title VII and the Americans with Disabilities Act, your small business may already have policies in place to ensure that discrimination does not occur. However, even if your business is not large enough to be subjected to these laws (Title VII, for instance, applies to companies with 15 or more employees), it still must abide by a strict policy of non-discrimination after it receives a federal contract award.

Exceptions to Your Company's Non-Discrimination Obligations

Occasionally—emphasis on *occasionally*—it is permissible to discriminate on the basis of one or more protected characteristics, but only if such discrimination is required by the nature of a particular job, and (in the cases of religious beliefs and disabilities) a reasonable accommodation cannot be made to allow the individual to perform the job.

The most common exception is for individuals with disabilities. Some jobs simply cannot be performed by someone with a certain disability, even if you make a reasonable accommodation. In these cases, you may refuse to hire someone or assign them to a certain job or task due to the disability.

Buck's Trucking, Inc., wins an Army contract to transport equipment between various Army bases. Buck's issues an advertisement seeking forklift operators to move the equipment between the trucks and warehouses. Barry applies for the job, but Buck's refuses to hire him when it learns he is legally blind, and his condition cannot be ameliorated by glasses or other measures.

Result: Barry's disability prevents him from safely operating a forklift and cannot be resolved with a reasonable accommodation. Buck's has not violated the law by refusing to hire him.

You may also discriminate based on an employee's religious belief if the belief would unduly interfere with the employee's ability to perform the job, and the situation cannot be resolved by making a reasonable accommodation.

In very rare cases, it is permissible to discriminate on the basis of sex. For instance, if the Department of Defense asked you to provide attendants for ladies' restrooms in the Pentagon, you need not interview or hire men (and probably should not, unless you're eager to face a sexual harassment lawsuit).

You may also discriminate on the basis of age in rare cases. For example, some occupations, such as pilots and firefighters, may be subject to mandatory retirement ages established by law. You need not hire anyone who does not qualify.

Simply put, you can *never* discriminate on the basis of race or color. Particular racial characteristics are not necessary to perform any job.

What Is a Reasonable Accommodation? Before discriminating on the basis of disability or religion, you must determine whether a *reasonable accommodation* can be made. A reasonable accommodation is a change to your company's facilities, equipment, policies, or practices that enables an individual to perform a particular job despite a disability or conflicting religious belief. You will violate the law if you fail to reasonably accommodate an employee's disability or religious belief.

QuickDri requires all employees to wear a standard uniform, including a baseball cap bearing the company's distinctive "QD" logo. During a job interview, a prospective employee, Horace, says that he must wear a traditional religious head covering whenever he is outside the home. Bob does not want to make an exception to QuickDri's uniform policy, so he does not hire Horace.

Result: Unless allowing Horace to wear the traditional head covering will somehow cause an undue hardship to QuickDri, Bob's decision violates the law.

As seen in this example, you must accommodate an employee's disability or religious belief unless the accommodation would cause an *undue hardship* to your business, that is, unreasonable financial costs or other problems. In QuickDri's case, allowing an employee to forgo the company hat for religious reasons is unlikely to harm the bottom line or cause any other problems significant enough to be deemed an undue hardship.

It is not an undue hardship to spend modest amounts of money on equipment. For instance, you may need to spend a few hundred dollars on a Braille reader or special software to allow a blind individual to perform an administrative position. On the other hand, you probably would not be required to buy a $100,000 forklift to enable a physically disabled person to perform a $10-per-hour job lifting boxes in a warehouse.

You should be especially sensitive when it comes to accommodating employees' requests for time off on a Sabbath or other holy day. The government expects you to make good faith efforts to adjust employees' schedules and shifts to accommodate absences for religious reasons.

Other Non-Discrimination Requirements

In addition to prohibiting your company from discriminating on the basis of protected characteristics, the government requires you to take other measures to demonstrate your commitment to non-discrimination, from the contents of your employment advertisements to (you guessed it) hanging another poster in your break room or another prominent location.

Employment Advertisements. Any time you issue an advertisement for employees to work on a government contract, you must expressly state that you are an "equal opportunity employer" or otherwise indicate that all qualified applicants will be considered without regard to race, color, religion, sex, or national origin.

Carefully review your employment advertisements before they go public to make sure they do not suggest, even inadvertently, that you will discriminate on the basis of one of the protected characteristics.

> Sleez-E wins a federal warehousing contract and issues an employment advertisement seeking employees to transport boxed items. Because Claude believes that men are physically stronger than women are, and thus better able to lift heavy items, Sleez-E's advertisement says that the company seeks "a few strong men" for the jobs.
>
> **Result:** Sleez-E must evaluate each prospective employee on his or her individual merit, rather than excluding applicants by sex. The advertisement violates Sleez-E's non-discrimination obligations.

The prohibition on discriminatory advertising does not mean that you have to hire applicants who cannot do the job. If lifting boxes weighing 80 pounds is an essential part of the job Sleez-E is trying to fill, and a reasonable accommodation cannot be made in cases of disability, Sleez-E is not required to hire candidates who cannot lift that amount of weight. However, you cannot prejudge an applicant's abilities based on protected characteristics. For all Claude knows, the first woman who walks in the door for an interview could be an Olympic weightlifting champion.

In addition to ensuring that your employee advertisements include equal opportunity provisions, you must list all job openings with the state workforce agency job bank or a local employment service.

> After CarFixers, Inc., signs a government automotive repair contract, one of CarFixers' best mechanics resigns. Without taking any other action to list the position, CarFixers' president, Skeeter, calls his nephew, Billy Ray, who was recently laid off, and offers him the position. Billy Ray accepts, and starts work the following day.

> **Result:** Because CarFixers hired Billy Ray without listing the opening, CarFixers has violated its equal opportunity obligations.

As the example demonstrates, as a government contractor, you cannot rely solely on word of mouth or posting on the company website to recruit employees. You can use these methods, but must also list all positions where individuals outside the company can see them and have the opportunity to apply for them. If you work with a "headhunter" to do your recruiting, make sure the headhunter will follow this requirement on your behalf.

Note that the job listing requirement applies to *all* job openings, not just openings for positions on government contracts. Even if Billy Ray would not be performing any work for the government, CarFixers would still be required to list the opening.

Selection Procedures. Generally, your small business cannot use any selection procedure, such as a test, if the procedure has an adverse impact upon the hiring, promotion, or other employment opportunities of members of any race, sex, or ethnic group. You may only use such a procedure if there is a legitimate business purpose for it and no workable alternative exists.

Sleez-E wins a federal warehousing contract and issues an employment advertisement seeking employees to perform computer data entry, logging the packages transported. Claude wants to hire men for the position because he thinks women "aren't good at computer stuff." Sleez-E's advertisement does not state a gender preference, but when prospective candidates arrive for their interviews, Claude asks them all to demonstrate the ability to lift 80-pound boxes, believing that the test will help weed out female candidates.

Result: No legitimate business purpose is served by the test, because lifting heavy boxes is not a requirement of the data entry position. Sleez-E's test violates the law.

Before requiring job applicants to complete any test or demonstration, think carefully about whether the procedure might adversely affect—even unintentionally—members of a particular racial, sex, or ethnic group. If so, it's time to find a new test.

Medical Examinations, Inquiries, and Confidentiality. You might be curious about a prospective employee's physical or mental condition. The problem is, you can't ask. In most cases, you cannot give a job applicant a medical examination or ask applicants questions about their medical histories. You may only ask medical questions of job applicants if they inquire into the applicant's ability to perform job-related functions.

> When Claude interviews Trina for an administrative position at Sleez-E, he notices that she walks with a pronounced limp. Concerned that he might have to install a ramp and make other updates to the office if one of his employees became wheelchair-bound, he asks, "Did you hurt yourself, or are you disabled?"
>
> **Result:** Claude's question is not based on Trina's ability to perform the job and is impermissible.

Be very careful on this front, because friendly chitchat during an interview may inadvertently lead to questions about the applicant's medical conditions. Instruct all your employees who conduct interviews to consider medical questions a "no fly zone," unless the question is strictly related to the applicant's ability to perform the job. Of course, if an applicant walks in and, without any prodding, announces something like "Sorry I'm late; the doctor kept me waiting for my chemotherapy treatment," you're off the hook. Applicants may volunteer their own medical information without causing you to violate the law.

You have a little more leeway when it comes to medical questions and examinations of employees (as opposed to applicants). For instance, you may require a new hire to undergo a medical examination, so long as all entering employees in the same job category are subjected to the same examination and the examination is not used to disqualify persons with disabilities. In addition, you can conduct *voluntary* medical examinations and activities (like the ever-popular workplace flu shot).

Any information you collect about your employees' medical conditions must be kept confidential. You should strongly consider keeping such information in locked file cabinets and/or password-protected electronic files.

Self-Identification. As we've seen, unless the question is job-related, you cannot ask a job applicant whether she is disabled. However, after you make an offer of employment, but before the applicant begins her job duties, you must invite the employee to tell you whether she is disabled or a disabled veteran, a process called *self-identification*. Your invitation must inform the employee that she may self-identify either immediately or anytime later in her employment.

Many employers fulfill the obligation by providing new hires with a "check the box" form to complete along with their initial employment paperwork. If the employee self-identifies, you may make follow-up inquiries to determine whether the employee requires any reasonable accommodations to perform her job.

You may ask a job applicant whether she is a veteran (as opposed to a disabled veteran). However, many contractors choose to wait until after hiring to inquire, including veteran status on a "check the box" form along with disabilities. You must also inform an applicant about her right to self-identify as a veteran before she begins her employment duties.

The Department of Labor's regulations include a sample invitation to self-identify as a disabled veteran at 41 C.F.R. § 60-300, Appendix B, and as a disabled individual at 41 C.F.R. § 60-741, Appendix B. You probably don't have a copy of the regulations sitting on your bookshelf, but just enter the regulatory citations above in Google or another search engine and the sample invitations should pop up.

Reporting on Form VETS-100A and Standard Form 100 (EEO-1).

If you hold a federal contract or subcontract of $100,000 or more, you must annually complete and submit a report, using Standard Form VETS-100A, on the number of covered veterans you employ. Visit the Department of Labor's website at http://www.dol.gov/vets/programs/fcp/main.htm for more information about the requirement and a copy of the form.

In addition, if your company is big enough, you must submit an annual non-discrimination report to the government, using Standard Form 100 (also known as the EEO-1). The reporting requirement applies if you have 50 or more employees and have any government contract worth $50,000 or more.

EEO-1 reports are typically due on September 30 each year. To file, go to the U.S. Equal Opportunity Commission's website at http://www.eeoc.gov/employers/eeo1survey/index.cfm.

Segregated Facilities.

Perhaps it should go without saying, but the government's nondiscrimination policies prohibit you from maintaining "separate facilities," including work areas, restrooms, waiting rooms, eating areas, and so on, that are segregated by race, color, religion, sex, or national origin.

Brett transforms BrettWorks' break room into a "man cave," complete with 60-inch televisions, kegs of beer, and framed posters of Yankees players and bikini-clad models. He tells female employees that they are not permitted to enter the room, which is to be a sanctuary for discussing "man stuff."

Result: By prohibiting female employees from entering the "man cave," BrettWorks has violated the prohibition on segregated facilities (and may face a sexual harassment suit for the swimsuit posters, to boot).

Although segregating facilities on the basis of race, color, religion, or national origin is never permitted, you may segregate restrooms, dressing areas, and sleeping areas (but not other facilities, like offices or break rooms) by sex.

Equal Opportunity Poster. Remember those E-Verify and Right to Work posters you hung in the lunchroom? It's time to give them some company. If you hold any federal or subcontract contract in excess of $10,000 over a 12-month period, you must prominently post an equal opportunity poster where it can be readily seen by employees and job applicants. You may download the poster from the Department of Labor's website at http://www.dol.gov/ofccp/regs/compliance/posters/pdf/eeopost.pdf.

What about Subcontractors?

You must flow down the FAR's equal opportunity clause, FAR 52.222-26, to your subcontractors, as well as FAR clause 52.222-21, which prohibits segregated facilities. For all subcontracts of $10,000 or more, you must flow down FAR 52.222-36, a special equal opportunity clause for individuals with disabilities. For all subcontracts of $100,000 or more, you must also flow down FAR 52.222-35, a special equal opportunity clause for veterans. Consider all four clauses "hot-button" flow downs you should specifically identify in your subcontracts, in addition to using a general incorporation by reference provision. For a discussion on flow downs, see Chapter 4.

Affirmative Action

Completed all your non-discrimination requirements? Don't breathe a sigh of relief just yet. As a government contractor, you also may be required to adopt *affirmative action programs*, that is, special programs to ensure the employment of women, minorities, individuals with disabilities, and certain veterans.

Am I Required to Adopt Affirmative Action Programs?

Your small business must adopt affirmative action programs if it:

1. Has 50 or more employees.
2. Has received a government contract or subcontract of $50,000 or more ($100,000 or more for affirmative action for veterans), and the contract is not for construction.

If your small business meets these criteria, read on. And if you are a construction contractor, don't think you'll be able to avoid affirmative action. Near the end of this section, we will briefly discuss the special affirmative action requirements for construction contracts.

When Must I Adopt My Affirmative Action Programs?

Once your company meets these two criteria, it must adopt affirmative action programs within 120 days, and they must be updated annually.

How Many Affirmative Action Programs Do I Need?

You must adopt at least three affirmative action programs, separately covering:

1. Women and minorities
2. Individuals with disabilities
3. Covered veterans

In addition, if your business has multiple offices or locations, you must adopt a separate affirmative action program for each office or location.

> Draper's Papers is headquartered in Omaha, Nebraska, and has a satellite office in Lawrence, Kansas. The company, which has more

than 50 employees and has not previously adopted affirmative action plans, wins a $1 million government contract.

Result: Draper's Papers must adopt *six* separate affirmative action programs within 120 days of award: programs for women and minorities, individuals with disabilities, and veterans for each of its two offices.

What Must My Affirmative Action Programs Include?

The government requires that your affirmative action programs include certain contents. The requirements differ based on the program: your program for women and minorities will include more detailed analysis, while your programs for individuals with disabilities and veterans (which have similar requirements) focus more on policy.

Women and Minorities. Your affirmative action program for women and minorities must include the following components:

Organizational Profile. Your organizational profile provides an overview of your entire workforce, identifying the gender and ethnicity of employees holding each job.

Job Grouping. In this component of your program, sort your jobs into larger groups. If your small business has a total workforce of fewer than 150 employees, you may use the same job groups used in the Standard Form 100. For instance, Jane's dry cleaning company, Dry Dry Again, might have "officials and managers," "administrative support workers," "operatives," and "laborers" among its job groups. See the U.S. Equal Employment Opportunity Commission website at www.eeoc.gov for additional guidance on placing your employees into the EEO-1 job categories.

If your company has more than 150 employees, you cannot use the EEO-1 categories. Instead, you must create your own categories based on each job's requirements, wages, and opportunities for advancement.

Placement of Employees in Job Groups. Once you establish the job groups, you must calculate the percentage of minorities and the percentage of women employed in each job group. The results can be illuminating. For instance, Dry Dry Again might discover that 90 percent of its administrative support workers are women, but only 10 percent of its operatives (in Dry Dry Again's case, primarily employees who run the dry cleaning equipment) are female.

Determination of Availability. Next, you must determine the availability of women and minorities, as prospective employees, for each job group. To do so, you may use U.S. Census data and data from local job service offices.

Comparison. In this portion of the program, you need to compare the percentage of minorities and women in each job group with the availability of minorities and women for that job group. Dry Dry Again might discover, for example, that 35 percent of operatives locally are women—much higher than the 10 percent it employs.

Placement Goals. If your comparison reveals a gap between available women or minorities and current women or minorities holding the job position, you must establish an *annual placement goal*, that is, an objective for hiring women or minorities for the job group. The placement goal must be at least equal to the availability numbers. In Dry Dry Again's case, it would be required to establish an annual placement goal of at least 35 percent women for the "operatives" job group.

Placement goals are *not* quotas and should not be considered a ceiling or floor on your hiring of women or minorities. In fact, the law prohibits the use of quotas. Meeting your placement goals should be a company-wide aspiration, but you are not required to hire an unqualified or lesser-qualified person in order to meet your goals.

After completing its affirmative action plan, Dry Dry Again concludes that 10 percent of its operatives are women, compared to 35 percent availability. Dry Dry Again establishes a 35 percent placement goal. A few weeks later, one of Dry Dry Again's dry cleaning operatives resigns and Dry Dry Again issues an advertisement for a replacement. Charlotte, who has six months' experience as an operative, applies. Mark, who has ten years' experience, also applies.

Result: Even though Dry Dry Again's goal is to hire more women operatives, it need not hire a less-qualified individual to meet the goal. In this case, Mark's significantly greater experience likely makes him better qualified than Charlotte, and Dry Dry Again is entitled to hire him.

Designation of Responsibility. You must assign responsibility and accountability for implementing and overseeing the affirmative action program to an employee with sufficient authority and resources. Consider assigning it to one of your top officers or your human resources director.

Identification of Problem Areas. In this portion of your program, you must analyze your existing employment processes to determine whether impediments to equal opportunity exist, such as unnecessary testing procedures or a tendency to hire "through the grapevine" rather than publicly listing job openings. If you identify any problems, you must develop and execute programs to correct them.

Audits. You must develop and implement an internal auditing system that periodically measures the effectiveness of your affirmative action program. The results of the audits should be reported to top management, together with recommendations for improvements.

Veterans and Individuals with Disabilities. Remember, you must create separate affirmative action programs for veterans and individuals with disabilities. However, since the requirements for the two programs are very similar, we have condensed the discussion to avoid unnecessary repetition.

Changes in the Disability Requirements? As of this writing, the Department of Labor is considering a number of changes to the nondiscrimination and affirmative action requirements with respect to individuals with disabilities. The proposed changes would require contractors to invite prospective employees to self-identify as disabled using language provided by the Department of Labor; set a goal that at least 7 percent of its workforce be individuals with disabilities; and impose a number of other requirements related to job postings, training programs, record keeping, and dissemination of information. Because these changes were still merely proposals of this writing, this book does not cover them in additional detail. However, be sure to visit the Department of Labor's affirmative action website at http://www.dol.gov/dol/topic/hiring/affirmativeact.htm to determine whether any new requirements, in addition to those described in this chapter, apply to you.

In order to create a compliant affirmative action program for covered veterans or individuals with disabilities, follow the steps below.

Develop a Policy Statement. You must develop a policy statement stating, among other things, that all employment and personnel decisions will be made without regard to disability or status as a covered veteran. The policy statement should be included in your employee handbook or policy manual and posted on company bulletin boards and other internal media (like newsletters).

Review Personnel Processes. You must review your personnel processes to ensure that they do not limit the access of disabled persons to jobs for which they are qualified. You should ensure that, when individuals with disabilities are screened out, it is due to business necessity for a particular job.

Make Reasonable Accommodations. Your affirmative action program must state that you will make reasonable accommodation to the physical or mental disabilities of an otherwise qualified individual unless the accommodation would impose an undue hardship on business operations. As you know, making reasonable accommodations is one of your non-discrimination obligations anyway. The affirmative action program merely puts this policy in writing.

Prohibit Harassment. You must develop and implement procedures to ensure that employees are not harassed because of their status as a covered veteran or an individual with a disability. Hopefully, none of your employees are so callous as to harass a veteran or disabled individual. However, in this part of your program, you should make clear that any such harassment will not be tolerated.

Undertake Recruitment Activities. In perhaps the "meatiest" part of your affirmative action program, you must undertake outreach and recruitment activities reasonably designed to recruit qualified veterans and individuals with disabilities. The nature and scope of your outreach effort will vary depending on your size and resources (the bigger and richer you are, the more extensive efforts the government will require), as well as the extent to which your existing employment practices already reach out to veterans and individuals with disabilities. Some efforts you might undertake include (but by no means are limited to) the following:

- Contact the local Department of Veterans Affairs (VA) regional office, veterans service centers, local veterans groups, state education agencies, and other potential recruiting sources serving veterans and individuals with disabilities.
- Establish relationships with local colleges, universities, and other educational institutions, including VA rehabilitation fa-

cilities and institutions with programs focusing on training individuals with disabilities.

- Encourage employees who are veterans or disabled individuals to participate in career days and other outreach and recruitment efforts on behalf of your company.

- Include individuals with disabilities when employees are pictured in advertising or other promotional materials (such as your company website).

Conduct Employee Training. You must train all personnel involved in recruitment, screening, promotion, and other human resources functions regarding your affirmative action programs and your company's efforts to implement them. As one way of meeting this requirement, consider requiring all affected employees to attend internal workshops and certify that they have attended and understand the affirmative action requirements.

Audits. As with your program for women and minorities, you must design and implement an audit and reporting system to measure the effectiveness of your affirmative action programs for covered veterans and individuals with disabilities.

Which Veterans Are Covered? Why do we keep talking about "covered" veterans? Because the affirmative action regulations do not apply to all veterans. First, and perhaps this goes without saying, to be covered, the individual must have served in the U.S. military. If a job applicant has a number of interesting tales from his years in the French Foreign Legion, he may be a lot of fun to chat with over lunch, but is not a covered veteran.

Not all U.S. veterans are covered. The affirmative action requirements apply to service-disabled veterans; veterans who served on active duty within the past three years; and veterans who participated in active duty during a war, campaign, or expedition. Other veterans are not covered. Of course, in recognition of the sacrifices all veterans have made for their country, you may choose to extend your affirmative action programs beyond the minimum requirements.

Special Rules for Construction Contractors. If you are a construction contractor, you are not subject to the same affirmative action requirements as other contractors, but this does not mean that you are off the hook when it comes to affirmative action. You will be required to sign a special affirmative action plan called a "Hometown Plan," "Imposed Plan," or "Special Plan." Although you must develop affirmative action goals and timetables, you need not put together the same type of extensive information required of other contractors, because the government writes most of your plan. This can save you a lot of work, but limits your flexibility.

Where to Get Help. Reading through the lengthy list of required affirmative action requirements may have you ready to throw up your hands and yell, "I give up!" But don't throw in the towel. Yes, putting together thorough and compliant affirmative action programs can be time-consuming and challenging, but there are resources available to help you.

Some contractors hire third-party consultants to assist them, but if you do not, the Office of Federal Contract Compliance Programs (OFCCP) offers compliance assistance—including, perhaps most helpfully, sample affirmative action programs. Visit OFCPP's website at http://www.dol.gov/ofccp/index.htm, or call toll-free at 1-800-397-6251.

What About Subcontractors? If your subcontractors meet the 50-employee and $50,000/$100,000 thresholds, they must develop affirmative action programs—even if your small business does not.

Amy's Caterers, Inc., which has 27 employees, wins a $600,000 small business set-aside contract. Amy's Caterers subsequently issues a $200,000 subcontract to Food Suppliers, Inc., which has 65 employees.

Result: Because Amy's Caterers has fewer than 50 employees, it is not required to adopt affirmative action programs. However, Food Suppliers has more than 50 employees and now holds a government subcontract of more than $100,000. Food Suppliers must develop affirmative action programs for women and minorities, individuals with disabilities, and covered veterans.

Although not required, you should consider requiring your subcontractors to certify whether they have developed and implemented the appropriate affirmative action plans. You can develop your own certification from scratch or simply use FAR clause 52.222-25 (which you will have to submit to the government as the prime contractor).

The Primary Rules: Where to Find Them

Here's where to find the primary rules discussed in this chapter:

- 41 C.F.R. ch. 60, FAR 22.9, FAR 52.222-26, FAR 52.222-35, and FAR 52.222-36 (non-discrimination)
- 41 C.F.R. ch. 60 and FAR 52.222-35 (employee advertisements)
- 41 C.F.R. ch. 60 (selection procedures, medical examinations, and self-identification)
- 41 C.F.R. ch. 60 and FAR 52.222-37 (VETS-100A Report)
- 41 C.F.R. ch. 60 and FAR 52.222-36 (EEO-1 Report)
- FAR 52.222-21 (segregated facilities)

- 41 C.F.R. ch. 60, FAR 52.222-23, FAR 52.222-25, FAR 52.222-27, FAR 52.222-35, and FAR 52.222-36 (affirmative action)

Compliance at a Glance: Non-Discrimination and Affirmative Action

❑ Treat all job applicants and employees without regard to any of the eight protected characteristics: race, color, religion, sex, disability, status as a veteran (including a disabled veteran), age, and national origin, unless such discrimination is required by the nature of a particular job and (in the case of religious beliefs and disabilities) cannot be remedied with a reasonable accommodation.

❑ Make reasonable accommodations—that is, changes to your company's facilities, equipment, policies, or practices—to enable individuals to perform particular jobs despite disabilities or conflicting religious beliefs.

❑ In all employee advertisements for work on a government contract, state that you are an "equal opportunity employer" or otherwise indicate that all qualified applicants will be considered without regard to race, color, religion, sex, or national origin.

❑ List all job openings with the state workforce agency job bank or a local employment service.

❑ Do not use any selection procedure, such as a test, if the procedure has an adverse impact upon the hiring, promotion, or other employment opportunities of members of any race, sex, or ethnic group, unless there is a legitimate business purpose for it and no workable alternative exists.

❑ Do not ask medical questions of a job applicant unless they inquire into the applicant's ability to perform job-related functions.

❏ Keep confidential all medical information you collect about employees.

❏ After making an offer of employment, but before the new employee begins work, invite the employee to self-identify as disabled or a disabled veteran.

❏ If you hold a government contract or subcontract of $100,000 or more, annually complete and submit the VETS-100A Report.

❏ If you have 50 or more employee and a government contract or subcontract of $50,000 or more, annually complete and submit a non-discrimination report on Standard Form 100 (EEO-1).

❏ Do not maintain any facilities segregated by race, color, religion, sex, or national origin, except that restrooms, dressing areas, and sleeping areas can be segregated by sex.

❏ Post an equal opportunity poster in a prominent location, such as a break room.

❏ Where appropriate, flow down the FAR's equal opportunity clauses, FAR 52.222-26, FAR 52. 222-21, FAR 52.222-36, and FAR 52.222-35, to subcontractors.

❏ If your business has 50 or more employees, adopt affirmative action programs for women and minorities and individuals with disabilities within 120 days after beginning a government contract of $50,000 or more.

❏ If your business has 50 or more employees, adopt an affirmative action program for covered veterans within 120 days after beginning a government contract of $100,000 or more.

❏ If you are a construction contractor, execute and follow a "Hometown Plan," "Imposed Plan," or "Special Plan" governing your affirmative action obligations.

❏ Ensure that your subcontractors adopt affirmative action programs if they meet the 50-employee and $50,000/$100,000 thresholds—even if your business does not.

CHAPTER 7

Uncle Sam, Union Boss: Employee Wages, Benefits, and Hours

YOU'VE RUN YOUR EMPLOYEES through E-Verify, followed the non-discrimination requirements, and implemented affirmative action programs (if your company is large enough). But for many of your employees—perhaps all of them—the most pressing question is not "are you an equal opportunity employer?" but rather "what are my wages and benefits?" And when you contract with the government, Uncle Sam has a thing or two (or maybe a thing or 20) to say about what the employees working on your government contracts earn and how much paid time off they receive.

Since 2009, the Department of Labor has added 250 new wage and hour inspectors (for a total of nearly 1,000 nationwide), whose sole mission is to ensure that contractors comply with the wage and hour requirements. Given the government's focus on wage and hour compliance, as well as the stiff penalties for violations (including the very real possibility of debarments), you should take extra care to ensure that your small business complies with the requirements we will discuss in this chapter.

Wages

What is the lowest amount of money you can pay your employees? If you answered "minimum wage," think again. As a government contractor, you will likely be required to pay many of your employees no less than the *prevailing wage*, that is, the hourly wage the Department of Labor has determined to be appropriate for a particular job in a certain geographical locality, based on wages paid by other employers in the region. The prevailing wage is often significantly higher than the federal minimum wage.

Am I Required to Pay Prevailing Wages?

To find out if you are required to pay prevailing wages, check the contract for FAR clause 52.222-6 or FAR clause 52.222-41. These clauses (together with other supporting clauses) implement the two federal prevailing wage statutes—the Davis-Bacon Act, for construction contracts, and the Service Contract Act, for service contracts. If either clause is present, you must pay prevailing wages to covered employees.

Which Employees Must Be Paid Prevailing Wages?

For service contracts covered by the Service Contract Act, you must pay prevailing wages to all employees working on the contract, except bona fide executive, administrative, and professional employees—commonly known as the "white-collar" exceptions.

An employee qualifies as an "executive" if:

- His primary duty is management.
- He earns at least $455 per week.
- He regularly directs the work of two or more other employees.
- He has the power to hire or fire other employees (or his hiring and firing suggestions are given particular weight by those who do have such power).

An employee qualifies as "administrative" if:

- His primary duty is the performance of office or non-manual work directly related to the management or general business operations of his employer or the employer's customers.
- He earns at least $455 per week.
- He exercises discretion and independent judgment with respect to matters of significance.

Be especially careful of the "matters of significance" factor. If you have not delegated any *significant* decision-making authority to an employee, the employee will not qualify for the exemption. Just because the employee can choose whether to take his lunch break at noon or one o'clock does not make him an "administrative" employee for Service Contract Act purposes.

The "professional" exemption, sometimes known as the "learned professional" exemption, covers employees with advanced degrees or creative talents. An employee is a "professional" if:

- His primary job duty requires knowledge of an advanced type in a field of science or learning customarily acquired by a prolonged course of specialized intellectual instruction, or invention, imagination, originality, or talent in a recognized field of artistic or creative endeavor.
- He earns no less than $455 per week.

The professional exemption covers individuals such as doctors, but most commonly applies to computer systems analysts, computer programmers, software engineers, and similar computer professionals.

In addition, an individual is exempt if she is a *highly compensated employee*, that is, someone who earns more than $100,000 annually and performs any of the functions of an executive, administrative, or professional employee.

For construction contracts, the Davis-Bacon Act stipulates that you must pay prevailing wages to laborers and mechanics working on the contract, or so-called "blue-collar" workers whose duties are primarily manual or physical in nature. White-collar employees whose duties are primarily mental or managerial are not covered.

Unlike service contracts, the duty to pay prevailing wages on construction contracts is limited by *where* an employee performs his duties. You must pay prevailing wages to a laborer or mechanic who works on a federal jobsite (such as a federal courthouse you are renovating). You must also pay prevailing wages to a laborer or mechanic who works on a *secondary jobsite*, that is, a separate jobsite established specifically for performance of the contract where a significant portion of the construction work is performed.

XPert Constructors wins a contract to renovate a federal office building. To minimize disruption to the building's workers, XPert rents a nearby warehouse, which it uses to assemble components for the construction project. Allen, a laborer, works at the warehouse assembling the components.

Result: The warehouse is a secondary jobsite. XPert must pay Allen prevailing wages for his work at the warehouse.

For construction contracts, employees who do not work at the federal jobsite or a secondary jobsite are *not* owed prevailing wages. For instance, an employee who works at your company' headquarters would not be covered. If an employee splits his or her time between onsite and offsite work, however, the employee must be compensated at prevailing rates for the time actually spent on the jobsite or secondary jobsite.

How Much Must I Pay My Covered Employees?

If the Davis-Bacon Act or Service Contract Act applies to your contract, you must pay every covered employee no less than the amount specified in the *wage determination* attached to the solicitation. A wage determination is a list of prevailing wages, organized by job category, and specific to a geographical region.

> QuickDri wins a government contract for dry cleaning services. The solicitation and contract include FAR clause 52.222-41. Brian, a QuickDri employee, will work as a dry cleaner on the contract. QuickDri typically pays its dry cleaners $10 per hour. The wage determination lists an hourly wage of $12.71 per hour for dry cleaners.
>
> **Result:** Because FAR clause 52.222-41 is included, the Service Contract Act applies to the contract. QuickDri must pay Brian no less than the prevailing wage, $12.71 per hour, for his work on the contract.

Read the wage determination carefully to make sure that you properly classify your employees. For instance, Brian might be better classified as a "machine washer" or a "hand presser," jobs that usually carry lower prevailing wages than dry cleaners. On the other hand, if Brian is better classified as a "tailor," he would probably be entitled to a higher hourly wage. Use the Department of Labor's *Directory of Occupations* (http://www.dol.gov/whd/regs/compliance/wage/) to help you classify your employees.

Do not be tempted to misclassify your employees in order to pay them less than they are owed. If you classify your bulldozer operator as a truck driver (a difference of perhaps $4.00 per hour), she may complain to the Department of Labor, and the resulting investigation could result in very tough sanctions—possibly even putting you out of business. We will discuss the penalties for wage and hour violations later in this chapter.

Can I Make Deductions from Prevailing Wages?

In a few cases, you can pay a covered employee less than the prevailing wage, but only if it is the result of a deduction permitted by law. You may deduct the following expenses from an employee's pay, even if the employee ends up earning less than the prevailing wage as a result:

- Taxes payable by the employee and required to be withheld by your small business

- Amounts due the employee that your small business is required by court order to pay a third party (such as a garnishment for child support)

- Amounts authorized by the employee or by a collective bargaining agreement to be paid to a third party for the employee's benefit, such as for health insurance

- Certain amounts paid by your small business for the employee's lodging, board, and other furnished facilities

- Amounts to pay union membership dues or initiation fees

Full Court Press, Inc., wins a government contract for court reporting services. The solicitation and contract include FAR clause 52.222-41. Stan, a Full Court Press employee, will work as a data entry operator on the contract. The wage determination lists an hourly wage of $12.71. Stan signs up for the company health plan and authorizes Full Court Press to deduct the expenses, which come to 75 cents per hour, from his pay. Full Court Press gives Stan four company uniforms, which cost the company $320, or $2 per hour Stan works in a month.

Result: Full Court Press must pay Stan no less than $11.96 per hour—the amount specified in the wage determination, less the healthcare deduction.

Did you notice that Full Court Press was not entitled to deduct the uniform costs in determining the minimum hourly wage due Stan? Uniforms are not a permitted deduction from prevailing wages, nor are any other expenses not expressly permitted by law—even if you think the employee should pick up the tab.

In addition to the permitted deductions, for construction contracts, you may pay lower wages to apprentices and trainees participating in programs recognized by the Department of Labor. However, you still must pay those employees a minimum wage specified by the government.

When Must You Pay Your Employees?

For service contracts covered by the Service Contract Act, you must pay covered employees at least twice per month. For construction contracts covered by the Davis-Bacon Act, you must pay laborers and mechanics no less often than weekly. If your small business currently pays its employees less frequently, you should adjust your payroll system before beginning work on the contract.

What If the Wage Determination Increases?

The Department of Labor sometimes issues new wage determinations to reflect current conditions in the market. While your small business is working on a government contract, the government may substitute the old wage determination for a new one. If this happens, you must comply with the new wage determination and give raises to any affected employees. The government will pick up the tab for the difference, but only if you act quickly. You must notify the contracting officer of your claim within 30 days of receiving the new wage determination. Otherwise, you're stuck paying the extra costs yourself.

What If My Employees Aren't Owed Prevailing Wages?

If an employee working on a federal contract is not covered by the Service Contract Act or Davis-Bacon Act, you must pay the employee no less than the federal minimum wage. Most businesses in the United States are obligated to pay the minimum wage, so chances are your small business already complies.

Health and Welfare Benefits

In addition to prescribing the hourly wages you must pay, your wage determination will specify a particular dollar amount you must spend to provide health and welfare benefits (sometimes called *fringe benefits*) to covered employees. For service contracts, the amount of health and welfare benefits is the same for every contract, no matter where you perform the contract work. Like wages, health and welfare benefits for construction contracts vary by geographic location.

What Qualifies as a Health and Welfare Benefit?

Many common benefits you may already offer your employees are considered health and welfare benefits, including:

- Health insurance
- Life insurance
- Vision and dental insurance
- Short- and long-term disability
- Pension plans
- Profit-sharing plans
- Educational reimbursement
- Vacation and holiday pay

Benefits you are required to provide under federal, state, or local laws, such as employer contributions under the Federal Insurance Contributions Act (FICA), do not help you fulfill your health and welfare benefit requirements. In addition, expenses that the Department of Labor believes primarily benefit your company—such as professional association dues, relocation expenses, and the costs of uniforms and tools—do not count toward the requirement.

How Do I Pay Health and Welfare Benefits?

The amount specified in your wage determination for health and welfare benefits refers to how much you must *spend*, per covered employee, on qualifying benefits, not how much the employee must *receive* in benefits (though the two can be the same if you "cash out" your benefits, as we will talk about below). If your expenditures meet or exceed the amount called for in the wage determination, you are compliant.

Mess Halls-R-Us, Inc., wins a contract for food preparation services. The wage determination calls for a wage of $7.98 for food service workers, and a health and welfare benefit of $3.50 per hour. Mess Halls-R-Us expends $3.25 per hour to provide its food service workers with health insurance, vision insurance, and dental insurance; 40 cents per hour to provide its food service workers with a pension plan; and $1.50 per hour to provide its food service workers with company uniforms.

Result: The amount spent on the uniforms is not a qualifying health and welfare benefit. However, the insurance and pension plan are qualifying benefits. Mess Halls-R-Us spends $3.65 per hour on qualifying benefits for its dry cleaners, exceeding the amount specified in the wage determination. The company meets its health and welfare benefit obligations.

What if your small business does not currently provide insurance, pensions, or other qualifying benefits? Do you have to rush out and start negotiating with insurance companies?

No. You may satisfy your health and welfare benefits—in whole or in part—by making cash payments to your covered employees.

BrettWorks wins a contract for administrative services. The wage determination calls for a wage of $20.69 for administrative assistants, and a health and welfare benefit of $3.50 per hour. BrettWorks spends $3.25 per hour to provide its administrative assistants with health, vision, and dental insurance, but does not provide any additional qualifying benefits to them. After receiving the wage determination, BrettWorks pays its administrative assistants an extra $0.25 per hour, on top of their $20.69 salaries, for a total of $20.94.

Result: BrettWorks' insurance benefits, alone, do not satisfy its health and welfare benefit requirement. But the additional cash payment solves the problem, because BrettWorks now spends $3.50 per hour, per covered employee, on a combination of qualifying benefits and cash payments.

If you decide to "cash out" all or part of your health and welfare benefits, record the fact as a separate line item on your payroll records (for instance, $20.69 in salary plus $0.25 in benefits, instead of $20.69 in salary). Although you might wonder what difference it makes (and truth be told, so do we), the government wants to see the breakdown.

What About My Other Employees?

If an employee is not covered by the Service Contract Act or Davis-Bacon Act, you generally are not required to provide her with health and welfare benefits simply because she works on a government contract. There are some limited exceptions. For example, if the employee works on an overseas military base, you likely will be required to provide her with workers compensation insurance under the Defense Base Act or War Hazards Compensation Act. Check your solicitation and contract. In addition, other federal or state laws might require you to offer certain benefits, or you may choose to provide them to recruit and retain qualified employees.

Vacation and Holidays

For service contracts covered by the Service Contract Act, you must provide your covered employees with paid vacation and holiday benefits. Further, for all government contracts, many of your employees are entitled to increased wages if they work more than 40 hours per week.

Paid Vacation

Your wage determination will tell you how much paid vacation you must offer your covered employees. Typically, the wage determination will state something like "two weeks paid vacation after one year of service with a contractor or successor; three weeks after five years, and four weeks after 15 years."

As you can see, you will owe your service employees different amounts of vacation based on their length of service. Employees with less than one year of service are typically not entitled to any vacation under the Service Contract Act (although you are free to offer them some, out of the goodness of your heart). After one year, employees begin to accrue vacation benefits.

For vacation purposes, you do not necessarily begin counting an employee's service on the day he started working for your company. You must also count time the employee worked for any predecessor contractor at the same facility, performing the same type of work.

Harr-Ball Limos wins an Air Force laundry services contract previously held by So-So Transport, Inc. Harr-Ball promptly hires Jenny, a former So-So Transport employee, to repair and maintain government-owned vehicles at an Air Force facility—the same job she held with So-So Transport. Jenny begins working for Harr-Ball on November 1. Jenny started working for So-So Transport the previous February 1. Harr-Ball's wage determination calls for two weeks' paid vacation after one year of service.

Result: Because of Jenny's work for the predecessor, So-So Transport, Harr-Ball will owe her two weeks' paid vacation on February 1, even though she will have worked only three months for Harr-Ball at that time.

Whenever you hire incumbent employees, be sure to find out when they were hired by the predecessor. Predecessors are supposed to provide this information, but if your predecessor is a sore loser and won't cooperate, don't hesitate to get the contracting officer involved.

Are Vacation Benefits Prorated? Vacation benefits are not prorated. The entire benefit vests upon an employee's annual anniversary date (whether with your company or the predecessor). If the employee does not reach an anniversary, he is not entitled to any vacation benefits for the partially completed year.

BrettWorks wins a federal administrative services contract. The wage determination calls for two weeks' paid vacation after one year of service. BrettWorks hires Fred, who did not work for the incumbent. Fred starts work on March 1. The following February 1, after catching Fred wearing a Boston Red Sox hat, Brett fires Fred, effective immediately.

Result: BrettWorks does not owe Fred a paid vacation because Fred never reached one year of service with the company.

Once an employee reaches an anniversary date, he is entitled to the entire vacation benefit. If Brett had fired Fred on March 15, Fred would have been entitled to two weeks' paid vacation as a parting gift.

What about Part-Time Employees? Part-timers earn vacation, too, but on a prorated basis. To figure out how much vacation a part-time employee has earned, first determine how much time the employee spent working on the government contract, and then apply the percentage to the vacation amount called for in the wage determination.

> After confirming that she is a Yankees fan, Brett hires Helen to work on BrettWorks' new administrative services contract. Helen, who did not work for the predecessor, works 20 hours per week over a 52-week period. Helen works 1,040 hours over the course of the year.
>
> **Result:** Helen worked 50 percent of a full-time schedule. Applying the percentage to the 80 hours (or two weeks) of vacation called for in the wage determination, Brett Works should give Helen 40 hours (or one week) of paid vacation after she reaches one year of service.

Can I "Cash Out" My Vacation Benefit Obligation? As with health and welfare benefits, you may "cash out" your vacation obligation by paying your employees the value of the vacation benefit rather than allowing the employee to take paid time off. You may also meet your vacation obligation by providing additional health and welfare benefits at a cost equal to or greater than the amount of paid vacation due the employee.

As a practical matter, your employees may be none too pleased if you unilaterally decide to increase the amount of their dental insurance (or even provide them cash) instead of providing them paid vacation. Many employees have come to expect vacation benefits as "standard," even if they have never heard of the Service Contract Act. However, some employees might appreciate the opportunity to *choose* whether to take paid vacation or receive their benefit (in whole or in part) in cash.

Paid Holidays

For service contracts covered by the Service Contract Act, you must give your covered employees a certain number of paid holidays, in addition to their vacation benefits. The wage determination will say something like "HOLIDAYS: A minimum of ten paid holidays per year: New Year's Day, Martin Luther King Jr.'s Birthday . . ." and so on.

Can I Substitute a Different Holiday? Even though wage determinations list specific holidays, you may substitute a different day for one named in the wage determination. However, your employees earn the right to a paid holiday as of the date named in the wage determination, even if you substitute a later day.

> Joey begins working on Harr-Ball Limo's transportation services contract on December 15. Harr-Ball's wage determination specifies that employees are entitled to ten paid holidays, including New Year's Day. However, Harry, who is a proud Irish-American, has decreed that all Harr-Ball employees will work on New Year's Day, but receive St. Patrick's Day as a paid holiday. Though slightly hung over, Joey works on New Year's Day. Upset at being made to work on the holiday, Joey quits in February, before St. Patrick's Day arrives.
>
> **Result:** Joey's entitlement to a paid holiday vested on New Year's Day, even though he did not get the day off. Because Joey quit before he was able to take his holiday, Harr-Ball owes Joey the value of the paid holiday.

If you substitute a different day for a holiday named in the wage determination, you must clearly communicate your decision to the affected employees in writing (such as in a company-wide memorandum). Keep in mind, too, that requiring your employees to work on widely celebrated holidays like Thanksgiving and Christmas without good reason may be legally permissible, but it is not a particularly effective means of boosting employee loyalty.

What If the Employee Has Not Worked for One Year? Unlike vacation, holiday benefits are not based on an employee's length of service. As seen in the example of Joey, who was hired on December 15 and earned a holiday a few weeks later, covered employees are entitled to holiday benefits immediately after they begin work.

What If the Employee Wouldn't Have Worked on the Holiday? Generally, an employee is entitled to a paid holiday if he performs *any* work during the workweek in which a named holiday occurs—even if the holiday falls on a day the employee would normally be off.

> Amanda, one of MaryIT, Inc.'s computer programmers, works a 40-hour schedule Wednesdays through Sundays with Mondays and Tuesdays off. Martin Luther King Jr.'s birthday falls on a Monday, and is named as a holiday in the wage determination. Amanda does not work that day, but resumes her usual schedule on Wednesday.
>
> **Result:** Because she worked during the workweek, Amanda is entitled to a holiday, even though she would have been off that day anyway.

If the employee did not work at all during the week the holiday occurred, the employee is still entitled to a paid holiday, as long as the absence was permissible (such as when the employee takes earned sick leave or vacation time). Of course, if your employees routinely leave work without permission, allocating their holiday benefits is probably the least of your concerns.

What about Part-Time Employees? Part-time employees are entitled to a prorated holiday benefit, based on the percentage of full time the employee works.

> Elmo, an employee of Buck's Trucking, works eight hours Wednesdays and Thursdays, with the remaining days off. Martin Luther

King Jr.'s birthday falls on a Monday, and is named as a holiday in the wage determination. Elmo does not work that day, but resumes his usual schedule on Wednesday.

Result: Elmo works 40 percent (16/40) of a full-time, 40-hour week. He is entitled to 40 percent of a paid holiday, or 3.2 paid hours off.

Can I "Cash Out" My Employees' Paid Holiday Benefits? As is the case for health and welfare benefits and paid vacation, you can "cash out" your employees' benefits rather than permitting them to take paid time off. Again, be careful about cashing out paid holidays, especially widely celebrated ones, without consulting the affected employees. Some employees may resent being forced to work on a holiday, even if they are paid extra for their time.

Other Wage and Hour Requirements

In addition to the requirement to pay prevailing wages and provide prevailing health and welfare, vacation, and holiday benefits, you must keep certain employment records, report your payroll information to the government (for construction contracts covered by the Davis-Bacon Act), hang some more posters on your walls, and take special care to flow down the wage and hour requirements to your subcontractors.

Record Keeping

You must keep detailed employment records about each employee working on a contract covered by the Service Contract Act or Davis-Bacon Act. These records should include, for each employee:

- Name, address, and Social Security number
- Number of daily and weekly hours worked

- Job classifications
- Wages paid and fringe benefits provided
- Total daily and weekly compensation
- Any deductions, rebates, or refunds from total daily or weekly compensation

If you employ apprentices or trainees under approved programs, you must also retain written evidence of the registration and certification of the programs, the registration of the apprentices and trainees, and the ratios and wage rates prescribed by the programs.

Good record keeping is critical. If the Department of Labor investigates or audits your business's wage and hour practices, the first thing it will do is ask to see your records. Offering the investigators thorough and well-organized records demonstrating compliance will go a long way toward avoiding any sanctions.

You must retain the records for a minimum of three years following completion of the contract.

Reporting Payroll Information

For construction contracts covered by the Davis-Bacon Act, it is not enough to keep employment records in your own files. For every week that you perform any contract work, you must submit a *certified payroll record* to the procuring agency.

A certified payroll record is a document that includes all of the information about each covered employee described in the "Record Keeping" section above, except that you should omit employees' Social Security numbers and home addresses (apparently, the government does not trust procuring agencies not to steal your employees' identities). Although it is not required, many contractors submit their payroll information on Standard Form WH-347. Using the form may make it less likely that you will inadvertently omit required information. Form WH-347 is available at http://www.dol.gov/whd/forms/wh347.pdf.

Together with each payroll submission, you must submit a signed "statement of compliance," certifying that:

- The payroll contains all required information.
- Your business is currently maintaining all such required information.
- The information provided is correct and complete.
- Each covered laborer or mechanic has been paid his or her full weekly wages earned, without deductions (except permissible deductions).
- Each laborer or mechanic has been paid not less than the applicable wage rates and fringe benefits or cash equivalents for the classification of work performed, as specified in the applicable wage determination incorporated into the contract.

Standard Form WH-347 includes an appropriate certification— yet another reason to use the form rather than trying to reinvent the wheel.

Your certified payroll records must include information about covered individuals employed by your subcontractors. Be sure to require your subcontractors to submit certified payroll reports to you each week, and insert the requirement for certified payroll records in your subcontracts.

Posting Requirements

You knew this was coming. It's time to hang a few more things on the walls in prominent locations in your office (like a break room or lunchroom).

If your contract is covered by the Service Contract Act, you must post the Department of Labor's Service Contract Act poster. The poster is available at http://www.dol.gov/whd/regs/compliance/posters/sca.htm. You must also post the wage determination itself near the poster. That way, covered employees can easily check for themselves to make sure they have been properly categorized and are receiving the appropriate wages and benefits.

The requirement is similar for construction contracts under the Davis-Bacon Act. Post the Davis-Bacon Act poster (available at http://www.dol.gov/whd/regs/compliance/posters/fedprojc.pdf), together with a copy of the wage determination.

What About My Subcontractors?

The wage and hour rules, including those implementing the Service Contract Act and Davis-Bacon Act, apply to your subcontractors. In addition to using a general incorporation by reference provision to flow down the applicable FAR clauses, be sure to specifically require the subcontractor to comply with the Service Contract Act or Davis-Bacon Act.

We've used the term "hot button" to describe particularly important provisions to flow down to your subcontractors. Consider the wage and hour clauses hotter than hot—scalding, maybe. Why? As a prime contractor, you are liable to the government for any violations your subcontractor commits. If you don't flow down the requirement, you could be forced to pay back wages to your subcontractor's employees, and be stuck with no way to recover the costs from the subcontractor. See Chapter 4 for an example drawn from real life.

For construction contracts covered by the Davis-Bacon Act, you need to go a step further by demonstrating to the government that you flowed down the requirement. Within 14 days after award of a Davis-Bacon prime contract, you must provide the procuring agency with a "statement and acknowledgment" from each subcontractor, confirming that the required clauses were flowed down in its subcontract.

You must prepare and submit the statement and acknowledgment using Standard Form 1413. The form is available on the General Services Administration's website at http://contacts.gsa.gov/webforms.nsf/.

If you hire any additional subcontractors after award, you have 14 days after executing the subcontract to submit a statement and acknowledgment from the new subcontractor.

The Mandatory Debarment Penalty

Yes, you read the heading correctly. Compliance with the wage and hour requirements under the Service Contract Act and Davis-Bacon Act is critical because violating either statute results in a *mandatory* three-year debarment from all government contracting unless you can prove that unusual circumstances exist to escape punishment. In other words, debarment for failing to comply with the Service Contract Act or the Davis-Bacon Act is the norm, not a special sanction for egregious violations. Especially because mandatory debarment is the rule, you owe it to yourself and your employees (as well as the government) to make sure that you follow your wage and hour obligations to a T.

The Primary Rules: Where to Find Them

Here's where to find the primary rules discussed in this chapter:

- FAR 52.222-6 and FAR 52.222-41 (prevailing wages)
- FAR 52.222-41 (paid vacation and holiday benefits)
- FAR 52.222-8 and FAR 52.222-41 (record keeping)
- FAR 52.222-8 (reporting payroll information)
- FAR 52.222-11 (subcontractors' statement and acknowledgment)
- FAR 52.222-6 and FAR 52.222-41 (posting requirements)
- 29 C.F.R. § 4.188 and 29 C.F.R. § 5.12 (mandatory debarment)

Compliance at a Glance: Wages, Benefits, and Hours

❑ If your contract includes FAR clause 52.222-6, implementing the Davis-Bacon Act, or FAR clause 52.222-41, implementing the Service Contract Act, pay prevailing wages to all covered laborers, mechanics, or service employees.

❑ Use the Department of Labor's Directory of Occupations to classify your employees for wage and hour purposes (recommended).

❑ Do not make deductions from prevailing wages unless permitted by law.

❑ Pay all employees covered by the Service Contract Act at least twice per month.

❑ Pay all laborers and mechanics covered by the Davis-Bacon Act no less often than weekly.

❑ If your wage determination increases during your performance of a contract, submit a claim for increased costs within 30 days (recommended—or you will lose your right to recover the costs).

❑ Pay all employees who are not covered by the Service Contract Act or Davis-Bacon Act at least the federal minimum wage.

❑ Provide qualifying health and welfare benefits (or their cash equivalent) to all employees covered by the Service Contract Act or Davis-Bacon Act, in the amount specified in the wage determination.

❑ Provide all employees covered by the Service Contract Act with paid vacation benefits (or their cash equivalent), in the amount specified in the wage determination.

❑ Provide all employees covered by the Service Contract Act with paid holiday benefits (or their cash equivalent), in the amount specified in the wage determination.

❑ Keep detailed employment records about each employee working on a contract covered by the Service Contract Act or Davis-Bacon Act, including name, address, Social Security number, daily and weekly hours worked, job classifications, wages paid and benefits provided, total daily and weekly compensation, deductions from compensation, and, for construction contracts, information about any apprentice or trainee programs you are using.

❑ For contracts covered by the Davis-Bacon Act, submit a certified payroll record, together with a signed statement of compliance, to the procuring agency each week. Consider using Standard Form WH-347 for the report.

❑ As applicable, post the Service Contract Act poster, Davis-Bacon Act poster, and the wage determination itself in prominent locations (like a break room or lunchroom) in your office.

❑ Flow down all FAR clauses implementing the Davis-Bacon Act and Service Contract Act to your subcontractors.

❑ Specifically require your subcontractors to certify that they will comply with the Davis-Bacon Act or Service Contract Act, as applicable (recommended).

❑ For construction contracts covered by the Davis-Bacon Act, provide the procuring agency with a "statement and acknowledgment" from each subcontractor, confirming that the required clauses were flowed down in its subcontract, within 14 days after award of the prime contract (or 14 days after executing the subcontract, if you execute the subcontract after award of the prime contract). Use Standard Form 1413 to obtain the statement and acknowledgment.

CHAPTER 8

PROHIBITED ACTIVITIES, ETHICAL VIOLATIONS, CONFLICTS OF INTEREST, AND DISCLOSURE RULES

WHAT DOES UNCLE SAM HAVE in common with Santa Claus? Sure, they both have white beards and wear funny hats. But for government contractors, the most important similarity goes back to the classic children's song, "Santa Claus Is Coming to Town." Like jolly old St. Nick, Uncle Sam wants to know if you have been naughty or nice—and has a lot of rules in place make sure government contractors are on the "nice" list.

As a government contractor, you must avoid specific prohibited activities and comply with a number of ethics requirements, including, in many cases, adopting a written code of compliance and hanging yet another poster. In addition, you should understand and follow the rules regarding conflicts of interest, which can affect your business's eligibility to receive federal contracts. And you may be required to inform the government of actual or suspected criminal or ethical violations, as in recent years the government has also adopted mandatory disclosure rules.

In this chapter, we'll discuss these important requirements, helping you avoid the contractor's version of a lump of coal—suspension, debarment, fines, and other penalties.

Prohibited Activities

In today's contracting climate, with its emphasis on regulatory enforcement, it is more important than ever that if you contract with the government, you run an honest, compliant small business. Although the government can penalize your business for just about any criminal act or other behavior demonstrating a lack of integrity, here are some of the most important behaviors to avoid.

Violations of the False Claims Act

The False Claims Act is one of the oldest procurement statutes on the books. It was originally signed into law by Abraham Lincoln to penalize Civil War profiteers who sold supplies (often of dubious quality) to the Union at exorbitant prices. The law has been updated and strengthened throughout the years, but still operates much the same as it did in Honest Abe's day: It imposes liability on any person or company that submits a monetary claim to the government that he or she knows (or should know) is false.

Sleez-E wins a contract to provide widgets to the government on an as-needed basis at the price of $10.50 per widget. A few weeks later, the government places an order for 100,000 widgets. Sleez-E only delivers 90,000, but invoices the government for the full 100,000.

Result: Sleez-E has violated the False Claims Act by claiming $105,000 for items it did not actually supply.

You probably do not need this book to tell you not to invoice the government for supplies or services you did not provide. But the reach of the False Claims Act is much longer. You may be liable for almost any untrue certification that you make to the government.

For a small government contractor, an incorrect certification about its size or eligibility to receive a set-aside contract, in particular, may lead to False Claims Act penalties. The bottom line: Double- (and triple-) check that every certification you make to the government is correct—especially those related to your small business's size (see Chapters 1–3 for guidance on calculating size) or eligibility to receive contracts set-aside for 8(a), HUBZone, service-disabled veteran-owned, or women-owned businesses (see Chapters 11–14).

Knowledge of Significant Overpayments

It is unethical to retain "extra" money received from the government if you know that it has significantly overpaid your business—even if you do not realize that there was an overpayment until long after the fact.

Sleez-E wins a contract to provide widgets to the government on an as-needed basis at the price of $10.50 per widget. A few weeks later, the government places an order for 100,000 widgets. Sleez-E delivers the full 100,000 and invoices the government. At year's end, when Sleez-E's accountant is doing the books, she discovers that Sleez-E's invoice contained an error—it charged the government $1,250,000 (or $12.50 per widget rather than $10.50). The government paid the bill without noticing the mistake. Sleez-E's owner, Claude, decides to "keep quiet" and not tell the government about the problem.

Result: Sleez-E has committed a violation by failing to report a significant overpayment made by the government. The company could be suspended, debarred, or face other significant penalties.

If you become aware of a significant overpayment, you should promptly report it to the government. Yes, you'll probably have to repay the money, but you didn't earn it anyway—and making a repayment is much better than being penalized for a failure to report.

Bribes, Gratuities, and Gifts

It should go without saying that attempting to bribe a federal official is a bad idea. Federal law provides stiff penalties for contractors who give something of value to a government employee with the intent of obtaining the award of a contract or other favorable treatment. If you're curious, run a quick Internet search and you'll discover plenty of articles about former government contractors who tried to commit bribery and are now residing in government-owned facilities—their jail cells.

The prohibition on bribery isn't always as cut-and-dried as slipping a contracting officer a briefcase full of unmarked bills. As a contractor, you are also prohibited from giving most *non-monetary gifts* to government employees, including gifts of entertainment, sporting tickets, and meals.

> In November, Full Court Press, Inc., bids on a federal solicitation for court reporting services. Hoping that a personal gesture will increase Full Court Press's chances of award, Gillian, the company's owner, sends Megan, the contracting officer, a Christmas card, and includes two tickets to the symphony, valued at $150.
>
> **Result:** Gillian and Full Court Press have violated the federal bribery statute.

A judge may not throw the book at Gillian for a $150 "bribe," but the gratuities statute does not have a minimum dollar number. As a worst-case scenario, Gillian could face up to 15 years in prison, and both she and the company could be made to pay large fines.

Gillian's gift is clearly improper because it is motivated by her hope that Megan will look more favorably upon Full Court Press's bid after she attends the symphony. But what if a gift is not motivated by the intent to obtain favorable treatment?

> BrettWorks wins a federal administrative services contract. Grateful that Annie, the contracting officer, took a chance by making award to his small business, Brett sends Annie a thank-you card and includes two tickets to the next Yankees game, valued at $100.
>
> **Result:** BrettWorks has given an improper gratuity. While not as serious as a violation motivated by the intent to obtain an advantage, Brett could nevertheless face up to two years in prison.

As the example demonstrates, gift restrictions apply even when not motivated by an effort to obtain favorable government treatment. Rather, the law penalizes anyone who gives or promises anything of value to a government official "because of or for" an official act.

This means that a gift to an agency official may be improper even if the official in question is not actively deciding whether to award you a contract or take any other action on your behalf. In the example, BrettWorks violated the gift rules even though it had *already won* the administrative services contract because Brett's gift to Annie was "because of" an action Annie had already taken.

What if your gift is not motivated by an effort to obtain favorable treatment and is not "because of or for" an official act? In that case, you are likely permitted to *give* the gift, but the agency official in question may be prohibited from *accepting* it.

As a general matter, a federal employee cannot accept a gift from an outside source (like you or your small business) if the source is seeking official action from the employee's agency, currently does business with the employee's agency, seeks to do business with the employee's agency, or may otherwise be affected by the employee's performance of her duties.

The government's rules for acceptance of gifts by its employees are stringent, but there are a few commonsense exceptions. First, government employees may accept non-monetary items worth less than $20. Government employees may also accept modest refreshments, such as coffee and bagels served at a presentation. However, a steak dinner or three-martini lunch is not considered a "modest" refreshment.

In addition, a government employee may accept more expensive gifts, as long as the government employee had a pre-existing personal relationship with the outside source. So, don't worry—if your family or friends work for the government, you may still give them birthday and Christmas gifts worth more than $20, as long as the personal relationship was pre-existing.

If you are in doubt as to whether a particular gift may be accepted by a government employee, consult the Department of Justice's guidelines, at http://www.justice.gov/jmd/ethics/generalf.htm#1, *before* offering the gift. If the guidelines do not help clear matters up, the wise course of action is to forgo the gift. The risk of embarrassment (or a violation, if the gift is perceived as a bribe or gratuity) just isn't worth it.

Kickbacks

As a prime contractor, you cannot solicit or accept anything of value (including non-monetary gifts) in exchange for providing favorable treatment with respect to a federal subcontract. Similarly, your subcontractors (or prospective subcontractors) are prohibited from offering anything of value in an attempt to induce favorable treatment from you.

> QuickDri wins a large federal dry cleaning contract. The day after the award is announced, Claude approaches Bob and asks him to award a subcontract to Sleez-E. When Bob seems unsure, Claude offers to "sweeten the deal" with a $10,000 cash payment to Bob, personally, if he awards a subcontract to Sleez-E.

> **Result:** Sleez-E has violated the prohibition on kickbacks. If Bob accepts the offer, QuickDri will also be in violation.

Claude's cash-for-subcontracts scheme is a blatant example, and (hopefully) uncommon in practice. But, like bribes, kickbacks need not take the form of cold cash, slipped under the table.

Commissions and fee-splitting can be deemed improper kickbacks. In one case decided by the U.S. Court of Federal Claims, a brokerage firm agreed to split its surety bond commissions with a construction contractor. The court found that the fee-splitting arrangement—which, of course, caused the contractor to use the surety to supply its bonds on several federal projects—was an improper kickback, even though testimony suggested that it was not an uncommon practice in the industry.[1]

The FAR's anti-kickback policy applies to all of your employees and agents, and the FAR directs contractors to put in place "reasonable procedures" designed to prevent and detect possible kickbacks. You should strongly consider including a section regarding kickbacks in your employee handbook, as well as in your company's official ethics policy.

Contingent Fees

As a federal contractor, your small business is generally prohibited from paying a contingent fee to a third party. A *contingent fee* is any commission, percentage, brokerage, or other fee that is contingent upon the third party's success in securing a government contract for your business.

> At his high school reunion, Claude runs into an old classmate, Jimmy. After a little small talk, Claude realizes that Jimmy is married to Tammy, a high-ranking procurement official with the Army.

Claude says that if Jimmy will sweet talk his wife about Sleez-E, Claude will give Jimmy 3 percent of the value of any contract Jimmy helps Sleez-E land with the Army.

Result: If Sleez-E and Jimmy follow through on the arrangement, they will have violated the prohibition on contingent fees.

When small government contractors first learn about the prohibition on contingent fees, they may become quite nervous. After all, it is relatively common for less-experienced contractors to pay "finders' fees," often a percent of the total contract amount or percent of contract profit. Fortunately, these fee arrangements are perfectly acceptable, provided they fall into one of the two exceptions to the prohibition on contingent fees.

First, you may enter into a contingent fee arrangement with a *bona fide employee*, that is, someone regularly employed by your business and subject to your supervision, as long as the employee does not exert (or propose to exert) any improper influence to obtain a government contract.

Buck's Trucking hires a new employee, Madelyn, who used to work in the procurement department of a large federal contractor. Recognizing that Madelyn understands the procurement process better than any of his current employees, the company's owner (not surprisingly, named Buck) puts Madelyn in charge of finding new federal opportunities for Buck's Trucking, and offers her 3 percent of the company's profit on any contract she brings in, on top of her salary.

Result: Provided Madelyn does not use or propose to use any improper influence to obtain contracts, the arrangement is acceptable.

To obtain contracts for Buck's Trucking, Madelyn may search the FedBizOpps website, network with her contacts at her previous employer, and even meet with government officials, so long as she does not use improper influence to obtain contracts.

Similarly, your small business may retain a *bona fide agency* on a commission or contingent fee basis. A bona fide agency is a commercial or selling agency retained by a contractor for the purpose of securing business.

> After losing several bids in a row, Amy decides that her company, Amy's Caterers, Inc., needs outside assistance to find viable federal opportunities. Amy's Caterers enters into an agreement with ContractFinders, LLC, a consulting company dedicated to helping federal contractors find business. Amy's Caterers promises to pay ContractFinders 5 percent of the profits on any contract Amy's Caterers is awarded due to ContractFinders' efforts.
>
> **Result:** Provided ContractFinders does not use or propose to use any improper influence to obtain contracts, the arrangement is acceptable.

Typically, a bona fide agency will have multiple clients, and finding procurement opportunities will be a major part of the agency's business. If a company does not fit this profile, it may not qualify as a bona fide agency. For example, if your large subcontractor sets you up with contract opportunities, but does not perform those services for anyone else, the arrangement may not pass muster.

As with bona fide employees, bona fide agencies cannot exert or propose to exert improper influence to help you obtain government contracts. That begs the question: What is *improper influence*?

The FAR defines it as any influence that would tend to cause a government official to make a contract award for reasons other than the merits of the situation. Think back to our previous example, in which Claude asked Jimmy to use his personal relationship with the contracting officer to influence her award decisions—something the government would consider an improper consideration, since it would not be based on the respective merits of the businesses competing for award.

Lobbying Restrictions

Government contractors are prohibited from using federal appropriated funds to lobby agency employees, members of Congress, or congressional employees with respect to the award, renewal, amendment, or extension of federal contracts, grants, loans, or cooperative agreements. In other words, the government doesn't want contractors using taxpayer funds for lobbying purposes.

> Buck's Trucking earns 100 percent of its revenues from federal prime contracts. Hoping to convince the Army to award it a sole source contract, Buck hires a lobbying firm to contact members of Congress on the Armed Services Committee about the contract.
>
> **Result:** Buck's lobbying funds necessarily come from federal appropriated funds, since Buck's has no other revenues. Buck's has violated the FAR's lobbying restrictions.

Note that the restriction applies to the use of federal appropriated funds. Government contractors are *not* prohibited from lobbying, even with respect to federal contracts, so long as the lobbying is not done with federal funds. If your small business intends to engage in any lobbying, you should consider establishing a separate bank account, funded by commercial work or other sources, from which to fund your lobbying activities.

Prior to being awarded any federal contract exceeding $150,000, your small business must certify that, to the best of its knowledge and belief, no appropriated federal funds have been used to attempt to influence an agency employee, member of Congress, or congressional employee with respect to award of the contract. If any registered lobbyists have made a lobbying contract on your behalf with respect to the contract, you must submit an OMB Standard Form LLL (Disclosure of Lobbying Activities) with your offer. (Download the form at http://www.whitehouse.gov/sites/default/files/omb/grants/sflllin.pdf.)

The lobbying restrictions apply to your subcontractors as well. You must also obtain lobbying certifications and disclosures from any subcontractor that will perform $150,000 or more of contract work. Your subcontracts should require your subcontractors to provide these certifications and disclosures.

Drugs-Free Workplace Requirements

Federal contractors must maintain drug-free workplaces—and take affirmative steps to communicate the drug-free policy to employees. If your small business is awarded any federal prime contract over $150,000, you must take the following actions to help ensure a drug-free workplace:

- Publish a statement notifying employees that the unlawful manufacture, distribution, dispensing, possession, or use of a controlled substance is prohibited, and stating that disciplinary actions will be taken against employees who violate the policy. You must provide a copy of the statement to all employees engaged in performance of the contract.

- Notify each employee in writing, as part of the statement provided to employees, that, as a condition of employment on the contract, the employee is required to abide by the drug-free policy and is required to notify you, in writing, within five days of any conviction under a criminal drug statute for a violation occurring in the workplace.

- Notify the contracting officer in writing within ten days after receiving notice (or otherwise learning) about an employee's conviction under a criminal drug statute for a violation occurring in the workplace. The written notice must contain the employee's title.

- Take action with respect to any employee who is convicted under a criminal drug statute for a violation occurring in the workplace. The action may be disciplinary (suspension, termination, etc.) or you may require the employee to satisfactorily participate in a drug abuse assistance or rehabilitation program approved by a federal, state, or local health or law enforcement agency.

- Establish an ongoing drug-free awareness program. The program should inform employees about: (1) the dangers of drug abuse in the workplace; (2) your business's policy of maintaining a drug-free workplace; (3) any available drug counseling, rehabilitation, and employee assistance programs; and (4) the penalties that you may impose upon employees for drug abuse violations in the workplace.

If you are awarded a contract with a performance period of 30 days or more, you must implement the appropriate drug-free workplace provisions within 30 days after award, unless the contracting officer agrees in writing to an extension. For shorter contracts, you must implement the provisions "as soon as possible," but in any case, prior to when performance is expected to be completed.

Practically speaking, there is no reason to wait until you win a contract to implement the FAR's drug-free workplace requirements. Assuming your business intends to perform federal contracts in excess of $150,000 (and you probably wouldn't be reading this book otherwise), you should consider implementing the FAR's drug-free workplace requirements as soon as possible.

Codes of Ethics

According to the FAR, all government contractors *should* adopt a written code of ethics and conduct. Because the FAR uses the term "should," your business may not be required to adopt a written code, so long as it does not perform particularly large government contracts.

However, if your small business is awarded a contract that is expected to exceed $5 million and will include a performance period of 120 days or more, it *must* adopt a written code of ethics within 30 days after award of the contract (unless the contracting officer approves a longer period).

> On March 1, Sleez-E Contractors, LLC, wins a $6 million construction contract with a one-year performance period.
>
> **Result:** Much to Claude's likely horror, Sleez-E must adopt a written code of ethics by March 31 (30 days after award).

Even if your business does not perform contracts in excess of $5 million, you should strongly consider adopting a written code of ethics. Adopting such a code can help create an ethical culture in your workplace and give your company a reputation as an honest contractor.

In addition, having a code of ethics in place can help protect your business should an employee do something unethical. When an ethics problem arises, one of the first questions the government will ask is "what did you do to prevent this?" If you can explain that you provided your employees with an ethics code and ethics training, it may go a long way toward convincing the government that you took reasonable precautions to prevent any ethical lapses.

What Should My Code of Ethics Include?

The FAR does not mandate any specific content for your written codes of ethics. However, this does not mean that simply directing your employees to act ethically will satisfy the government. If you adopt an ethics code, you should take it seriously. Spend some time creating a code that educates employees about specific ethical issues (contingent fees, kickbacks, gratuities, and so on), requires employees to disclose suspected ethical violations, and calls for disciplinary action against employees who violate the code.

In creating your company's written code of ethics, you should consider including:

- A general statement of your company's ethics policy (for example, "QuickDri believes in honesty and fairness in all aspects of our business . . .")

- A statement that the ethics policy applies to all personnel, including independent contractors, subcontractors, all employees, and the company's officers

- Prohibitions on specific activities, such as false claims, bribery, and kickbacks

- A policy of internal and external (government) disclosure of ethics violations

- Identification of the company officials responsible for implementing the code

- Identification of at least two company officials to whom violations should be reported by employees (multiple officials should be identified, in case an employee believes a particular official is involved in a violation)

- Disciplinary action to be taken against employees who commit violations

- Reference to your business's training and compliance program (see below)

- A signature page for employees to acknowledge receiving and reading the code

If your business wins a $5 million-plus contract with a 120-day period of performance or longer, you must provide a copy of the code to all employees engaged in performance of the contract. However, regardless of whether you win such large contracts, the best practice is to provide every employee with a copy of the code—preferably on the employee's first day of work. After all, a corporate policy of honesty and ethics won't do much good if it is locked up in your desk drawer and never sees the light of day.

Ethics Training and a System of Internal Controls

In addition to a written code of ethics, the FAR states that all contractors should have an employee business ethics and compliance program and a system of internal controls. Although the compliance program and system of internal controls sound similar to the code of ethics, they are actually separate (albeit related) requirements.

Like the code of ethics, the compliance program and system of internal controls are mandatory whenever your company is awarded a contract that is expected to exceed $5 million and has a performance period of 120 days or more. However, a compliance program and system of internal controls are not required when your business has self-certified as small for the procurement, or if the procurement is for commercial items.

Just because your business self-certifies as small does not mean that it is a good idea for you to avoid implementing a compliance program and system of internal controls. Having a system in place may help prevent ethical breaches (or help avoid suspension or debarment by persuading the government that you did everything reasonably possible to prevent a breach).

Unlike the code of ethics, you must include certain provisions in your compliance program and system of internal controls. At a minimum, the system must:

- Assign responsibility for implementing and auditing the code of ethics at a sufficiently high level to ensure effectiveness.

- Assign adequate resources to implementing and auditing the code of ethics to ensure effectiveness.

- Implement reasonable efforts not to include an individual as a principal of the business if due diligence would indicate that the person has engaged in conduct contrary to the code of ethics.

- Implement periodic reviews of the company's business practices, policies, and procedures, including monitoring to detect criminal conduct, periodic evaluation of the effectiveness of the ethics code and the control system, and periodic assessment of the risk of criminal conduct.

- Establish an internal reporting mechanism, such as a hotline, that allows for anonymity or confidentiality, whereby employees may report suspected incidents of improper conduct, and instructions to employees encouraging them to make such reports when appropriate.

- Provide for disciplinary action for improper conduct or the failure to take reasonable steps to prevent or detect improper conduct.

- Provide for the disclosure obligations discussed below in the "mandatory disclosures" section.

- Establish a policy of full cooperation with any government agencies responsible for audits, investigations, or corrective action.

The FAR provides that an employee business ethics and compliance program and a system of internal controls should be reasonably suitable to the size of the business and the extent of its involvement in government contracting. While they should adopt robust and thorough systems of internal controls, small businesses are not expected to expend the same resources as their larger counterparts on compliance efforts.

Hotline Poster

Is there any space left on your office walls? If not, you better make room, because you have another poster to hang.

If your small business wins a government contract over $5 million, you must prominently display in common work areas an agency fraud hotline poster or Department of Homeland Security fraud hotline poster. In addition to displaying the poster in common areas, if you maintain a company website as a means of providing information to employees, you must display an electronic version of the poster on the website.

The contracting officer should specify which poster to hang (and where to obtain it). Look for the clause at FAR 52.203-14 in your contract. If the contracting officer fails to fill out the section, you should ask for guidance.

The hotline poster provides a toll-free number by which employees may report suspected criminal violations, misconduct, wasteful conduct, and allegations of civil rights or civil liberties abuses. You cannot retaliate against any employee who chooses to use the hotline, though you can encourage employees to report violations or suspected violations internally before contacting the government.

What About Subcontractors?

You must flow down the FAR's code of ethics clause, FAR 52.203-13, to all subcontractors holding subcontracts valued in excess of $5 million with a period of performance exceeding 120 days. But even if a particular subcontractor does not meet the $5 million/120 day threshold, it is still wise to require the subcontractor to adopt an ethics code and system of internal controls—including a requirement that the subcontractor promptly report any suspected ethical violations to you and the government.

Remember that, as the prime contractor, you are ultimately responsible for your subcontractors, including any unethical behavior. "Don't ask, don't tell" is not a smart policy when it comes to your subcontractors' ethics.

Organizational Conflicts of Interest

The government will not award a contract if the award would create an actual, apparent, or potential *organizational conflict of interest*, or OCI, unless the OCI can be mitigated. OCIs come in three distinct types: unequal access to information, biased ground rules, and impaired objectivity.

Unequal Access to Information

An *unequal access to information* OCI arises if a contractor has access to confidential or other nonpublic information as part of its performance of a government contract, and the information may provide the contractor with a competitive advantage in a future competition for a government contract.

> Acquisition Consultants, Inc., under a prime contract, assists an agency in the procurement planning for an administrative services solicitation. As part of its work, Acquisition Consultants receives nonpublic information regarding the solicitation. Acquisition Consultants subsequently signs on as a subcontractor to BrettWorks, which submits a bid on the solicitation.
>
> **Result:** BrettWorks, through its subcontractor, has an unequal access to information OCI.

As the example indicates, even if your small business does not have access to any nonpublic information, there may be an OCI if one of your subcontractors has access to such information. You should consider including a provision in your subcontracts requiring your subcontractors to disclose potential OCIs, including those related to unequal access to information.

Biased Ground Rules

A *biased ground rules* OCI occurs when, as part of its performance of a government contract, a contractor helps set the ground rules for a procurement, such as by writing the statement of work or specifications. The government's concern with biased ground rules OCIs is that the contractor could skew the competition, whether intentionally or not, in its favor.

> Acquisition Consultants, Inc., under a subcontract with another company, drafts a feasibility study, which the agency subsequently uses to prepare a solicitation for engineering services. AC Engineers, Inc., a sister company of Acquisition Consultants, Inc., attempts to bid on the solicitation.
>
> **Result:** AC Engineers has a biased ground rules OCI and is not eligible to participate in the competition.

If your small business assists a federal agency in any form of acquisition planning, it may have a biased ground rules OCI. It may be possible to mitigate the conflict (which we will discuss in a moment), but mitigation is not always an option. Before engaging in acquisition planning work for a federal agency, you should carefully consider whether your small business might wish to compete for any underlying procurement. If so, you may be forced to choose between the two.

Impaired Objectivity

The third type of OCI, *impaired objectivity*, arises when a contractor's work under a government contract could result in the contractor evaluating itself (or an affiliate). In "impaired objectivity" cases, the government's primary concern is that the contractor's ability to provide impartial advice to the government could be undermined by virtue of the contractor's relationship with the company being evaluated.

Sleez-E, whose business includes selling widgets to the government, submits a proposal on a government procurement. The procurement calls, in part, for the successful offer to advise the government on which brand of widgets to purchase.

Result: Sleez-E has an impaired objectivity OCI because its recommendations could affect its own sales to the government.

How Can I Mitigate OCIs?

The FAR's prohibition on OCIs extends beyond actual OCIs, like the ones discussed in the previous examples. It also applies when a contractor has an *apparent* or *potential* OCI. According to the GAO, which decides a number of bid protests each year involving OCIs, even the appearance of an OCI may compromise the integrity of the procurement process, thus requiring agencies to avoid, neutralize, or mitigate potential or apparent OCIs—even if an actual OCI does not exist.

So, besides avoiding situations that could create conflicts, how can you prevent OCIs? Your small business should adopt a written *OCI mitigation plan*, which contains your internal policy on OCIs and explains how you will mitigate any actual, potential, or apparent conflicts that may arise.

Contracting agencies have broad discretion to award contracts, even in the face of an OCI, as long as the agency reasonably determines that the problem has been mitigated. In other words, possessing a strong OCI mitigation plan may make the difference between winning a contract and being conflicted out.

The FAR does not specify any contents for an effective OCI mitigation plan, but you should consider including:

- An indication that your business understands the FAR definitions of OCIs, including the three types of OCIs
- A policy statement indicating that it is your business's policy to promptly identify and mitigate any OCIs

- A strategy for identifying actual, potential, or apparent OCIs in connection with solicitations, including an identification of the employees (by name or job title) primarily responsible for OCI identification

- An indication that your business will promptly report all actual, potential, or apparent OCIs to the appropriate government official(s)

- A list of potential strategies for avoiding, neutralizing, or mitigating OCIs, which may include such actions as employee firewalls, document and information control

- A company policy of refraining from bidding on solicitations where OCIs cannot be mitigated

- A commitment to training employees to identify OCIs and report them to their superiors

- A commitment to including OCI mitigation requirements in all of your company's government subcontracts

- A commitment to periodically review and audit the company's OCI policy

! Identification (by name or job title) of the persons primarily responsible for implementing the company's OCI plan, and for answering employees' questions about the plan

Creating a thorough OCI mitigation plan is only the first step. The plan is useless if it is not effectively implemented. If the plan calls for employee training, you should follow through with seminars, meetings, and so on. If it indicates that subcontracts will contain OCI mitigation clauses, be sure to alter the company's standard subcontracts to provide for OCIs (something you should do anyway).

And keep in mind that the broad OCI plan may need to be tweaked to take into account the particulars of a procurement. If you identify an OCI with respect to a particular contract, you should consider drafting an addendum to the OCI plan for use on the specific procurement, naming the individualized mitigation measures to be used.

Disclosure Rules

Your employees have the option of deciding whether or not to pick up the phone and call the government hotline, but your small business is *required* to report certain violations and suspected violations of ethics rules or criminal law to the government. The FAR includes two disclosure rules—a mandatory disclosure requirement for certain matters deemed extremely serious, which applies to all contractors, and a broader disclosure requirement if you earn enough federal contracting revenue.

The Mandatory Disclosure Requirement

As a government contractor—of any size—you may be suspended or debarred from government contracting if you do not inform it whenever you have credible evidence that a principal, employee, agent, or subcontractor has violated the False Claims Act; committed a violation of criminal law involving fraud, conflict of interest, or bribery; or if the company has received a significant overpayment.

If you make a mandatory disclosure, it must be in writing and must be addressed to the appropriate agency's office of inspector general, with a copy to the contracting officer. You must provide specific details and certify to the accuracy of the account. If you want the government to treat the information as confidential (and you almost certainly will), you should mark your submission as "proprietary" or "confidential."

The disclosure obligation includes a three-year *"look-back" provision*. This means that you must report credible evidence of one of the above violations if you become aware of the evidence within three years after final payment on a government contract.

XPert Constructors wins a federal construction contract and hires Sleez-E as a subcontractor. The contract winds up and the government makes final payment in November 2012. In January 2015,

> XPert's owner, Erik, has dinner with Sharon, a former Sleez-E vice president, who tells Erik that although Sleez-E invoiced XPert (and through XPert, the government) for six employees on the contract, it only had three people actually working, and that Claude pocketed the difference.
>
> **Result:** XPert has credible information of false claims and significant overpayments on the dry cleaning contract, and final payment was less than three years earlier. XPert must promptly make a written disclosure.

You do not need to *immediately* report the information, but merely report it in a "timely" manner. Many contractors interpret the requirement to allow a grace period to investigate the matter internally. For instance, Erik might contact other former Sleez-E employees to see if they will confirm Sharon's story—or if they will say that Sharon is disgruntled and merely trying to "take down" an ethical company.

Do not delay too long, though. The government takes the mandatory disclosure requirement very seriously, and you do not want to create the appearance that you are trying to sweep a problem under the rug. As students of political history know, the fallout from a cover-up is almost always worse than the crime.

The FAPIIS Disclosure Rule

In addition to the mandatory disclosure obligation, your small business may be required to report additional information to the Federal Awardee Performance and Integrity Information System (FAPIIS)—colloquially known in government contracting circles as the "Bad Boys List." FAPIIS is meant to be a one-stop information source for agencies, collecting data from a variety of sources about contractors' ethics and past performance.

Does the FAPIIS Disclosure Rule Apply to My Small Business?

The FAPIIS disclosure obligation applies if your small business wins a new federal contract exceeding $500,000 and subsequently holds federal contracts and grants—in the aggregate—valued at $10 million or more, including all priced options.

> Dry Dry Again wins a federal dry cleaning contract valued at $4 million, including options. Dry Dry Again also holds four other federal contracts, valued at $500,000, $3 million, and $2.75 million, respectively.
>
> **Result:** Because Dry Dry Again's new contract award puts it over the $10 million threshold, it must begin reporting information to FAPIIS.

What Information Must I Report to FAPIIS?

If your small business is required to make FAPIIS reports, you must submit a report anytime your business, or one of its principals (defined as owners, officers, and others having primary management or supervisory authority over a segment of business), has, in connection with the award or performance of a federal contract or grant, in the last five years, been subject to:

- Criminal conviction (whether misdemeanor or felony)
- A civil proceeding (such as a lawsuit) that resulted in a finding of fault or liability and required the payment of $5,000 or more as a result
- An administrative proceeding (such as a hearing before the Securities and Exchange Commission or the Armed Services Board of Contract Appeals) that resulted in a finding of fault or liability and required the payment of at least $5,000
- Any settlement of an administrative proceeding that resulted in the acknowledgment of fault and payment of $5,000 or

more, or the payment of a reimbursement, restitution, or damages in excess of $100,000

- In a criminal, civil, or administrative proceeding, a disposition of the matter by consent or compromise, with an acknowledgment of fault, if the proceeding could have led to any of the above outcomes

If this list looks familiar, it's because you've been paying attention to the previous chapters. The information you must report to FAPIIS is similar to the information the government may use to find your small business "non-responsible," as we discussed in Chapter 5. So, be wary: To paraphrase the venerable Miranda warning, anything you say to FAPIIS can and will be used against you. Unfortunately, unlike a criminal defendant, your small business does not have the right to remain silent.

How Do I Make My FAPIIS Reports? You should submit your FAPIIS information online by logging into your Central Contractor Registration (CCR) profile at http://www.ccr.gov. Once your business is subject to FAPIIS reporting requirements for a particular contract, you must update your FAPIIS information semiannually, through the life of the contract, to ensure that the information remains current, accurate, and complete.

The Primary Rules: Where to Find Them

Here's where to find the primary rules discussed in this chapter:

- 31 U.S.C. §§ 3729-3733 (False Claims Act)
- FAR 3.1003, FAR 9.406-2, and FAR 9.407-2 (significant overpayments)
- 18 U.S.C. § 201 (bribery)

- 5 U.S.C. § 7353 and 5 C.F.R. §§ 2635.201-205 (gifts)
- FAR 3.502-2 and FAR 52.203-7 (kickbacks)
- FAR 3.4 and FAR 52.203-5 (contingent fees)
- FAR 3.8, FAR 52.203-11, and FAR 52.203-13 (lobbying restrictions)
- FAR 23.5 and FAR 52.223-6 (drug-free workplace)
- FAR 3.10, FAR 52.203-13, and FAR 52.203-14 (codes of ethics)
- FAR 52.203-13 (training and internal controls)
- FAR 9.5 (organizational conflicts of interest)
- FAR 9.406-2, FAR 9.407-2, and FAR 52.203-12 (mandatory disclosure)
- FAR 52.209-7 and FAR 52.209-9 (FAPIIS disclosure)

Compliance at a Glance: Ethics, Conflicts, and Disclosure

❑ Ensure that all claims and certifications made to the government are accurate, including certifications relating to your business's size and eligibility for set-aside contracts.

❑ Inform the government of any significant overpayments received by your company.

❑ Avoid monetary and non-monetary gifts to government employees, including gifts of entertainment, sporting tickets, and meals, unless an exception applies.

❑ Do not solicit or accept anything of value (including non-monetary gifts) in exchange for providing favorable treatment with respect to a federal contract or subcontract.

☐ Put in place reasonable procedures designed to prevent and detect possible kickbacks (consider updating your employee handbook and ethics policy).

☐ Do not use federal appropriated funds to lobby a government official or employee with respect to a federal contract.

☐ Implement a drug-free workplace policy, including publishing a policy statement, notifying employees of the policy, and establishing a drug-free awareness program.

☐ Notify the contracting officer within ten days after receiving notice or learning about an employee's conviction under a criminal drug statute for a violation occurring in the workplace.

☐ Take disciplinary action against any employee who is convicted under a criminal drug statute for a violation occurring in the workplace.

☐ Adopt a written code of ethics (recommended for all contractors; required if your business is awarded a contract that is expected to exceed $5 million and will include a performance period of 120 days or more).

☐ In your code of ethics, educate employees about specific ethical issues, require employees to disclose actual or suspected ethical violations, and implement a policy of disciplinary action against violators (recommended).

☐ Adopt a compliance program and system of internal controls including at a minimum the contents called for in FAR 52.203-13 (recommended for all contractors; required if your business is awarded a contract that is expected to exceed $5 million and will include a performance period of 120 days or more).

☐ Flow down FAR 52.203-13 to all subcontractors holding subcontracts valued in excess of $5 million with a period of performance exceeding 120 days.

☐ Display an agency fraud hotline poster or Department of Homeland Security fraud hotline poster (required if your small business holds a federal contract of more than $5 million).

☐ Put in place procedures to identify and, if necessary, mitigate organizational conflicts of interest (recommended).

❑ Adopt a written OCI mitigation plan (recommended; may be required by the government for a particular procurement).

❑ Include a provision in your subcontracts requiring disclosure of potential organizational conflicts of interest and personal conflicts of interest (recommended).

❑ Inform the government in a timely manner, in writing, whenever you have credible evidence that a principal, employee, agent, or subcontractor has violated the False Claims Act; committed a violation of criminal law involving fraud, conflict of interest, or bribery; or where the company has received a significant overpayment.

CHAPTER 9

USA! USA! DOMESTIC PREFERENCES AND OVERSEAS CONTRACTS

IT SHOULD COME AS NO SURPRISE that the government prefers buying products made in the good ol' USA. Although commercial stores are flooded with items manufactured in other countries, Uncle Sam knows that it doesn't look good if the federal government buys too many foreign-made goods. Plus, buying domestic products helps American companies (like your small business) earn the lion's share of federal contracting dollars.

If your business sells products or supplies to the government (including construction materials), you should understand how the government's so-called *domestic preferences* operate. A domestic preference, like the name implies, provides an incentive for contractors to sell the government items produced in the United States. In this chapter, we will discuss how to ensure that you comply with the domestic preferences established by the Buy American Act.

In addition, we will discuss an important rule that applies when your government contract requires you to perform work overseas—something many small businesses have found themselves doing in the years following the September 11, 2001, terrorist attacks.

The Buy American Act

Contrary to popular belief, the Buy American Act does not (in most cases) prohibit the government from buying products produced outside the United States. After all, the government has competing policy interests in mind: It wants to support domestic business, but also does not want to pay extravagant sums of taxpayer money for domestic products if foreign products are much cheaper.

So why do you care whether you sell the government foreign or domestic products? Two reasons.

First, the Buy American Act encourages contractors to provide products "Made in the USA" by establishing a *price premium*, that is, an upward adjustment to the actual prices of foreign goods in its evaluation of contractors' proposals—6 to 12 percent for civilian agencies, and a whopping 50 percent for the Department of Defense. For civilian agency procurements, small businesses get the full 12 percent price premium for offering domestic products. Offering domestic products can make your offer more competitive, even if foreign products are less expensive without the premium.

> The Department of Defense issues a solicitation seeking 10,000 handheld radios. Pickle Bytes, Inc., a purveyor of electronics (whose owner really loves dill pickles), offers the government domestic radios at a price of $22 each, for a total bid of $220,000. Claude, hoping to get Sleez-E into the electronics business, offers foreign-made radios at a price of $18 each, or $180,000.
>
> **Result:** In evaluating the competing offers, the Department of Defense will add 50 percent, or $90,000, to Sleez-E's offer, resulting in a total evaluated price of $270,000. Pickle Bytes' offer becomes the lower priced—by quite a bit.

In order to determine whether it is getting homegrown products or something from overseas, the government will require you to certify whether each product you intend to provide is a "domestic end product," made in the United States. If you are providing non-U.S. end products, you must specifically identify each one and its country of origin.

As with all certifications you make to the government, the consequences of a false certification can be devastating, including suspension, debarment, and even False Claims Act liability (see Chapter 8 for a discussion of the False Claims Act). It is critical, then, to know where your products come from and get your certifications right.

How Do I Complete My Buy American Act Certification?

To complete your Buy American Act certification, you must determine whether your products are considered domestic or foreign under the act. The first step is to think about whether your products are unmanufactured or manufactured.

Unmanufactured Products

An *unmanufactured product* is one that is provided to the government in its original form—typically, agricultural products or minerals. Under the Buy American Act, an unmanufactured end product is considered "domestic" if it is mined or produced in the United States.

Johnny's Bananas, Inc., supplies bananas to the government. The bananas come from trees located in Hawaii.

Result: Johnny's Bananas is supplying a domestic end product. Johnny should certify under the Buy American Act that the bananas are domestic.

As you can see, for unmanufactured products, completing your Buy American Act is straightforward. Since Johnny gets his bananas from Hawaii, they are domestic. If they came from Nicaragua, or another foreign country, they would not be domestic.

Manufactured Products

The rule for manufactured products is a little more complex. A *manufactured product* is considered "domestic" if the end product (the completed item actually sold to the government) is manufactured in the United States and one of two other criteria is met:

- The cost of the components manufactured in the United States is greater than the cost of the components manufactured in foreign countries.
- The end product is a commercially available off-the-shelf item.

Are My Products Manufactured in the United States?

Generally, it does not take much for an end product to be "manufactured" in the United States. As long as the final assembly of the product occurs in the United States, the government will likely consider it manufactured domestically.

ComfortFeet, LLC, sells shoes to the government. The company acquires shoe leather from an Argentine company, rubber from a supplier in Brazil, and insoles from a domestic firm, and then puts the whole product together in its facility in Raleigh, North Carolina.

Result: Because the final assembly occurs domestically, Comfort-Feet's shoes are "manufactured" in the United States for purposes of the Buy American Act. (Note, however, that domestic manufacture, by itself, does not mean that ComfortFeet is supplying domestic end products—it still has to meet one of the other two criteria we will discuss below.)

In most cases, any final assembly done domestically meets the "manufactured in the United States" test. However, if your business does little if anything to transform the product during the "assembly," it may not qualify.

While on vacation abroad, Claude acquires some foreign-made computer processors at discount prices. Upon returning to the United States, Claude buys some domestic monitors and key-boards, and then plugs them into the processors. Sleez-E attempts to sell the resulting desktop computers to the government, certi-fying that they were manufactured domestically.

Result: Simply plugging the monitors and keyboards into the processors is not enough for the government to deem the com-puters manufactured in the United States. Sleez-E's Buy American Act certification is improper.

How Do I Determine the Cost of Components?

Once you determine that your end products were manufactured in the United States, you must figure out whether the cost of the components manufactured in the United States is greater than the cost of the components manufactured in other countries (except in the case of commercially available off-the-shelf products, which we will discuss below).

First things first: What counts as a "component" for Buy American Act purposes? A *component* is considered an item directly incorporated into the end product itself—not subcomponents or materials making up the components directly incorporated into the end product.

ComfortFeet, LLC, wants to sell shoes to the government. The company acquires shoe leather from an Argentine company, rubber from a supplier in Brazil, and insoles from a domestic firm. The insole manufacturer acquires the materials it uses to produce the insoles from Mexico.

Result: In completing its Buy American Act certification, Comfort-Feet will count the shoe leather, rubber, and insoles as components. The materials that go into the insoles are not components, so the fact that the materials come from Mexico is irrelevant for Buy American Act purposes.

Once you determine what components make up your end product, you should determine where those components were manufactured, using the same "final assembly" test you apply to your own products. Then, allocate the entire acquisition cost of that component (including transportation costs and duties, but excluding profit for components you manufacture yourself) into one of two categories— domestic or foreign. Repeat the process for each component, and then determine whether the total greater costs were incurred for domestic or foreign components.

ComfortFeet intends to bid on a contract to sell boots to the Marine Corps. The company plans to spend $500,000 to obtain the components for the boots, broken down as follows: $300,000 for leather from an Argentine firm, $50,000 for rubber from a supplier in Brazil, and $150,000 for insoles from a domestic manufacturer.

Result: The acquisition costs of ComfortFeet's components are $350,000 (70 percent) foreign and $150,000 (30 percent) domestic. The majority of ComfortFeet's acquisition costs are for foreign components, so ComfortFeet cannot certify that it is providing domestic products.

As the example demonstrates, just because your company is located in the United States does not mean that it is offering domestic products for Buy American Act purposes. ComfortFeet probably believed that its boots were domestic products—after all, the company assembles the boots at its facility in North Carolina. If it wants, ComfortFeet can fix the problem by buying its leather from a domestic source, allowing it to certify that its shoes are domestic end products.

What if ComfortFeet didn't know where its leather came from? Could the company just remove leather from the calculation and claim to be offering domestic products?

No. If you do not know the origin of any component, you must assume that it was manufactured outside the United States for purposes of your Buy American Act certification. In ComfortFeet's case, the result would have been the same.

What Are Commercially Available Off-the-Shelf Items?

You do not need to perform a cost comparison of components if your end product is a "commercially available, off-the-shelf" item. A commercially available, off-the-shelf-item is an item that is:

- Customarily used by the general public or non-governmental entities for purposes other than government purposes
- Sold in substantial quantities to the commercial marketplace
- Offered to the government, without modification, in the same form in which it is sold in the commercial marketplace

Let's look at how the "commercially available, off-the-shelf" exception can affect your Buy American Act certification:

ComfortFeet intends to bid on a contract to sell athletic shoes to the Army. Last year, the company sold more than a million of its popular "Big Comfort Cross-Trainer" shoes to the public. ComfortFeet produces the Big Comfort using leather from its favorite

Argentine supplier, rubber from an Indonesian company, and plastics from a company located in India, and then assembles the shoes at its Raleigh plant. ComfortFeet plans to offer the Big Comfort to the Army without modification.

Result: Because all three criteria are met, the Big Comfort qualifies as a commercially available, off-the-shelf item. ComfortFeet need not run a cost comparison of components. The Big Comfort is manufactured in North Carolina, which qualifies it as a domestic product for Buy American Act purposes.

The result would be different if ComfortFeet sold a modified version of its shoes specifically for a government customer—say, a special shoe designed in camouflage colors and known as the "G.I. Comfort." In that case, because the G.I. Comfort would not be commercially available, ComfortFeet would have to run the cost comparison, leading to a "non-domestic" certification.

Special Buy American Rules for Construction Materials

Some special Buy American Act rules apply to construction contracts. Most important, as a general matter, you cannot offer foreign construction materials unless the cost of domestic materials exceeds the cost of foreign materials by more than 6 percent.

XPert Constructors submits a $1.5 million bid on a procurement to renovate a Department of Veterans Affairs hospital. XPert proposes using drywall from Canada, which will cost XPert a total of $500,000. Obtaining the same drywall domestically would have cost $515,000.

Result: XPert's bid does not comply with the Buy American Act because the cost of domestic material does not exceed the cost of foreign material by more than 6 percent (in fact, here, the price difference is only 3 percent). The procuring agency will likely reject XPert's bid.

If the price differential is not at least 6 percent, there are a few other cases in which you may offer foreign construction materials, but they occur less frequently—such as if a particular material is not available domestically in reasonable quantities.

If you intend to use foreign construction materials because they are cheaper, you must submit a written justification to the procuring agency, comparing the domestic and foreign prices. See FAR clause 52.225-9 for the pricing table you should complete in support of your justification. If FAR clause 52.225-10 is included in the contract, you may hedge your bets and submit *two* offers—one using foreign materials, the other domestic.

For larger construction contracts (those valued at $7,804,000 as of this writing), you have a little more leeway when it comes to acquiring your construction materials. For these contracts, you can provide materials from so-called "designated countries" (generally, countries with which the United States has established free trade agreements or other special trade relationships), and count those materials as domestic for purposes of your Buy American Act certification.

XPert Constructors submits a $10 million bid on a contract to build a school on an Air Force base. XPert proposes using drywall from Canada, which will cost XPert $1,125,000. Using domestic drywall would have cost $1,135,000.

Result: Thanks to the North American Free Trade Agreement (NAFTA), Canada is a designated country under the Buy American Act. Although the price differential does not meet the 6 percent rule, it doesn't matter—since the contract exceeds the $7.8 million threshold, XPert can count Canadian materials as domestic for purposes of its certification.

If you are thinking about using non-domestic construction materials, check your solicitation for FAR clause 52.225-11. If it's included, you can use designated country materials and count them as domestic materials.

So which countries are "designated," anyway? As you might imagine, the list shifts from time to time along with the political winds. Check FAR clause 52.225-11 for the current list of designated countries.

What Is the Trade Agreements Act?

A statute called the Trade Agreements Act includes a list of designated countries for non-construction contracts, and sets up a framework allowing contractors to count products from designated countries as domestic for Buy American Act purposes. But here's the hitch—the Trade Agreements Act does not apply to small business set-aside contracts. If your company bids exclusively on set-asides, you should not be running into the Trade Agreements Act anytime soon.

However, if you bid on an *unrestricted procurement*, that is, a procurement not set-aside for small businesses or any subcategory of small businesses (like 8(a) or women-owned firms) you'll likely see the Trade Agreements Act clause, FAR 52.225-6, included in the solicitation and in your contract. If this clause is included, you must submit a separate certification, informing the government where each of your products originates. Confusingly, though, the Trade Agreements Act uses a different test than the Buy American Act to determine whether a product is foreign or domestic. Forget about comparing the cost of components. Instead, according to the Trade Agreement, a product is considered to come from a country when one of two circumstances exists:

- The product is wholly the growth, product, or manufacture of that country.
- Within the country, the product has been substantially transformed into a new and different article of commerce with a distinct name, character, or use.

Johnny's Bananas, Inc., sells bananas to the government. The bananas come from trees located in Hawaii.

Result: The bananas are wholly grown in the United States. Johnny's Bananas is supplying a domestic end product.

Just like the Buy American Act, if the product comes entirely from one country, it is a product of that country for purposes of the Trade Agreements Act.

If the product is manufactured from components coming from different countries, the product is considered to come from the country where the final assembly occurred, as long as that assembly considerably altered the product.

ComfortFeet wants to sell boots to the Marine Corps. The company intends to acquire shoe leather from Argentina, rubber from a supplier in Brazil, and insoles from a Canadian firm, then put the whole product together in its facility in Raleigh, North Carolina.

Result: ComfortFeet's shoes are considered a domestic product for Trade Agreements Act purposes because they have been substantially transformed in the United States.

Note that in this case, the shoes are a domestic product under the Trade Agreements Act, but *not* under the Buy American Act (unless the boots are commercially available, off-the-shelf items), because none of the components come from the United States.

Because the Trade Agreements Act does not apply to small business set-asides, we have kept our discussion intentionally brief. But if you bid on a solicitation containing the Trade Agreements Act clause, be sure to look at the clause to determine which countries are designated. Who knows—you may be able to acquire products much cheaper abroad, but still count them as domestic when you submit your bid to the government.

What are the FAR's "Prohibited Sources?"

Do you do a lot of business in North Korea, Iran, and other international pariahs? Probably not, which means you have nothing to worry about when it comes to the FAR's *prohibited sources list*. The prohibited sources list is simply a list of a handful of countries from which you cannot acquire products to sell to the government—no matter the price difference.

As of this writing, most transactions involving Cuba, Iran, Sudan, Burma, and North Korea were prohibited. But keep an eye on the FAR and the contracting headlines, because the prohibited sources list is not set in stone. Cuba may be removed from the list when the Castro regime finally falls, and political changes in other nations could lead to their addition or removal from the prohibited sources list. For a current list of prohibited sources, see FAR 25.701.

The Foreign Corrupt Practices Act

While we're on the topic of foreign countries, we want to draw your attention to a very important statute you should know about if your company does any government contracting work abroad—like working at an overseas military base. This statute, called the Foreign Corrupt Practices Act (FCPA), is not the only special requirement that applies when you do government contract work overseas (for example, the Defense Base Act may require you to provide special workers compensation insurance to your employees working abroad). We recognize that most small government contractors don't work overseas, so we have not covered these other requirements in this book. The Foreign Corrupt Practices Act, however, is too important not to discuss because the potential penalties for violations are so severe.

The Foreign Corrupt Practices Act broadly prohibits bribing foreign officials in order to obtain a business advantage—even if bribery is the norm in the country where you are working.

BigTime Construction wishes to bid on a contract to provide construction services to a U.S. embassy overseas. The contract requires BigTime to ship construction equipment abroad. To avoid the expensive fee the host country charges on all products arriving in the country (and thus, provide a lower-priced proposal), BigTime offers $10,000 to a foreign customs official, who accepts the payment and waives the customs fee.

Result: BigTime has violated the FCPA.

A foreign official need not accept a bribe in order for it to violate the FCPA: The FCPA applies to offers or promises to make illicit payments, as well as to the payments themselves.

Anytime you or one of your employees makes a payment to a foreign official, you may risk a FCPA violation. However, while the FCPA prohibits bribes of the type BigTime made, it permits so-called *grease payments*, that is, payments made to a foreign official to expedite or secure the performance of a routine governmental action—something the government official would have or should have done anyway.

XPert Constructors, LLC, wishes to bid on a contract to provide construction services to the U.S. embassy in the nation of Slowland. The contract requires XPert to ship construction equipment to Slowland and commence work immediately. Understanding that Slowland's customs officials ordinarily delay large shipments for months at the docks before they review them for transport within the country, XPert pays a foreign customs official $10,000 to review XPert's shipment the day it arrives.

Result: So long as it is part of the foreign official's routine duties to review such shipments, XPert's payment qualifies as a permissible "grease payment" and will not result in a FCPA violation.

XPert's payment is permissible because XPert merely paid the official to expedite an act he was already obligated to perform—the review of XPert's shipment. But XPert is walking a very fine line. If XPert's payment was in exchange for the official's review and *approval* of the shipment, it would probably have violated the FCPA. After all, Slowland's customs officials are not required to approve every shipment.

And remember that this exception applies only to *foreign* officials. You cannot make "grease payments" to U.S. government officials, no matter how slowly it seems they may be performing their jobs. If you do, you will run afoul of the bribery laws we discussed in Chapter 8.

In recent years, the government has dramatically increased Foreign Corrupt Practices Act enforcement, resulting in the payment of millions of dollars in penalties. For example, in 2011, Tyson Foods, Inc., the well-known purveyor of chicken, agreed to pay more than $5 million in penalties to settle claims that it bribed meat-processing inspectors at its plants in Mexico.

Given the government's increasing emphasis on Foreign Corrupt Practices Act enforcement, if your company does any work overseas, you should educate your employees about this act and strictly prohibit violations as part of your firm's code of ethics and employee handbook. Even if an employee believes that a particular payment is a permitted grease payment or qualifies for another exception, he or she should obtain a review and authorization for the payment at your company's highest levels.

The Primary Rules: Where to Find Them

Here's where to find the primary rules discussed in this chapter:

- FAR 25.2, FAR 52.225-1, and FAR 52.225-2 (Buy American Act—supplies)
- FAR 25.2, FAR 52.225-9, FAR 52.225-10, FAR 52.225-11, and FAR 52.225-12 (Buy American Act—construction materials)

- FAR 25.4, FAR 52.225-5, and FAR 52.225-6 (Trade Agreements Act)
- FAR 25.7 and FAR 52.225-13 (prohibited sources)
- 15 U.S.C. § 78 (Foreign Corrupt Practices Act)

Compliance at a Glance: Domestic Preferences and Overseas Contracts

☐ When pricing your offers to the government, apply the Buy American Act price preference to determine whether it is less expensive to offer foreign or domestic products (recommended).

☐ Accurately complete your Buy American Act certification whenever the Buy American Act is included in your contract.

☐ If you sell unmanufactured products to the government, do not certify that they are domestic unless they are mined or produced in the United States.

☐ If you sell manufactured products to the government, do not certify that they are domestic unless the end product is manufactured in the United States and either (1) the cost of the components manufactured in the United States is greater than the cost of the components manufactured in foreign countries; or (2) the end product is a commercially available off-the-shelf item.

☐ For construction solicitations including the Buy American Act clauses, do not offer foreign construction materials unless the cost of domestic materials exceeds the cost of foreign materials by more than 6 percent or another exception applies.

☐ Whenever you offer foreign construction materials because they are cheaper, submit a written justification, comparing the domestic and foreign prices, using the table at FAR clause 52.225-9.

- ❑ For larger construction contracts valued at $7,804,000 or above, treat materials from designated countries named in FAR clause 52.225-11 as domestic.

- ❑ For unrestricted contracts containing subject to the Trade Agreements Act, accurately complete a certification telling the government where each of your products originates.

- ❑ When completing your Trade Agreements Act certifications, state that a product comes from a country if the product (1) is wholly the growth, product, or manufacture of that country; or (2) has been substantially transformed into a new and different article of commerce, with a distinct name, character, or use, within the country.

- ❑ Do not attempt to sell the government any products originating from a prohibited source identified in FAR 25.701.

- ❑ When performing contracts overseas, do not bribe or attempt to bribe foreign officials.

- ❑ Educate your employees about the Foreign Corrupt Practices Act and prohibit violations in your company's handbook and code of ethics (recommended).

CHAPTER 10

UNDER THE HOOD:
THE NUTS AND BOLTS OF A
GOVERNMENT CONTRACTOR

LET'S TAKE A BREAK from ethics, eligibility, and other hot-button issues to discuss a few fundamental matters that arise "under the hood" when you contract with the federal government. We can't promise that this chapter will be the most exciting portion of the book, but like the rest of the material we have covered, the topics we will discuss are important to your small business's success in the federal marketplace.

First, this chapter covers the registration numbers you must obtain and the databases you must enter in order to receive a government contract. If you're an experienced contractor, you might be tempted to skip this section, but give it a read anyway—it's not too long, and you might learn a thing or two about just how important these registrations can be.

Next, the chapter delves into what happens when your company's ownership changes in the middle of contract performance, and how to go about transferring a government contract from one company to another.

Finally, we briefly discuss where to get help to ensure that your accounting system is compliant, and how long you must preserve your contract-related records.

Registration Numbers and Databases

To be awarded a government contract, your small business must obtain two different registration numbers and register in two independent databases (as well as a third, recommended database).

What Registration Numbers Do I Need?

Your small business cannot be awarded a government contract without a Taxpayer Identification Number (TIN). A TIN is used to identify your company for Internal Revenue Service purposes, including your tax returns. (Note that the FAR refers to the number as a TIN, while the IRS calls it an Employer Identification Number, or EIN.)

Unless your company is brand-new, you probably already have a TIN. So why are we discussing the requirement here? Small government contractors sometimes form joint ventures with other companies, and often structure their joint ventures as limited liability companies (LLCs). Because an LLC is a new legal entity, you must obtain a new TIN for your joint venture, even if both partners to the joint venture already have their own TINs.

Harry's company, Harr-Ball Limos, forms a joint venture with Jane's business, Dry Dry Again. The companies intend for Dry Dry Again to perform dry cleaning services for federal agencies, while Harr-Ball transports the clothing between government buildings and Dry Dry Again's facilities. Harry and Jane structure their joint venture as an LLC and name it The Ol' Ball & Jane, LLC. The new company submits a bid on a government contract.

Result: Because The Ol' Ball & Jane is a new legal entity, it must obtain its own TIN before it can be awarded a federal contract—even though Harr-Ball and Dry Dry Again presumably already have TINs of their own.

The IRS makes it easy to obtain a TIN. You can apply online at https://sa1.www4.irs.gov/modiein/individual/index.jsp and receive your TIN immediately.

Once you have a TIN, you must obtain a second identification number, called a Data Universal Numbering System (DUNS) number. You may obtain a DUNS number through Dun & Bradstreet online at http://fedgov.dnb.com/webform/pages/CCRSearch.jsp. Although Dun & Bradstreet is a private company, it provides DUNS numbers for free to all businesses required to register with the government for contracting purposes. Again, even if you already have a DUNS number, you should obtain a new one if you form a new legal entity (like a joint venture) to bid on government contracts.

What Databases Do I Need to Join?

After you obtain both a TIN and DUNS, you must register your company in the Central Contractor Registration (CCR) database. Except in unusual circumstances (such as for classified contracts or contracts made to support urgent and compelling needs), the government cannot award contracts to companies not listed in the CCR database. To register, go to www.ccr.gov.

The CCR registration page will ask you for information about your company's address, contact persons, and—perhaps most importantly—its size status under your company's primary and secondary NAICS codes. If you plan to bid on small business set-aside contracts, it is essential that you fill out the CCR profile correctly, especially the size information. When competitors are considering whether to file a size protest challenging a set-aside award to your small business, your

CCR profile will be one of the first places they will look. Don't give them any unnecessary ammunition.

> When Bob fills out QuickDri's CCR profile, he is in a hurry, and answers that QuickDri is not a small business under any of the dry cleaning NAICS codes (even though he should know better). He intends to correct the information when he has more time, but never gets around to it. Several months later, QuickDri wins a set-aside dry cleaning contract.
>
> **Result:** One of QuickDri's competitors uses QuickDri's CCR profile as "Exhibit A" in a size protest challenging QuickDri's eligibility.

Of course, it's even worse to do the opposite: state in the CCR that your company is a small business under a particular size standard when in fact your company is not small. If you do so, the government might accuse you of misrepresentation or even fraud. Carefully monitor your CCR profile and update it regularly to make sure the information is current and accurate.

As part of your CCR profile, you should complete your SBA Dynamic Small Business Search (DSBS) profile. Contracting officers often look to the DSBS to locate eligible small businesses, and—like the CCR—competitors may use an incorrect DSBS profile against you. Unlike CCR, you are not required to register in the DSBS in order to obtain government contract awards, but failing to register, or neglecting your DSBS profile, is not a good idea. Create your DSBS profile by following the link from your CCR account.

In addition to your CCR profile, you must complete an Online Representations and Certifications (ORCA) profile, at https://orca.bpn.gov/. As with the CCR, do not treat your ORCA profile like just another bit of bothersome paperwork to rush through. Your ORCA profile is a potential minefield of compliance issues, because you will be asked not only to certify your size, but also your eligibility for special contracting programs, like those reserved for women-owned businesses and service-disabled veteran-owned small businesses.

Do not check "yes" unless you are certain that you qualify, even if you do not intend to bid on contracts set-aside for service-disabled veteran-owned or women-owned small businesses. The government may suspend or debar your company from all government contracting if you incorrectly certify that you are eligible—even if you make a good faith mistake. See Chapters 12 and 14 to determine whether your small business qualifies as service-disabled-owned or women-owned.

Update your ORCA profile as often as necessary to ensure that the information is current and accurate. Even if nothing changes, you must update your profile at least annually.

What Is the SAM?

Though CCR and ORCA still existed as stand-alone databases as of this writing, they may not by the time you read this book. The government has announced plans to consolidate many of its electronic databases, including CCR, ORCA, and several others (such as the Excluded Parties List System we discussed in prior chapters) into a single database known as the System for Award Management, or SAM. The new SAM database will be rolled out in stages between 2012 and 2015, and the stand-alone databases it replaces will gradually disappear. However, the web addresses we provide in this chapter and elsewhere in this book should still work. The government has stated that after the transition, those addresses will simply reroute visitors to SAM.

Ownership Changes

Imagine that you've been a successful government contractor for many years (due in large part to your company's strong reputation for compliance) and start thinking about retirement. Thanks to your hard work, your company is worth much more than it was when you began government contracting. But before you put your company up for sale and start negotiating to buy that beach house you've always dreamed about, you need to make sure you handle the transaction right.

If FAR clause 52.215-19 is included in any ongoing government contract, you must provide written notice to the administrative contracting officer if:

- Your company has changed ownership, or is certain to change ownership, and

- The ownership change could result in changes in the valuation of your company's capitalized assets in its accounting records

You should provide the written notification within 30 days of the ownership change or the date you knew the change of ownership was certain to occur, whichever is earlier.

> Harry wants to sell a controlling interest in Harr-Ball Limos so that he can spend more time vacationing in Ireland. On May 1, he and Buck's Trucking sign a stock purchase agreement, in which Buck's Trucking agrees to buy 51 percent of Harr-Ball. The deal closes two weeks later, on May 15.
>
> **Result:** If the transaction could result in a change in the value of Harr-Ball's capitalized assets in its accounting records, Harry should submit notifications to all of Harr-Ball's contracting officers by May 31—30 days after Harry knew the ownership change was certain to occur.

How do you know if an ownership change may result in a change in value of your capitalized assets in your accounting records? Don't try to figure it out yourself. Talk to your accountant. If your accountant isn't certain, err on the side of caution and submit the notifications.

Ownership Changes and Size Recertification

If your company qualified as a small business for any government contracts it is performing at the time an ownership change occurs, you must submit a separate size recertification to the procuring agencies within 30 days after the transaction becomes final.

> Amy's Caterers is performing government contract work under two small business set-aside contracts, for which the company qualified as small, and one unrestricted contract, for which the company did not qualify as small. On May 1, Amy signs a stock purchase agreement, in which International Food, Inc., a large business, agrees to buy 51 percent of the company's stock. The deal closes two weeks later, on May 15.
>
> **Result:** Amy's Caterers must submit size recertifications for the two set-aside contracts by May 14—30 days after the deal was finalized. The company does not need to submit a size recertification for the unrestricted contract because it did not qualify as small for that contract.

Just because a contract is not set-aside for small business does not mean that you can forgo a size recertification. If you self-certified as a small business for the contract, you must recertify, even if the contract was not set-aside for small business.

What if My Company Is No Longer Small? If the change in ownership causes your company to lose its "small" status for a particular contract, the procuring agency need not terminate the contract (except for 8(a) contracts, which we will discuss below). However, the agency may no longer count option years or task order awards toward its small business contracting goals. Depending on the agency, the inability to take small business credit for option years or task order awards may cause the agency to decide not to award them. Consider this possibility—and if possible, try to get a feel for the contracting officer's intentions—before following through with an ownership change.

Size Recertification and the 8(a) Program. If your small business is a participant in the SBA's 8(a) Program and is working on 8(a) set-aside contracts, you may want to think twice about selling your ownership interest. Unlike other set-aside contracts, the procuring agency must terminate an 8(a) contract if the disadvantaged individual upon whom 8(a) eligibility was based (typically, the majority owner) relinquishes or agrees to relinquish ownership, such that the company would no longer be 51 percent owned by disadvantaged individuals. (See Chapter 11 for an explanation of when an individual is considered disadvantaged.)

> XPert Constructors, Inc., is a participant in the 8(a) program and is currently performing work under three 8(a) set-aside contracts. On November 1, Erik, the disadvantaged individual upon whom XPert's 8(a) status is based, signs an agreement to sell 51 percent of the company to BigTime Construction. The deal closes on November 30.
>
> **Result:** Erik's deal to sell the company triggers the termination requirement. The procuring agencies should terminate XPert's 8(a) contracts, even before the deal closes.

The SBA may waive the termination requirement in rare cases, such as when the disadvantaged owner dies or becomes incapacitated or the head of the procuring agency certifies that termination would severely impede the agency's program objectives. However, except in cases of death or incapacity of the disadvantaged owner, you must request a waiver in writing before the change in ownership occurs. If the disadvantaged owner dies or becomes incapacitated, the company must submit a waiver request within 60 days.

Selling or Transferring a Government Contract

Unlike most of your business's assets, you cannot sell or transfer a government contract at your whim. The government believes that it is anti-competitive for "Company A" to win a contract and then transfer it to "Company B," which may not have had the qualifications to win the contract in the first place. To implement this policy, a federal law called the Anti-Assignment Act prohibits contractors from selling or transferring their government contracts—unless the government gives its permission.

> After International Food purchases a majority interest in Amy's Caterers, Amy recognizes that her company is no longer eligible to win new small business set-aside contracts due to its affiliation with International Foods. Amy decides to pull Amy's Caterers out of the government marketplace and focus on commercial work. With International Foods' permission, she signs an agreement with Buster's Bakers, Inc., selling all of her company's government contracts to Buster's Bakers, but does not obtain the government's permission for the sale.
>
> **Result:** Government contracts cannot be transferred or sold without the government's consent. The sales agreement is invalid (unless and until the government signs off on it) and Amy's Caterers is still responsible for performing the government contracts.

Do I Need to Request the Government's Permission?

You do not need to request the government's permission to transfer or sell a contract if there is a change in ownership as the result of a stock or ownership purchase, with no change in the legal identity of the contractor.

> While BrettWorks is performing an administrative services contract for the Navy, Brett receives a job offer from the New York Yankees. Brett, who has always dreamed of working for the Yankees, sells 100 percent of BrettWorks' stock to Mark—who is not a baseball

fan, but offers the highest price. BrettWorks continues performing the contract under Mark's leadership.

Result: BrettWorks does not need to request permission from the Navy to transfer the contract because BrettWorks remains the contractor, despite Mark's purchase of the company.

If there is a change in your small business's ownership, you may need to notify the government (see the discussion above), but do not need to obtain the government's permission to transfer your contracts. However, if the identity of the contractor will change—such as through a merger or asset purchase agreement—the government must approve the transfer.

When Will the Government Approve a Transfer or Sale?

The government may agree to a *novation* of a government contract, that is, a transfer or sale of the contract with the government's consent, if one of two circumstances exist:

- Your small business transfers all of its assets to another company.
- Your small business transfers all of the assets involved in performing the contract to another company.

Happy Security, Inc., which prides itself on the cheery demeanor of its employees, provides security services to a government office building. The contract requires Happy Security to supply its security guards with uniforms, handcuffs, and guns. After working under the contract for six months, Happy Security signs an agreement to sell its contract to ToughGuards, Inc. However, Happy Security does not agree to sell the uniforms, handcuffs, and guns.

Result: The government will not approve Happy Security's novation request because Happy Security has not sold all of its assets involved in performing the contract to ToughGuards.

Even though the government *may* approve your novation request does not mean that it *will* approve it. The government has essentially unlimited discretion to approve or deny a request. Although procuring agencies will ordinarily approve a good faith novation request made in accordance with the rules, they may deny the request if the new contractor lacks qualifications or resources, if the new contractor has an organizational conflict of interest (see our discussion in Chapter 8), if there is little time remaining on the contract, or for other reasons.

How Do I Request Approval for a Transfer or Sale?

In order to obtain the government's approval of a transfer or sale of your government contracts, you must submit a novation request containing the following information:

- Three copies of a *novation agreement*, a three-way contract between your small business, the new contractor, and the government (a standard form novation agreement is available at FAR 42.1204)
- The document describing the proposed transaction, such as a merger agreement or asset purchase agreement
- A list of all contracts you wish to transfer, including the contract number and type, name and address of the contracting officer, total dollar value, and approximate remaining unpaid balance
- Evidence of the new contractor's ability to perform, such as a capabilities statement and past performance references

In addition, either together with your initial request or as soon as possible after the initial request is submitted, you must provide:

- An authenticated copy of the document effecting the transaction
- Certified copies of resolutions of each company's board of directors and stockholders approving the transaction

- A legal opinion letter by attorneys for each company stating that the transfer was properly effected

- Balance sheets for each company as of the dates immediately before and after the transfer of assets, audited by independent accountants

- Evidence that any security clearance requirements have been met

- The consent of any sureties if bonds are required (typically for construction contracts), or a statement that no surety consent is necessary

As you can see, putting together a novation request is not an exercise to take lightly. It requires putting together a substantial amount of paperwork and obtaining outside assistance from legal counsel and an independent accountant. If you want to transfer or sell a contract, get started on the novation request early in the process—perhaps while you are still negotiating the parameters of the underlying merger or asset sale—so that you will be able to submit your request to the government as soon as possible.

What If I Am Transferring More Than One Contract?

If you want to transfer or sell more than one contract, you do not need to submit multiple novation requests. If any of the contracts you wish to novate have been assigned to an administrative contracting officer (ACO) you should submit the novation request to the ACO. Otherwise, submit your novation request to the contracting officer responsible for the contract with the largest outstanding dollar balance.

After further negotiations, Happy Security's owners agree to sell all of the company's government contracts, together with all the assets used in performing the contracts, to ToughGuards. Happy Security is performing three government contracts: a contract with the Army, which has a $250,000 outstanding balance; a contract with the Department of the Treasury, which has a $1 million out-standing balance; and a contract with the Department of Health and Human Services, which has a $100,000 balance. None of the contracts has been assigned to an ACO.

Result: Happy Security should submit its novation request to the contracting officer responsible for its Department of State con-tract, which has the largest outstanding balance. That contracting officer may approve the novation of all three contracts—including those between Happy Security and other agencies.

Name Changes

What if you don't want to sell your company or its contracts, but just change your company's name? You still must obtain the government's agreement, but as long as you follow the appropriate procedure, the government is very unlikely to deny your request.

Claude hears through the grapevine that the name of his company, Sleez-E, is not well received by government officials. Claude files paperwork with the state, changing the company's name to Angelic Contractors, Inc.

Result: Claude must obtain the government's agreement to the name change. Until he does so, the government will continue to call the company Sleez-E and issue payments in Sleez-E's name.

If you want to change your company's name, you should complete a Change-of-Name Agreement, using the template provided at FAR 42.1205. Then, submit three copies of the agreement to the govern-ment, together with one copy each of the following:

- The document effecting the name change, authenticated by an official of the state with jurisdiction, such as an amendment to your articles of organization or articles of incorporation

- A legal opinion letter from your attorney, stating that the change of name was properly effected under applicable law, and showing the effective date of the change of name
- A list of all affected contracts and purchase orders remaining unsettled between the contractor and the government, showing for each the contract number and type, and name and address of the contracting office

As is the case for novation requests, you need not submit more than one change-of-name agreement if you are performing multiple contracts. Instead, submit the change-of-name agreement to the same person you would submit a novation request: either the ACO or the contracting officer responsible for the contract with the largest outstanding balance.

Accounting

As we mentioned in the introduction, this book does not cover the accounting rules set forth in the FAR. Discussing the government contracts accounting rules in sufficient detail would require its own book. In fact, books have been written on the topic.

But just because we have not spent hundreds of pages talking about accounting does not mean that it's not important to adopt a compliant accounting system. At some point in your small business's government contracts work—quite possibly in connection with your first contract award, depending on the type of contract—the Defense Contract Audit Agency (DCAA) will audit your accounting system. Failing to fix problems the DCAA identifies can (and will) cause you to lose out on contracts.

Many government contractors turn to experts to help them establish and maintain DCAA-compliant accounting systems. If your accountant is not familiar with the FAR and the DCAA's rules, consider working with someone else. In addition, if your small business is part of a government-sanctioned mentor-protégé relationship with a larger, more experienced company (such as the 8(a) mentor-protégé program we will discuss in Chapter 11), consider asking your mentor to assist you in setting up and maintaining a DCAA-compliant accounting system. For more information on the accounting rules and audits, including a free informational handbook for contractors, visit the DCAA's website at www.dcaa.mil.

Record Keeping

When your small business generates records related to a government contract, you can't just toss them out as part of your spring cleaning the next year. The government requires you to keep your contract-related records for a period of two to four years following final payment on a contract.

The records may just sit there gathering dust, then eventually get thrown out. But the government makes you keep them for a reason: Uncle Sam has the right, at any reasonable time, to ask you to make the records available in connection with an investigation or audit, or for any other purpose. For instance, if a disgruntled former employee complains that your company has been falsely billing the government, you can expect investigators to show up at your doorstep asking to see your records.

How Long Must I Preserve My Records?

Different records must be preserved different lengths of time. The simplest solution is to simply hold all records for at least four years following the end of the fiscal year in which final payment on the government contract occurred, unless a contract provision or special regulation requires you to keep certain records longer.

If you are eager to dispose of records as soon as possible, however, the following records need only be kept for two years:

- Labor cost distribution cards or equivalent documents
- Petty cash records
- Clock cards or other time and attendance cards
- Paid checks, receipts for wages paid in cash, or other evidence of payments for services rendered by employees
- Store requisitions for materials, supplies, equipment, and services

Do I Need to Preserve Original Records?

The "paperless" office is in vogue these days, and understandably so—electronic data storage can be much cheaper and easier to manage than box upon box of yellowing paper files. If you prefer storing your records electronically, you're in luck, because the FAR allows you to maintain electronic copies or photocopies of your records in lieu of the originals.

If you choose to maintain copies of your records instead of the originals, you must ensure that your imaging process preserves accurate images (including signatures and any graphic images appearing in the originals) and that your imaging process is reliable and secure. In addition, you must maintain an effective indexing system to permit government investigators or auditors to quickly and conveniently access the records.

Even if your imaging system produces perfect copies, you cannot immediately dispose of the original records. You must keep them for at least one year after imaging them. Still, one year is a lot less than four, so making electronic copies may save you a lot of storage space.

The Primary Rules: Where to Find Them

Here's where to find the primary rules discussed in this chapter:

- FAR 4.9, FAR 52.204-3, and FAR 52.204-6 (registration numbers)
- FAR 4.11, FAR 4.12, FAR 52.204-7, and FAR 52.204-8 (databases)
- FAR 15.408, FAR 52.215-19 (ownership changes)
- 13 C.F.R. § 121.404, 13 C.F.R. § 124.515 (size recertification)
- FAR 42.12 (transferring or selling a government contract, name changes)
- FAR 4.7, FAR 52.214-26, FAR 52.215-2 (record keeping)

Compliance at a Glance: The Nuts and Bolts of a Government Contractor

❑ Register your business for a Taxpayer Identification Number and Data Universal Numbering System number prior to the award of any government contract.

❑ If you establish a limited liability company or other new legal entity with a joint venture partner, obtain separate TINs and DUNS numbers for the new company.

❑ Register your company in the CCR and ORCA databases prior to award of any government contract.

❑ Regularly update your CCR and ORCA databases to ensure that they are current and complete. In all cases, update your ORCA profile annually.

- ☐ If FAR clause 52.215-19 is included in your contract, provide written notice to the administrative contracting officer for every ongoing contract if your company has changed ownership or is certain to change ownership, and the ownership change could result in changes in the valuation of your company's capitalized assets in its accounting records.

- ☐ If your company qualified as a small business for any government contracts it is performing at the time an ownership change occurs, submit a separate size recertification to the procuring agencies within 30 days after the transaction becomes final.

- ☐ If your company is a participant in the 8(a) program, and the disadvantaged individual upon whom eligibility was based relinquishes or agrees to relinquish majority ownership or control, obtain an SBA waiver of the transaction (the procuring agencies will terminate ongoing 8(a) contracts without a waiver).

- ☐ If you transfer or sell a government contract to a third party, obtain the government's consent, if required.

- ☐ If the government's consent to the transfer or sale is required, submit a novation request using the standard form available at FAR 42.1204, together with the supporting information described in FAR 42.12.

- ☐ To change your company's name, complete and submit a Change-of-Name Agreement, using the template provided at FAR 42.1205, together with the supporting documentation described in the same FAR provision.

- ☐ Work with an accountant familiar with the intricate government contracting rules to ensure that your accounting system is compliant with the FAR and will pass an audit (recommended).

- ☐ Preserve all government contracting records between two and four years, as described in FAR 4.7, unless another rule or regulation provides for a longer period.

- ☐ If you make copies of government contracting records, preserve the originals for one year after the copies are made.

CHAPTER 11

THE 8(A) BUSINESS
DEVELOPMENT PROGRAM

NOW THAT WE'VE LOOKED at the key rules and regulations all small government contractors must follow, it's time to discuss the government's programs for special types of small businesses: the 8(a) Business Development Program, the Service-Disabled Veteran-Owned Small Business Program, the HUBZone Program, and the Women-Owned Small Business Program. Participating in these programs can give your company access to special contracting opportunities and benefits. But (and this should come as no surprise) each program comes with unique rules and compliance hurdles.

First up: the granddaddy of the four special programs, the 8(a) Business Development Program, or 8(a) Program. Participating in the 8(a) Program allows your company to win contracts set-aside exclusively for 8(a) participants, as well as the potential to obtain *sole source contracts*, that is, contracts awarded without any competition at all.

Over the years, many 8(a) participants have used the 8(a) Program as a springboard to grow and develop their businesses—in some cases, into multinational companies with hundreds of millions of dollars in revenues. Even if your company has more modest goals, it can benefit from its participation, but in either case, you must take care to follow the rules. Failure to comply with the regulations will land you in hot water—from termination of your 8(a) certification to much more severe penalties, including suspension and debarment.

If your small business has been admitted to the 8(a) Program or is considering applying, this chapter will help keep you on the straight and narrow.

The 8(a) Program Term

Before applying to the 8(a) Program, you should understand that 8(a) status does not last forever. The government's intent in creating the program was to provide a temporary vehicle for disadvantaged individuals to "catch up" with their non-disadvantaged peers. For that reason, a company is only permitted to participate in the 8(a) Program for a single, nine-year term. Once that term expires, a company "graduates" from the 8(a) Program and is no longer entitled to obtain new benefits under the program (though a company may continue to perform existing 8(a) contracts even after it graduates from the program).

Although nine years sounds like a long time, it can go by very quickly, and before you know it, your company could be in its last years of 8(a) Program participation. Before you apply, consider whether your company is well poised to take full advantage of the benefits the program offers. Ask yourself questions such as whether you have a strategy in place for winning 8(a) set-aside contracts and whether you have a prospective mentor in mind to enable you to take advantage of the 8(a) mentor–protégé program (which we will discuss later in this chapter). If not, it is wise to spend a little more time laying the groundwork before you submit your 8(a) application.

Initial 8(a) Program Eligibility

Unlike qualifying for small business set-aside contracts, for which you may self-certify your size, you cannot participate in the 8(a) Program unless the SBA certifies your company as an 8(a) participant. In order to be certified, your company must:

1. Qualify as a small business in its primary NAICS code.
2. Demonstrate potential for success.
3. Be unconditionally owned and controlled by one or more socially and economically disadvantaged individuals who are United States citizens and possess good character.

The third requirement applies to businesses owned by individuals. Indian tribes may also own 8(a) companies, but the rules are a little different. We will discuss the special 8(a) rules for Indian tribes in Chapter 15.

Let's examine each of the three requirements: size, potential for success, and ownership and control.

Does My Business Qualify as "Small" for the 8(a) Program?

Remember our initial discussion of size way back in Chapter 1? When it comes to small business set-aside procurements, whether or not you are "small" is based upon the NAICS code assigned to a particular procurement. Not so for 8(a) Program eligibility. To gain admission to the 8(a) Program, your small business must be deemed small under the size standard corresponding to its *primary industry classification*, typically, the NAICS code in which you did the most business in the prior fiscal year.

Mark, the new owner of BrettWorks, Inc., is interested in applying to the 8(a) Program. Over the past year, BrettWorks has earned most of its revenues under NAICS code 561110 (Office Administrative Services), which carries a $7 million size standard. BrettWorks recently outgrew the $7 million standard, but Mark notices that several agencies are issuing 8(a) set-aside procurements under NAICS code 561320 (Temporary Help Services), which carries a $13.5 million size standard. Mark would like to bid on those contracts, for which BrettWorks still qualifies as small.

Result: Assuming that the SBA deems NAICS code 561110 to be BrettWorks' primary NAICS code, the company will not qualify for the 8(a) Program, because it is not small under that NAICS code—even though it is small under the NAICS code for the contracts it wants to bid on.

After you gain admission to the 8(a) Program and begin bidding on contracts, you must be small *both* under your primary NAICS code and the NAICS code assigned to each 8(a) set-aside solicitation. For instance, if the numbers above were reversed so that BrettWorks' primary NAICS code carried a $13.5 million size standard, and the solicitation's NAICS code had a $7 million size standard, BrettWorks would qualify as small for purposes of program admission, but could not bid on set-aside contracts carrying the $7 million code once it was admitted.

As with all SBA evaluations of size, the concept of affiliation applies to initial and ongoing 8(a) eligibility. In order to qualify as small for purposes of the 8(a) Program, and for any 8(a) procurement you bid on, your company, together with any affiliates, cannot exceed the applicable size standards. Affiliation is discussed in Chapters 2 and 3.

Does My Business Have Potential for Success?

It seems like a silly question, doesn't it? After all, you wouldn't have started a company if you did not believe in its prospects to succeed. But, for 8(a) Program purposes, "potential for success" means convincing the SBA that your business stands a good chance of thriving.

The SBA has a great deal of discretion to evaluate potential for success, but tends to focus most heavily on your company's financial health. It does not expect you to be raking in huge profits (this is a program for disadvantaged companies, after all), but will look for modest success. If your balance sheets are bathed in red ink, you're unlikely to be admitted to the program.

The SBA will also examine the experience of your company and its managers. Generally, if a company has not been in business for at least two years, the SBA will deny the application and tell the applicant to come back later. Waivers are available in rare cases, but especially in recent years, the SBA has been very hesitant to waive the "two years in business" standard. If your company is brand-new, consider holding off on your 8(a) Program application until you have reached the two-year mark.

Am I Socially and Economically Disadvantaged?

In order to be admitted to the 8(a) Program, your small business must be at least 51 percent owned and controlled by one or more "socially disadvantaged" individuals. A person is considered "socially disadvantaged" for 8(a) purposes if he or she has been subjected to racial or ethnic prejudice or cultural bias within American society due to the person's identity as a member of a particular group. Social disadvantage must stem from circumstances beyond your control.

Members of certain groups, including African Americans, Hispanic Americans, Native Americans, and certain Asian Americans[1] are presumptively socially disadvantaged, so long as they hold themselves out, and are identified by others, as members of the group. However, despite popular misconception, you do *not* need to be a racial or ethnic minority in order to be socially disadvantaged. Rather, any individual can be deemed socially disadvantaged so long as he or she demonstrates that social disadvantage to the SBA's satisfaction.

If you are not "presumptively disadvantaged," you must show the SBA that you have a distinguishing feature that has contributed to social disadvantage and explain how the feature has had a negative impact on your entry or advancement in the business world. For example, in one case, a veteran who walked with a limp was able to demonstrate that his handicap contributed to bias against him—particularly since his company was in the construction industry.[2]

The SBA has also admitted companies owned by women, religious minorities, and ethnic minorities whose country of origin is not on the "presumed disadvantaged" list. But you should use common sense in identifying a distinguishing feature. In one instance, the SBA denied an application when the individual claimed that he was discriminated against for being short (he was five-foot-five).[3]

Even if you are socially disadvantaged, the SBA will not admit your small business to the 8(a) Program if it believes your income or net worth is too high. The SBA only admits companies owned by "economically disadvantaged" individuals. Fortunately, the SBA takes a pretty broad view of what it means to be economically disadvantaged—you do not need to be living in a "van down by the river," like Matt Foley, Chris Farley's memorable *Saturday Night Live* character. However, if you own a yacht and a couple of island vacation homes, it's probably best to move on to the next chapter of this book, because the SBA won't deem you economically disadvantaged.

To qualify as economically disadvantaged for 8(a) Program purposes, you must have a net worth of less than $250,000, not including your ownership interest in your small business and your primary residence. You may also exclude funds invested in a retirement account, but only if the funds are unavailable until retirement age without significant penalty. Other assets, including savings and checking accounts, as well as the value of personal property (electronics, jewelry, and so on) are included in your net worth. To determine whether you qualify, fill out SBA Form 413, which is available on the SBA's website (www.sba.gov/sites/default/files/tools$$ussbf$$usfinasst413.pdf).

In addition, you must have an adjusted gross income (AGI) of $250,000 or less, averaged over the three years prior to the 8(a) application. If you file taxes jointly with your spouse, the SBA will exclude your spouse's income from the calculation, but you will have to provide evidence (such as W-2s) indicating which of you was responsible for the income.

SalCo applies to the 8(a) Program in October 2012. Its owner, Sally, had an AGI of $150,000 in 2009, $260,000 in 2010, and $280,000 in 2011. So far, Sally has earned $300,000 in 2012. Sally's husband, Jerome, had an AGI of $120,000 in each of 2009, 2010, and 2011, and expects to earn the same amount in 2012.

Result: Sally's three-year average AGI is $230,000, which falls beneath the $250,000 threshold. Her 2012 income does not count, nor does Jerome's income for any year (provided Sally and Jerome can show which spouse earned what). Sally's AGI qualifies her as economically disadvantaged.

Do I Meet the 8(a) Program's Citizenship and Residency Requirements?

In addition to being socially and economically disadvantaged, all individuals applying for 8(a) Program eligibility must be United States citizens currently residing in the country. If you were born outside the country, you must provide proof of citizenship in the form of a passport or naturalization papers. The citizenship requirement is limited to the socially and economically disadvantaged individual (or individuals) who control the company. Other employees, officers, and minority owners may be non-citizens.

Do I Meet the 8(a) Program's "Good Character" Requirement?

All individuals upon whom 8(a) Program eligibility is based, as well as all minority owners of 10 percent or more of the company, partners, members, directors, and key employees, must possess "good character" in the SBA's eyes. In evaluating character, the SBA will examine your criminal record (if any), as well as any civil judgments, debarments, or suspensions from government contracting, and failure to repay federal monetary obligations, such as income taxes or SBA loans.

A blemish or two on your record will not necessarily preclude your admission to the 8(a) Program, even if you have been convicted of a crime. Rather, the SBA will examine the severity of the offense, when the matter occurred (a long-ago conviction is less relevant than a recent one), and the overall context. For instance, the SBA has sometimes found that individuals who were convicted several years earlier of driving under the influence possessed "good character," so long as they promptly complied with all court-ordered sanctions and candidly disclosed the incident to the SBA.

Candor is always important when dealing with the SBA, but is absolutely critical when it comes to the "good character" requirement. Failing to disclose an arrest, conviction, or other problem to the SBA will almost certainly result in a denial of your application when the SBA discovers it through its background check—even if the incident, had it been disclosed, would not have precluded your company from gaining admission to the 8(a) Program.

Does My Small Business Meet the 8(a) Program's Ownership Requirements?

In order to participate in the 8(a) Program, your small business must be at least 51 percent unconditionally and directly owned by one or more economically and socially disadvantaged individuals. In addition, your company must meet the so-called *overlapping ownership restrictions*, which limit the extent to which one person can own interests in multiple 8(a) companies.

Unconditional Ownership. To qualify for the 8(a) Program, a disadvantaged individual must own at least 51 percent of the company, with no strings attached. If a non-disadvantaged individual has an option to purchase an interest in the company—even if the option is unexercised—your small business may fail the unconditional ownership test.

> Sally, a disadvantaged individual, owns 100 percent of SalCo. Dry Dry Again's wheeler-dealer owner, Jane, who serves as SalCo's vice president and is not a disadvantaged individual, holds an unexercised option to purchase 51 percent of SalCo.
>
> **Result:** The SBA will treat Jane's option as exercised. In the SBA's eyes, SalCo is already 51 percent owned by Jane, causing the company to be ineligible for the 8(a) Program.

Direct Ownership. In order for a business to qualify for the 8(a) Program, the disadvantaged individual must also directly own the company. Indirect ownership, such as through a parent company, generally will not satisfy the test (although the SBA makes a narrow exception in the case of certain revocable trusts).

The "Overlapping Ownership" Restrictions. The SBA does not want the same handful of people to benefit from the 8(a) Program through multiple companies. To that end, it will prevent a small business from entering the program if either the company or its owners do not satisfy one of the three overlapping ownership restrictions.

First, a disadvantaged individual cannot use his or her status to qualify a company for the 8(a) Program if an immediate family member has used his or her status to qualify another company for the program. The SBA may waive this restriction, but only if you can present clear and compelling evidence that there are no ties between the companies. As a general matter, the rule is "one 8(a) company per family."

Second, a non-disadvantaged individual, in the aggregate with all immediate family members, who owns at least 10 percent of one 8(a) company cannot own more than 10 percent of a second 8(a) company in the first four years of participation in the program (the so-called "developmental" stage), or more than 20 percent of an 8(a) firm in its last five years of participation (the "transitional" stage). If an 8(a) firm has a corporate owner, the same rule applies.

Third, a non-8(a) company in the same or similar line of work as an 8(a) company cannot own more than 10 percent of an 8(a) company in the developmental stage or 20 percent of an 8(a) company in the transitional stage. The rule also applies to principals of non-8(a) companies. There are two exceptions to the rule. A former 8(a) participant may own an additional 10 percent at each stage—up to 20 percent in the first four years and up to 30 percent in the last five. In addition, an SBA-approved mentor may own up to 40 percent of its protégé. We will discuss the 8(a) mentor–protégé program later in this chapter.

Does My Small Business Meet the 8(a) Program's Control Requirements?

Even if your small business is owned by a socially and economically disadvantaged individual, it will not be admitted to the 8(a) Program unless the same individual also controls the business. As the SBA sees it, "control" means that both the long-term decision making and the day-to-day management and administration of business operations must be conducted by a disadvantaged individual.

> Jerry, a disadvantaged individual, owns 100 percent of Pretty Good Cleaners, Inc. Semi-retired, Jerry spends most of his time on the golf course, while his brother, Larry, serves as the company's day-to-day manager. Larry is not a disadvantaged individual.
>
> **Result:** Pretty Good Cleaners is ineligible for the 8(a) Program because its day-to-day operations are not managed by a disadvantaged individual.

Before submitting your 8(a) application, carefully review your bylaws, operating agreement, or other governing documents to make sure that the disadvantaged individual unconditionally controls the company. A unanimous consent provision or any other provision that allows non-disadvantaged individuals the right to "veto" the disadvantaged individual's business decisions may cause the SBA to find that your business does not meet the control requirement.

In evaluating whether a disadvantaged individual controls your small business, the SBA will also consider four distinct subfactors: the disadvantaged individual's managerial position in the company, degree of relevant experience, working hours, and compensation.

Managerial Position. In order for your company to gain admission to the 8(a) Program, a disadvantaged individual must hold the highest officer position in the company (usually president or chief executive officer). If a non-disadvantaged individual holds the highest officer position, your small business is ineligible.

Degree of Relevant Experience. The SBA will not consider your business to be controlled by a disadvantaged individual unless the individual has sufficient managerial experience to effectively run the business. The SBA's concern is that an inexperienced business owner will necessarily lean on others to help him or her run the business—to the extent that the owner does not truly control the company.

> Lola, a disadvantaged individual, forms a new company, NewtCo, Inc., which specializes in medical equipment leasing. Prior to forming NewtCo, Lola spent most of her career in the restaurant industry. NewtCo's vice president, Matt, has 20 years' experience in the medical equipment leasing industry. NewtCo applies to the 8(a) Program three months after Lola forms it.
>
> **Result:** The SBA will likely deny NewtCo's 8(a) application because Lola lacks sufficient experience to effectively control the company, particularly in light of Matt's extensive industry experience. (NewtCo also fails to meet the "two years in business" standard.)

As Lola's example shows, the experience subfactor is most likely to be a problem if you form a new company in a completely unfamiliar industry. However, the SBA does not require the disadvantaged individual to be the *most* experienced in the company, as long as the individual has sufficient experience to understand the industry and effectively direct the company's operations.

Working Hours. The disadvantaged owner of an 8(a) company must work full-time during the normal working hours of firms in the same or similar line of business. Because working for the 8(a) firm must be a full-time job, if you are the disadvantaged owner of an 8(a) applicant or participant, you cannot work outside the small business, unless the SBA grants prior written permission.

If you currently hold a second job, you should take one of two steps: Resign before you submit your application (and provide the SBA with copies of your resignation letter and the other company's acceptance of your resignation), or explain to the SBA why your second job does not interfere with your management and control of your small business.

Compensation. The disadvantaged owner of an 8(a) company typically must be the highest-compensated person in the company. Compensation includes salary, as well as other distributions or benefits (such as dividends) made available to owners, officers, or employees.

Trina, a disadvantaged individual, owns Meridian Books, Inc., a bookbinding company. In order to obtain government contracts, Trina hires Liz, a veteran proposal writer with an enormous Rolodex of government and industry contacts. In negotiations, Liz demands an annual salary of $135,000. Trina agrees, even though she only pays herself $120,000.

Result: The SBA will deny Meridian's application, unless Trina can convince the SBA to grant an exception.

The SBA may allow an exception to the "highest compensation rule" if you can demonstrate that paying another individual more than the disadvantaged owner will be beneficial to the business. In Trina's case, she might explain that she requires someone with Liz's skills to market Meridian to the government, but cannot hire her unless she pays the going market rate of $135,000. If Trina can present compelling evidence to support her position, the SBA might admit Meridian to the 8(a) Program despite the compensation difference between Trina and Liz. Still, the best bet is to simply make yourself the highest compensated employee in the company—if you aren't already.

Maintaining 8(a) Eligibility

Once you've been admitted to the 8(a) Program, don't let down your guard. With the exception of the net worth and income requirements, which we will discuss below, all of the initial eligibility factors apply throughout your nine-year program term. Your company must continue to be owned and controlled by a socially and economically disadvantaged individual, who is the highest officer, highest compensated, works full-time, and so on. Your company's participation in the 8(a) Program may be terminated if you fail to maintain any aspect of your eligibility.

Net Worth and Income

First, the good news: Once your business has been admitted to the 8(a) Program, you no longer need to ensure that your net worth remains below $250,000. However, you must still monitor your net worth—if it exceeds $750,000 during your program term, the SBA may end your program term early (a process known as *early graduation*).

As for income, you may increase your salary above the $250,000 initial eligibility mark. But if your three-year average income exceeds $350,000 at any point during your 8(a) Program term, the SBA may begin the early graduation process.

Excessive Withdrawals

The SBA expects 8(a) participants to use most of their revenues to develop the business. If your 8(a) company uses its funds for certain other purposes, the SBA deems it a "withdrawal" of money that could have otherwise been used to benefit the company. Withdraw too much money and your business may be deemed ineligible for continued participation in the program.

A *withdrawal* occurs whenever your business uses its funds for things such as cash dividends, bonuses, loans, advances, payments to family members not working for the business, charitable contributions, or any other expenditure the SBA believes does not materially benefit the company. Not every expenditure is a withdrawal: Salaries paid to employees and officers do not count (unless the SBA believes that you are "gaming" the system to avoid the excessive withdrawal rule), nor do the ordinary bills your company must pay, such as the lease payments on your office.

Annually, withdrawals are considered "excessive" and improper, if they exceed:

- $250,000 if your company has sales of $1 million or less
- $300,000 if your company's sales are between $1 million and $2 million
- $400,000 if your company's sales exceed $2 million

After Trina addresses her compensation problem, the SBA admits Meridian into the 8(a) Program. During its third year in the program, Meridian grows spectacularly and earns revenues of $10.4 million. Pleased at her firm's profitability, Trina rewards herself with a $50,000 bonus. She bestows $25,000 bonuses on her top four officers and $10,000 bonuses on six other employees. To bolster Meridian's community profile (and because she has a good heart), Trina authorizes Meridian to make $20,000 in contributions to local charities. When Trina's brother, Ryan, approaches Trina with an idea to start a new business, Trina authorizes Meridian to make a $200,000 loan to Ryan.

Result: Meridian's withdrawals total $430,000—$30,000 above the $400,000 limit for companies with more than $2 million in sales. Meridian has violated the excessive withdrawal rule.

You should closely monitor your bonuses, advances, loans, and the like yearly to ensure that they fall beneath the appropriate threshold. If you aren't sure whether a particular expenditure will be treated as a withdrawal, the best bet is to discuss it with your SBA representative—before you spend the money.

Business Activity Targets

The purpose of the 8(a) Program is to help disadvantaged businesses gain the resources and skills they need to compete on a level playing field with other companies. Although 8(a) contracts are an essential ingredient of the 8(a) Program, the SBA does not want your company to become too dependent on 8(a) set-aside and sole source contracts, only to lose the ability to obtain those contracts after nine years.

To that end, the SBA requires 8(a) companies to obtain non-8(a) revenues during their last five years of program participation. These so-called *business activity targets*, also known as *business mix targets*, require your 8(a) company to earn no less than a certain percent of its overall revenues from non-8(a) sources, as follows:

8(a) Program Year	Non-8(a) Revenue
5	15%
6	25%
7	35%
8	45%
9	55%

It is important to understand that the business activity targets require you to obtain *non-8(a)* revenues, not *non-federal* revenues. You may meet your non-8(a) revenue requirement by obtaining federal small business set-aside contracts, as well as HUBZone, service-disabled veteran-owned small business, or women-owned small business contracts (if you qualify). Revenues from unrestricted federal contracts, subcontracts, and commercial contracts also count.

If you do not meet your business activity targets for a given year, the SBA will not terminate you from the program. However, it will suspend your eligibility to receive 8(a) sole source contracts (a vital source of revenues for many 8(a) businesses) until you correct the problem.

The best way to avoid a business activity target problem is to continually focus some of your efforts on obtaining non-8(a) work, even in your first few years of 8(a) participation. That way, you will not have to scramble at the last minute to obtain non-8(a) revenues in your fifth year.

The 8(a) Mentor–Protégé Program

Once your small business has been admitted to the 8(a) Program, you should strongly consider finding an experienced firm to serve as your *mentor*. A mentor is another business (often, but not always, a large business, but any business with sufficient resources and skills can serve as a mentor) that the SBA allows to have a special relationship with an 8(a) company, with the goal of aiding the 8(a) company's business development. Pairing with a mentor can help your 8(a) company develop valuable business skills—and take advantage of an important exception to the normal affiliation rules we discussed in Chapter 2.

How Do I Get a Mentor?

The SBA does not recognize informal mentor-protégé relationships. Instead, you and your mentor must sign a written mentor-protégé agreement and submit it to the SBA for approval. The agreement must contain a number of required terms—see 13 C.F.R. § 124.520(e) for a full list. In addition, speak with your SBA representative before submitting the agreement to see what other information the SBA may require to evaluate your request.

If the SBA approves the mentor-protégé agreement, it takes effect immediately for a period of one year. The SBA must renew its approval annually in order for the agreement to continue in effect. Each year, you must provide the SBA with information about the ongoing mentor-protégé relationship to help the SBA determine whether to renew the agreement (assuming you wish to have the agreement renewed). If the agreement lapses, the affiliation "shield" lapses, too.

What Is the 8(a) Mentor-Protégé Affiliation "Shield"?

Once the SBA approves a mentor-protégé agreement between your company and your mentor, you may receive almost any type of assistance from your mentor—including loans, contracts, bonding assistance, and so on—without risk of affiliation. You may even sell an ownership stake of up to 40 percent to your mentor in order to raise revenues. It's worth repeating: The mentor-protégé program essentially acts as an affiliation "shield," allowing you and your mentor to take many of the actions we spent so much time discussing in Chapter 2—risk-free.

After Lola spends two years successfully running NewtCo's medical equipment leasing business, the SBA admits the company to the 8(a) program. NewtCo then enters into a mentor-protégé relationship with Helton, Inc., a large medical supply company. After the SBA approves the mentor-protégé agreement, Lola sells 40 percent of NewtCo to Helton. In addition, Helton provides NewtCo with three subcontracts, guarantees two bid bonds obtained by NewtCo, and uses its "war room" resources to help prepare NewtCo's proposals for 8(a) contracts.

> **Result:** NewtCo and Helton are not affiliated. The mentor-protégé agreement allows Helton to provide these types of assistance to NewtCo without risk of affiliation.

As nice as loans, subcontracts, and similar assistance can be, the most popular use of the mentor-protégé affiliation "shield" is to create joint ventures. A joint venture between an 8(a) protégé and its mentor can bid on any government contract as a small business, as long as the protégé qualifies as small—no matter how large the mentor may be.

> NewtCo's average annual receipts are $3 million. Its mentor, Helton, has average annual receipts of $500 million. NewtCo and Helton form a joint venture to bid on an 8(a) set-aside contract carrying a $19 million size standard.
>
> **Result:** The joint venture is eligible for award, notwithstanding the fact that Helton exceeds the size standard by some $481 million.

On its own, NewtCo may not have had much luck bidding on a $19 million contract, but with Helton's participation, its chances rise considerably. As NewtCo's example suggests, joint venturing with your 8(a) mentor can significantly increase your odds of success when competing for contracts. Not only will your mentor bring much-needed resources to the table, but also some agencies may be more likely to award to your firm, knowing that a larger, more established company is involved in your bid.

Joint Venturing on 8(a) Set-Aside Procurements

Now that you understand why joint venturing is so popular among 8(a) companies, it's time to make sure that you do it right. In order to form a joint venture for an 8(a) procurement (or any other government contract for which you want to compete using a mentor-protégé joint venture), you must follow the SBA's 8(a) joint venture rules.

How Do I Form an 8(a) Joint Venture?

To form a joint venture between your 8(a) company and another firm for an 8(a) set-aside procurement or other procurement on which you intend to use the special mentor-protégé joint venture exception from affiliation, you must enter into a *joint venture agreement*, a special contract creating the joint venture. Your joint venture must contain a number of mandatory provisions. For a full list, see 13 C.F.R. § 121.513(c).

Your joint venture agreement should be more than a regurgitation of the regulatory requirements. After all, it is a binding contractual document, establishing the framework of your working relationship with your teammate. A strong joint venture agreement will address issues such as the confidentiality of proprietary information, non-solicitation of employees, the resolution of disputes, and other matters that may arise as the parties compete together for federal contracts.

If your joint venture will bid on non-8(a) contracts, you're set once you adopt the joint venture agreement. For 8(a) procurements, though, you must obtain the SBA's approval of the joint venture agreement prior to award of the contract. If the joint venture agreement omits any of the required terms, the SBA will refuse to approve it.

In addition to submitting your proposed joint venture agreement for approval, you must provide the SBA with a substantial amount of additional information about you and your joint venture partner. Unfortunately, this additional information is not called for in the regulations, so 8(a) companies are sometimes surprised when the SBA returns their joint venture applications, along with a request for more documentation. For a list of the additional information the SBA will require to approve your joint venture agreement, review the SBA's 8(a) Standard Operating Procedure (an internal document instructing SBA employees how to administer the 8(a) Program). The SBA's Standard

Operating Procedures are available online at http://www.sba.gov/about-sba-services/7481.

Because you must obtain the SBA's prior approval, you should submit your proposed joint venture agreement to the SBA as early as possible in the procurement process. Although the SBA makes every effort to process joint venture agreements quickly, you may lose out on a contract if you submit your agreement at the last moment and the SBA does not have sufficient time to review it. Allow time for some back-and-forth if the SBA has questions about your agreement or wants you to submit a revised version.

What If My Joint Venture Partner Is Not My Mentor?

Thanks to the exception from affiliation, when 8(a) companies form joint ventures, it is often with their mentors. But you may form a joint venture for an 8(a) procurement with another company, so long as the joint venture meets certain size requirements.

As a general matter, you must add your company's size to your joint venture partner's size to determine whether your joint venture qualifies as small for the procurement. For some competitive procurements, your joint venture will qualify as small as long as each joint venture member, individually, is small under the NAICS code assigned to the contract. The special "individual size treatment" rule applies when:

- Your 8(a) company's size is less than half the size standard corresponding to the NAICS code.

- For a procurement with a revenue-based size standard, the procurement exceeds half the size standard corresponding to the NAICS code.

- For a procurement having an employee-based size standard, the procurement exceeds $10 million.

NewtCo, an 8(a) firm with $3 million in average annual receipts, forms a joint venture with New Bids on the Block, Inc., a non-8(a) firm with $6 million in average annual receipts. The companies name the joint venture Newt Bids on the Block JV, LLC. The joint venture submits an offer on a competitive 8(a) set-aside procurement carrying a $7 million size standard. The government estimates the contract's value at $5.5 million.

Result: NewtCo's size is less than half the size standard, and the contract's expected value is greater than half the size standard. Newt Bids on the Block JV qualifies as small, even though its partners' combined sizes are $9 million—$2 million above the size standard.

If any of the requirements described above are not met, the SBA will aggregate the sizes of the joint venture partners. In the example, if NewtCo's average annual receipts were $4 million, the SBA would add its revenues to New Bids on the Block's and deem the joint venture ineligible for award.

Subcontracting on 8(a) Procurements

Like ordinary small business set-aside procurements, your small business can only subcontract so much of an 8(a) contract. For most procurements, the 8(a) program's subcontracting limitations are the same as those applicable to small business set-aside contracts. See Chapter 4 for a full discussion. If your 8(a) company wins an indefinite delivery/indefinite quantity (IDIQ) 8(a) set-aside, a special rule requires you to perform the applicable percentage of work for each six-month increment of the contract, except the first six months. Unlike in the HUBZone and service-disabled veteran-owned small business programs, you cannot meet your own performance obligations by subcontracting to another 8(a) company.

If your 8(a) small business joint ventures with another company, the subcontracting limits apply to the joint venture, not your small business. However, if the joint venture is *unpopulated*, that is, has no employees on its own payroll, or only a handful of administrative employees on its payroll, your small business must perform 40 percent of the work performed by the joint venture.

> Newt Bids on the Block JV, LLC, the joint venture between NewtCo and New Bids on the Block, bids on an 8(a) set-aside contract. The joint venture intends to perform 70 percent of the work and subcontract the remaining 30 percent to a large business.
>
> **Result:** NewtCo must perform 40 percent of the 70 percent of the work performed by the joint venture, or 28 percent of the overall contract.

If your joint venture is *populated*—staffed with employees on the joint venture's own payroll—the 40 percent rule does not apply. But you will have to convince the SBA before it will approve the joint venture arrangement that the work split will assist your 8(a) company's business development.

The Primary Rules: Where to Find Them

Here's where to find the primary rules discussed in this chapter:

- 13 C.F.R. § 124.102 (size requirements)
- 13 C.F.R. § 124.107 (potential for success)
- 13 C.F.R. § 124.103 (social disadvantage)
- 13 C.F.R. § 124.104 (economic disadvantage)
- 13 C.F.R. § 124.101 (citizenship and residency)
- 13 C.F.R. § 124.108 (good character)

- 13 C.F.R. § 124.105 (ownership)
- 13 C.F.R. § 124.106 (control)
- 13 C.F.R. § 124.112 (excessive withdrawals)
- 13 C.F.R. § 124.598 (business activity targets)
- 13 C.F.R. § 121.103 and 13 C.F.R. § 124.520 (mentor-protégé program)
- 13 C.F.R. § 124.513 (joint ventures)
- 13 C.F.R. § 124.510 and 13 C.F.R. § 125.6 (subcontracting)

Compliance at a Glance: The 8(A) Business Development Program

❑ When you apply to the 8(a) Program, and throughout your nine-year term, remain small in your primary NAICS code.

❑ When you apply to the 8(a) Program, and throughout your nine-year term, ensure that your small business is at least 51 percent owned by one or more socially disadvantaged individuals.

❑ When you apply to the 8(a) Program, ensure that your small business's owner is economically disadvantaged in that he or she has a net worth of less than $250,000 (less permitted exclusions) and average adjusted gross income over the last three years of $250,000 or less.

❑ Throughout your nine-year program term, ensure that your small business's owner is economically disadvantaged in that he or she has a net worth of less than $750,000 (less permitted exclusions) and average adjusted gross income over the last three years of $350,000 or less.

❑ When you apply to the 8(a) Program, and throughout your nine-year term, ensure that your small business's disadvantaged owner is a citizen of and resides in the United States.

❑ When you apply to the 8(a) Program, and throughout your nine-year term, ensure that your small business's disadvantaged owner unconditionally and directly owns his or her interest in the company.

❑ When you apply to the 8(a) Program, and throughout your nine-year term, ensure that your small business complies with the so-called "overlapping ownership" restrictions, which cap certain types of minority ownership interests in the company.

❑ When you apply to the 8(a) Program, and throughout your nine-year term, ensure that a socially and economically disadvantaged individual holds the highest officer position and is the highest-compensated employee.

❑ When you apply to the 8(a) Program, and throughout your nine-year term, ensure that the disadvantaged individual holding the highest officer position works full-time during normal business hours and does not accept outside employment without the SBA's approval.

❑ During your nine-year program term, avoid excessive withdrawals for expenditures such as dividends, bonuses, loans, payments to family members not working for your company, and charitable contributions.

❑ In years five through nine of your participation in the 8(a) Program, obtain sufficient non-8(a) revenues to meet your business activity targets.

❑ To participate in the 8(a) mentor-protégé program, execute a written agreement containing the mandatory terms found in 13 C.F.R. § 124.520(e) and submit it to the SBA for approval.

❑ Provide the SBA with information about the mentor-protégé relationship annually, and obtain the SBA's annual reapproval if you wish to continue the relationship.

- ❑ To form a joint venture for an 8(a) set-aside procurement or other procurement on which you intend to use the special mentor-protégé joint venture exception from affiliation, enter into a joint venture agreement containing the mandatory provisions in 13 C.F.R. § 121.513(c).
- ❑ For 8(a) procurements, obtain the SBA's approval of your joint venture prior to award of the contract.
- ❑ Do not subcontract 8(a) contract work in excess of the subcontracting limitations, which are the same as for small business set-aside contracts (except for IDIQ contracts).
- ❑ If your 8(a) small business joint ventures with another company, perform at least 40 percent of the joint venture's work if the joint venture is unpopulated.

CHAPTER 12

THE SERVICE-DISABLED VETERAN-OWNED SMALL BUSINESS PROGRAMS

IF YOU ARE A SERVICE-DISABLED VETERAN of the United States military, your small business may be eligible to participate in the Service-Disabled Veteran-Owned Small Business Programs, or SDVO Programs. Yes, that's "programs," in the plural—the SBA administers one special program for companies owned and controlled by service-disabled veterans and the Department of Veterans Affairs (VA) administers a second such program.

Why participate in the SDVO Programs? The government strives to award 3 percent of prime contract dollars—more than $15 billion annually—to qualified SDVO small businesses. To reach that 3 percent goal, it sets aside many procurements exclusively for competition among SDVO small businesses, and even awards some smaller contracts on a sole source basis, that is, without any competition at all.

Participation in these programs can help your small business grow and thrive, but it comes with strict (and sometimes complex) compliance strings attached. Incorrectly certify that your company is an eligible SDVO small business, and you could face a successful eligibility protest, or even debarment from all government contracting. This chapter will help you stay on the straight and narrow.

Verification as a SDVO Small Business

The SBA's SDVO Program, which applies to procurements issued by most federal agencies, does not currently require your small business to obtain a certification before submitting an offer as an SDVO small business (though, as of this writing, legislation was making its way through Capitol Hill to eventually require participants in the SBA's SDVO Program to obtain certifications). Instead, you may self-certify your eligibility for most SDVO set-aside contracts. Self-certification lessens the amount of red tape you must wade through to obtain set-aside contracts, but it also heightens your burden of ensuring that your self-certification is accurate. As described above, an incorrect SDVO self-certification could land you in very hot water. Carefully read the next section regarding SDVO eligibility, and make sure you fully comply, before self-certifying.

The VA's SDVO Program only applies to VA procurements. A contracting program limited to a single federal agency doesn't sound like much, until you consider that the VA has special rules favoring awards to SDVO small businesses. Unlike other federal agencies, the VA prioritizes SDVO small businesses above all other contractors, including 8(a), HUBZone, and women-owned firms. Due to this relatively new policy, VA awards to SDVO small businesses have skyrocketed in recent years. However, unlike for other agencies, if your small business wants to win a VA SDVO set-aside contract, it must be verified as an eligible SDVO small business and listed as verified in the Vendor Information Pages (VIP), a VA database of contractors, before submitting its offer.

As noted above, as of this writing, Congress was considering legislation to require all SDVO small businesses, for both the SBA and VA SDVO Programs, to obtain certification through the VA. Thus, if you intend to pursue non-VA SDVO set-aside contracts, you should check to see if this legislation has become law before attempting to self-certify as a SDVO small business. Even if it has not, the days of self-certification on non-VA SDVO set-aside contracts are likely numbered. The wise move is to get "ahead of the curve" and obtain your VA SDVO certification as soon as possible.

How Do I Obtain My VA SDVO Verification?

To obtain a VA SDVO verification, you must apply through the VA's Center for Veterans Enterprise (CVE), using the web portal at www.vetbiz.gov. You will be asked to provide a substantial amount of documentation, such as your corporate bylaws and meeting minutes, so be sure that your documents are up to snuff before you click "submit." If your application is denied, the VA may make you wait up to six months before reapplying, which can cost you valuable contract opportunities. We will discuss the eligibility requirements in the next section of the chapter.

How Long May I Remain in the SDVO Programs?

Unlike the 8(a) Program, for which participation is limited to a single, nine-year term, you may participate in the SDVO Programs indefinitely, as long as you continue to meet the eligibility requirements. But for the VA's SDVO Program, you must renew your verification each year in order to remain eligible to bid on and win VA SDVO set-aside contracts. If your verification lapses, you will not be eligible until you renew it, even if you meet all of the eligibility requirements.

What About Joint Ventures?

If your small business forms a joint venture with another company to compete for a VA SDVO set-aside procurement, *the joint venture itself* must be verified and included in the CVE's database.

VetCo, Inc., a verified SDVO small business listed in the VIP database, forms a joint venture with Off Road Adventures, Inc., which is not verified or listed in the VIP database. VetCo is the lead venturer and the joint venture complies with the requirements identified in 13 C.F.R. § 125.15. The new joint venture, called All Vets Are Off JV, LLC, submits an offer on a VA set-aside procurement.

Result: The VA will reject All Vets Are Off JV's offer because the joint venture is not separately verified and listed in the VIP database.

Don't worry about the example's references to the joint venture requirements in 13 C.F.R. § 125.15. We will discuss the special rules for creating a SDVO joint venture later in this chapter. But for now, just remember: Even if you follow all the regulatory requirements, the joint venture will not be eligible to win a VA SDVO set-aside contract unless it is verified and listed in the VIP database.

Can a Competitor Challenge My SDVO Status?

Once your small business is verified and listed in the VIP database, you're guaranteed to be eligible for SDVO set-aside contracts, right? Not so fast. Even if you are verified, a competitor may still challenge your eligibility to receive a SDVO set-aside procurement by way of an eligibility protest, filed either with the SBA or the VA, depending on the identity of the procuring agency. The protest could result in an adverse eligibility decision if the SBA or VA discovers that the CVE overlooked something in processing your application, or that something has changed since the application was submitted.

After VetCo wins a VA small business set-aside contract, a competitor files an eligibility protest with the VA. During its evaluation of the protest, the VA discovers that, following its verification,

VetCo adopted new bylaws, and that the bylaws contain a provision restricting the ability of VetCo's service-disabled veteran owner to sell his stake in the company.

Result: The VA sustains the eligibility protest, because VetCo's owner does not unconditionally own the company. VetCo loses the contract.

The bottom line is that verification is not a magic pill inoculating you from the allegation that your company is not an eligible SDVO small business. Don't rely on the CVE to do the work of figuring out if you are compliant. Carefully review the next section on eligibility for the SDVO Programs to ensure that you comply with every requirement.

Eligibility for the SDVO Programs

Your business qualifies for the SDVO Programs if it is:

- A small business under the NAICS code assigned to a particular procurement
- At least 51 percent unconditionally owned by one or more service-disabled veterans
- Unconditionally controlled by one or more service-disabled veterans

This basic definition is a good starting point, but complying with the eligibility requirements means understanding how the SBA and VA interpret it. For instance, "unconditional ownership," in the government's eyes, precludes several provisions commonly found in companies' bylaws, like right of first refusal clauses and certain quorum provisions. But before we delve deeper into the eligibility requirements, let's find out whether you satisfy the baseline requirement for participating in the SDVO Programs: qualifying as a service-disabled veteran.

Do I Qualify as a Service-Disabled Veteran?

You served in the military and incurred a disability during your service. So you are a service-disabled veteran, right? Probably, but read a little further before making any assumptions, because there are three important limits you should understand.

First, in order to qualify for the SDVO Programs, your disability must have been incurred or aggravated in the line of duty in the active army, naval, or air service. So, though there are some nuances in the regulatory language, if your disability was incurred while you were in the Reserves, you may not be eligible.

Second, you cannot qualify for the SDVO Programs if you were dishonorably discharged from the military, no matter how serious your service-connected disability.

Third, you cannot self-certify as a service-disabled veteran (as opposed to self-certifying as a service-disabled veteran-owned *small business* which, as we discussed, is currently acceptable for non-VA procurements). Instead, you must obtain appropriate documentation from the VA or the Department of Defense certifying you as a service-disabled veteran, such as a VA letter or a DOD Form 214 (Certificate of Release or Discharge from Active Duty). If you do not possess the appropriate documentation, you must go get it *before* bidding on any SDVO contracts.

Mark, the new owner of BrettWorks, was wounded during Operation Desert Storm and walks with a slight limp as a result. However, Mark has never obtained DOD or VA paperwork certifying him as a service-disabled veteran. He notices a new administrative services procurement set-aside for service-disabled veteran-owned small businesses. Because Mark is certain that he is a service-disabled veteran, he decides to submit a proposal.

Result: Mark may well be a service-disabled veteran, but until he obtains DOD or VA documentation, he does not qualify as one for purposes of the SDVO Programs. BrettWorks is vulnerable to an eligibility protest and may face significant penalties for submitting its offer in the absence of appropriate documentation.

What Disability Rating Must I Have? No particular disability rating is required to be a service-disabled veteran. The Department of Defense has confirmed that even a zero percent disability rating will suffice.

What Net Worth and Income Restrictions Apply? Unlike the 8(a) Program, you need not meet any net worth or income restrictions to qualify for the SDVO Programs. Even billionaires may qualify as service-disabled veterans (though, if you have a few billion in the bank, you probably have more interesting hobbies than government contracting to fill your time).

Is My Company Small Enough for SDVO Program Purposes?

Your company qualifies as a small business as long as it falls beneath the size standard corresponding to the NAICS code assigned to a particular SDVO set-aside procurement. See Chapter 1 for a full discussion of how to calculate your company's size.

Unlike in the 8(a) Program, your company need not be small in its primary NAICS code in order to participate in the SDVO Programs. Of course, if you exceed the NAICS code in your primary industry, you can no longer bid on SDVO contracts carrying that code.

As with all SBA considerations of size, the concept of affiliation applies to SDVO eligibility. In order to qualify as small for purposes of the SDVO program, your small business, together with any affiliates, cannot exceed the applicable size standard. Affiliation is discussed at length in Chapters 2 and 3.

Does a Service-Disabled Veteran Own My Company?

To qualify as a SDVO small business, your company must be at least 51 percent "unconditionally and directly owned" by one or more service-disabled veterans. It sounds like an easy requirement to meet, but this is not necessarily so, due to the strict manner in which the SBA and VA interpret the word "unconditional." As the SBA's Office of Hearings and Appeals has stated, "unconditional ownership means that the service-disabled veterans must immediately have an absolute right to do anything they want with their ownership interest or stock, whenever they want."[1]

Because of the strict interpretation, so-called *right of first refusal provisions*, which restrict an owner's ability to sell his or her interest in the company, do not pass muster when they apply to service-disabled veteran owners. Right of first refusal provisions are commonly found in corporate bylaws, shareholders' agreements, and buy/sell agreements, and have torpedoed an untold number of companies' SDVO eligibility in recent years.

Mark obtains VA documentation certifying that he is 20 percent service-disabled. To raise capital, Mark sells a 25 percent interest in BrettWorks to Ramanjit, who is not a service-disabled veteran. Mark continues to own the remaining 75 percent of BrettWorks. The company's bylaws state that if either owner wishes to sell his ownership interest, he must first offer it to the other owner, and can only sell it on the open market if the other owner declines to purchase it.

Result: The right of first refusal provision prohibits Mark, the service-disabled veteran, from doing whatever he wants with his ownership interest, because he cannot sell it to anyone other than Ramanjit without Ramanjit's permission. The provision negates Mark's unconditional ownership of BrettWorks and renders the company ineligible for the SDVO Programs.

Right of first refusal provisions and similar restrictions on ownership transfers commonly appear in standard corporate documents, including those prepared by seasoned attorneys (many very good corporate attorneys are simply unaware of the special rules governing

SDVO small businesses). Give your corporate documents a thorough review and, if necessary, amend them to revise any problematic provisions, before self-certifying for a SDVO contract or applying for VA SDVO verification.

"Unconditional" ownership also means that there cannot be any other strings attached to the service-disabled veteran's ownership rights. An option to purchase an interest in the company held by a non-service-disabled veteran, even if it is unexercised, will prevent your small business from meeting the ownership requirement if the option, if exercised, would cause service-disabled veterans to own less than 51 percent of the company.

Horace, a service-disabled veteran, owns 51 percent of Ace Contractors, Inc. Amanda, who is not a veteran, owns the remaining 49 percent. In exchange for a capital contribution of $50,000, Horace grants Amanda an option to purchase an additional 20 percent of the company and become its majority owner for a one-time payment of $1,000. Amanda has not exercised the option.

Result: The SBA and VA will deem Amanda the majority owner of Ace Contractors, even though she has not exercised the option. Because Amanda is not a service-disabled veteran, Ace Contractors is ineligible for the SBVO Programs.

One or more service-disabled veterans must also *directly* own your small business in order for it to qualify. Indirect ownership, such as through a parent company, does not count.

Does a Service-Disabled Veteran Control My Company?

The term "Service-Disabled Veteran-Owned Small Business Programs" is misleading because it suggests that a company may qualify for the SDVO Programs solely on the basis of its ownership. In fact, the programs would be more accurately described as the "Service-Disabled

Veteran Owned *and Controlled* Programs," because even if your small business is 51 percent (or 100 percent) owned by service-disabled veterans, it will not qualify for the programs unless it is also unconditionally controlled by those veterans.

If you read the previous chapter, the control requirements may seem familiar, because the SBA and VA borrowed liberally from the 8(a) Program in establishing their SDVO control guidelines. As in the 8(a) Program, generally, "control" means that both the long-term decision making and the day-to-day management and administration of business operations must be conducted by service-disabled veterans.

Let's look at two examples of how the control requirement can affect your small business:

Virginia, a service-disabled veteran, unconditionally owns 100 percent of Dahl House Builders, Inc., a construction company. Semi-retired, Virginia spends most of the year at her beach home in St. Lucia, while her brother, Wayne, who is not a service-disabled veteran, manages Dahl House's day-to-day affairs.

Result: Dahl House is ineligible for the SDVO Programs because its day-to-day operations are not managed by a service-disabled veteran.

Elvis, a service-disabled veteran, owns 75 percent of Blue Suede Shoes Cleaners, Inc. Summer, who is not a service-disabled veteran, owns the remaining 25 percent. The company's bylaws require unanimous consent of the owners to enter into contracts, take out loans, or make capital expenditures of $5,000 or more.

Result: The unanimity provision prevents Elvis from unconditionally controlling the company, because Summer can veto a number of Elvis's business decisions. The unanimity provisions prevent Blue Suede Shoes from being eligible for the SDVO Programs.

As the second example demonstrates, common provisions in by-laws and other corporate documents can cause your small business to be ineligible for the SDVO Programs. Carefully review your governing documents, paying special attention to voting provisions and quorum provisions, to ensure that the service-disabled veterans have the absolute right to control the company without interference by others. If it helps, picture your company as a banana republic and the service-disabled veteran as its bandoleer-wearing dictator, because representative democracy, while a wonderful thing in national governance, is a no-no when it comes to the SDVO Programs.

In evaluating whether a service-disabled veteran controls your company, the SBA and VA will examine a number of subfactors, including the veteran's position in the company and level of experience.

Managerial Position. In order for your company to qualify for the SDVO Programs, a service-disabled veteran must hold the highest officer position in the company (usually president or chief executive officer). If a non-service-disabled veteran holds the highest officer position, your small business is automatically ineligible.

Degree of Relevant Experience. The SBA and VA will not consider your business to be controlled by a service-disabled veteran unless the veteran has sufficient managerial experience to run the company, without undue reliance on others. The government's concern is that an inexperienced veteran will necessarily lean on others to help him or her run the business—to the extent that the veteran will not truly control the company.

> Don, a service-disabled veteran, spent most of his non-military career in the restaurant industry, working in a pizza parlor. After learning of opportunities in government contracting, Don starts a construction company, which immediately bids on a SDVO set-aside construction contract.

Result: Because Don lacks any experience in the construction industry, the SBA and VA will likely conclude that Don does not control his company.

The service-disabled veteran need not be the most experienced person in the company, but must have enough knowledge and experience to understand the industry and effectively direct the company's operations. Unfortunately, the vague regulations do not provide a clear-cut answer as to when a service-disabled veteran has enough experience to qualify. Use your best judgment, and hope that the government agrees.

Economic Dependence. The SBA and VA may find that a service-disabled veteran does not control your company if your company heavily relies on another business for its revenues. In the government's eyes, such an arrangement prevents the veteran from effectively controlling the company because the veteran cannot take positions adverse to the other business without great economic risk.

After repealing the unanimity provision in its bylaws, Blue Suede Shoes Cleaners plans to begin bidding on SDVO set-aside procurements. Over the past three years, Blue Suede Shoes has earned 90 percent of its revenues from Dry Dry Again, Jane's juggernaut cleaning company.

Result: Because Blue Suede Shoes Cleaners relies so heavily on Dry Dry Again for revenues, the SBA and VA are likely to conclude that Elvis does not effectively control the company.

As you may remember, economic dependence is a risk factor for affiliation, too. See Chapter 2 for a discussion. In Blue Suede Shoes' case, if it is affiliated with Dry Dry Again, it may be ineligible for SDVO set-aside contracts for size reasons, too. But even if an affiliation based on economic dependence does not result in a size problem, economic reliance on the other company can lead to a lack of appropriate control, in the eyes of the government, for purposes of the SDVO Programs.

Geographic Location. If the service-disabled veteran does not live near your small business's headquarters or the locations where your contracts are performed, it may present a control problem. The problem is likely to be especially acute if your company performs work that requires on-site supervision, such as construction or other work on a federal facility. In these cases, the SBA and VA are likely to conclude that the veteran cannot effectively manage the company from afar.

In other industries, you may be able to satisfy the government's concern by demonstrating that the veteran controls the company from a distance. Be prepared to show that the veteran is in constant contact with officers and employees using the telephone, e-mail, or videoconferencing technology.

VA-Specific Requirements

In addition to the size, ownership, and control requirements common to both SDVO Programs, the VA goes a little further, imposing five additional subfactors, largely borrowed from the 8(a) Program. Although these five subfactors are not necessarily required for non-VA SDVO procurements, satisfying them is recommended even if your company does not intend to bid on VA contracts.

Good Character. The service-disabled veteran, and the company itself, must be of "good character" to gain admission to the VA's SDVO Program. Of course, as we discussed in Chapter 8, criminal convictions and serious ethical lapses can hamper your small business's ability to obtain federal contract work of any type.

Federal Debts. Your company cannot be admitted to the VA's SDVO Program if the company or the service-disabled veteran has failed to pay significant financial obligations owed to the federal government, such as unpaid taxes or payments due on SBA loans. Again, as we learned in Chapter 8, such debts can be problematic when it comes to all federal procurements, not just VA SDVO contracts.

Full-Time Employment. A service-disabled veteran must manage your small business on a full-time basis during normal working hours of firms in the same or similar line of business. If the service-disabled veteran owner works a second job or owns other companies, the VA may find that the full-time employment requirement has not been met.

Work performed for a wholly owned subsidiary of the small business may satisfy the requirement. For this reason, if you are a service-disabled veteran and currently own two companies, you may wish to consider making one company a subsidiary of the other. Just be aware that if you do so, the subsidiary will not be able to qualify as a SDVO small business in its own right, because it will not meet the "direct ownership" requirement we previously discussed.

Highest-Compensated Employee. For both SDVO Programs, a service-disabled veteran must serve as the company's highest officer. For the VA's program, however, that highest officer must also be the highest-compensated employee in the company. The service-disabled who serves as the highest officer can only take a lower salary if he or she can demonstrate to the VA that taking a lower salary benefits the business.

Right to Profits. The service-disabled veteran's right to share in your small business's profits must be commensurate with his or her ownership share, and in no event may the veteran receive less than 51 percent of the annual distribution of profits.

Nina, a service-disabled veteran, owns 60 percent of Lake Tahoe Builders, Inc. Two non-service-disabled veterans each own 20 percent. Lake Tahoe Builders' bylaws call for profits and losses to be split equally among the three owners.

Result: Nina does not earn profits commensurate with her ownership share, and earns less than 51 percent of Lake Tahoe Builders' profits. Lake Tahoe Builders is not eligible for the VA's SDVO Program.

Joint Venturing on SDVO Procurements

You may form a joint venture with another company to submit a proposal for a SDVO set-aside procurement. Your joint venture partner need not be another SDVO small business. But the joint venture must meet certain size requirements, adopt a joint venture agreement containing a number of mandatory provisions, and (for the VA's SDVO Program) be created as a separate legal entity, like a limited liability company. And remember, as discussed earlier in this chapter, for VA SDVO set-aside procurements, the joint venture itself must be verified and listed in the VIP database.

Size Requirements for SDVO Joint Ventures

As a general matter, you must add your company's size to your joint venture partner's size to determine if your joint venture qualifies as small for a SDVO set-aside procurement. For some competitive procurements, your joint venture will qualify as small only as long as each joint venture member, individually, is considered small under the NAICS code assigned to the contract. The special "individual size treatment" rule applies when:

- Your SDVO small business's size is less than half the size standard corresponding to the NAICS code.

- For a procurement with a revenue-based size standard, the procurement exceeds half the size standard corresponding to the NAICS code.

- For a procurement having an employee-based size standard, the procurement exceeds $10 million.

If any of the requirements described above are not met, the SBA will aggregate the size of your company and your joint venture partner's company (confusingly, the SBA, not the VA, decides matters of size for VA SDVO procurements, while the VA has jurisdiction over other aspects of eligibility).

Does the rule look familiar? If so, it's because it is identical to the "individual size treatment" rule for 8(a) contracts. See Chapter 11, page 240, for an example of how the rule works.

Mandatory SDVO Joint Venture Provisions

As in the 8(a) Program, the parties to a joint venture bidding on a SDVO set-aside procurement must adopt a written joint venture agreement containing a number of mandatory terms. The terms are similar, but not identical, to those required in the 8(a) Program, and are designed to ensure that the SDVO small business controls the joint venture and benefits from it. For a full list of the required terms, see 13 C.F.R. § 125.15(b)(2).

For non-VA procurements, there is no requirement that the SBA give its prior approval of the joint venture arrangement. Nevertheless, it is critical that you include all of the mandatory provisions. Failure to do so may lead to a successful eligibility protest, and may lead to harsher sanctions (such as suspension, debarment, or False Claims Act liability), especially if the SBA believes that you and your teammate intentionally executed a non-compliant joint venture agreement.

For VA procurements, the CVE will ask to see the joint venture agreement as part of the verification process.

The VA's "Separate Legal Entity" Requirement

The VA requires a joint venture to be a "separate legal entity," that is, officially organized under the auspices of a particular state. The limited liability company is probably the most common, but a corporation or (depending on the corporate forms available in a particular state) other type of formal entity will also work.

Between 2007 and early 2011, the SBA's Office of Hearings and Appeals held that a joint venture could not be a separate legal entity for non-VA SDVO set-aside procurements, but instead had to be an "informal" entity created only by contract. You may still hear someone tell you that you cannot create a non-VA SDVO joint venture as a separate legal entity, but fortunately, this is no longer the case. In 2011, OHA reversed itself, holding that a joint venture for a non-VA SDVO set-aside procurement may be either a separate legal entity or an informal entity, whichever the parties choose.[2]

Subcontracting on SDVO Procurements

Like ordinary small business set-aside procurements, your small business can only subcontract so much of a SDVO contract—unless you subcontract to another SDVO small business. If you subcontract to a non-SDVO business, the subcontracting limitations are the same as those applicable to small business set-aside contracts. See Chapter 4 for a full discussion.

Subcontracting to Other SDVO Small Businesses

A special rule applies if you subcontract to one or more other SDVO small businesses: You may subcontract in excess of the ordinary subcontracting limits as long as the work performed by your small business, plus any SDVO small business subcontractors, meets the applicable limitation.

Lake Tahoe Builders submits a proposal on an Army SDVO set-aside procurement for general construction. Lake Tahoe Builders performs 10 percent of the cost of the contract with its own employees, subcontracts 10 percent to another SDVO small business, and subcontracts the remaining 60 percent to a large company.

Result: Lake Tahoe Builders' subcontracting plan is compliant because, together, Lake Tahoe and its SDVO small business subcontractor will perform 20 percent of the cost of the contract with their own employees—5 percent more than the 15 percent performance of work requirement for general construction contracts.

Wait a second—isn't Lake Tahoe Builders ineligible for SDVO set-aside contracts because it doesn't split its profits correctly? Not for this procurement. Remember, the profit-splitting restriction is a special VA rule. In the example, the procurement falls under the SBA's SDVO Program, which does not include a similar requirement.

As the example demonstrates, you have a little more flexibility to satisfy the subcontracting limits on SDVO set-aside procurements than on ordinary small business set-aside procurements because you can count SDVO subcontractors' work toward the requirement. But be careful: This special rule only applies to SDVO procurements. Had the Army's contract been a small business set-aside rather than an SDVO set-aside, Lake Tahoe would have violated the subcontracting limits.

In addition, keep in mind that satisfying the subcontracting limits does not necessarily mean that you will avoid ostensible subcontractor affiliation. If your small business will perform very little of the contract work itself, the SBA may be more likely to deem you affiliated with your subcontractors. For a thorough discussion of ostensible subcontractor affiliation, see Chapter 3.

What About Joint Ventures?

If your SDVO small business forms a joint venture with another company, the subcontracting limits apply to the joint venture, not your small business individually. Unlike in the 8(a) Program, there is no requirement that your small business perform 40 percent (or any other defined percent) of the joint venture's work. Nevertheless, use common sense when you decide how to allocate the work between your small business and your joint venture partner. If your small business will perform very little of the work, the SBA or VA could decide that your SDVO small business does not truly control the joint venture—a prerequisite for the joint venture to be eligible for SDVO set-aside contracts.

The Primary Rules: Where to Find Them

Here's where to find the primary rules discussed in this chapter:

- 38 C.F.R. § 74.10, 38 C.F.R. § 74.11, and 38 C.F.R. § 74.12 (VA SDVO verification)
- 38 C.F.R. § 74.15 (VA renewal requirement)
- 13 C.F.R. § 125.8 and 38 C.F.R. § 74.1 (status as a service-disabled veteran)
- 13 C.F.R. § 125.11 and 48 C.F.R. § 819.7003 (size status)
- 13 C.F.R. § 125.9 and 38 C.F.R. § 74.3 (ownership)
- 13 C.F.R. § 125.10 and 38 C.F.R. § 74.4 (control)
- 38 C.F.R. § 74.2, 38 C.F.R. § 74.3, and 38 C.F.R. § 74.4 (VA-specific requirements)
- 13 C.F.R. § 125.15 and 48 C.F.R. § 819.7003 (joint venturing)
- 13 C.F.R. § 125.6 (subcontracting)

Compliance at a Glance: The Service-Disabled Veteran-Owned Small Business Programs

☐ Obtain a VA SDVO verification prior to bidding on any VA SDVO set-aside contracts, using the web portal at www.vetbiz.gov.

☐ Renew your VA SDVO verification annually.

☐ If you form a joint venture for a VA SDVO procurement, obtain VA verification for the joint venture itself.

☐ To qualify as a service-disabled veteran, obtain appropriate documentation from the VA or Department of Defense certifying your service-connected disability.

☐ Ensure that your company qualifies as a small business for any SDVO set-aside procurement for which you submit an offer.

☐ Ensure that your company is at least 51 percent unconditionally and directly owned by one or more service-disabled veterans.

☐ Review your bylaws, operating agreement, shareholders' agreements, and other governing documents and amend them to eliminate right of first refusal provisions or similar provisions restricting the service-disabled veteran owner's ability to sell his or her interest in the company to anyone at any time.

☐ Avoid any options held by non-service-disabled veterans to purchase an interest in the company if the options, if exercised, would cause service-disabled veterans to own less than 51 percent of the company.

☐ Ensure that service-disabled veterans control both the long-term decision making and day-to-day management of your company.

☐ Review your bylaws, operating agreement, shareholders' agreements, and other governing documents and amend them to eliminate unanimity provisions or any other provisions preventing service-disabled veterans from enjoying absolute control of the company.

- ❑ Ensure that a service-disabled veteran holds the highest officer position in the company (usually president or chief executive officer).

- ❑ Ensure that a service-disabled veteran manager has sufficient managerial experience to run the company, without undue reliance on others.

- ❑ Avoid undue economic reliance on another company (such as obtaining all or most revenues from a single other company).

- ❑ If the veteran manages the company or its contracts remotely, ensure that the veteran has the appropriate technology to do so, and that remote management is effective and feasible in the industry.

- ❑ For VA SDVO verification, ensure that your company and its service-disabled veteran owners are of good character and do not have significant federal debts.

- ❑ For VA SDVO verification, ensure that a service-disabled veteran manages your small business on a full-time basis during normal working hours of firms in the same or similar line of business.

- ❑ For VA SDVO verification, ensure that a service-disabled veteran serves as the company's highest officer.

- ❑ For VA SDVO verification, ensure that the service-disabled veteran's right to share in your small business's profits is commensurate with his or her ownership share, and in no case less than 51 percent of annual distributions of profits.

- ❑ To form a joint venture for a SDVO set-aside procurement, enter into a joint venture agreement containing the mandatory provisions in 13 C.F.R. § 125.15(b)(2).

- ❑ For VA set-aside procurements, form all joint ventures as separate legal entities.

- ❑ Do not subcontract SDVO set-aside contract work in excess of the subcontracting limitations, which are the same as for small business set-aside contracts, except that you may count subcontracts to other SDVO small businesses toward your own performance of work requirements.

CHAPTER 13

THE HUBZONE PROGRAM

THREE OF THE FOUR special small business contracting programs require your company to be owned and controlled by a certain person: a disadvantaged individual, service-disabled veteran, or woman. Not so for the Historically Underutilized Business Zone, or HUBZone Program. HUBZone eligibility depends on whether your company and its employees are located in a *HUBZone*, that is, an area of the country classified by the government as economically disadvantaged due to high unemployment, poverty, or similar conditions. For this reason, participating in the HUBZone Program can be a particularly good option if your small business does not qualify for one of the other three programs (although if it does, you can still participate in this program).

The HUBZone Program offers important contracting advantages to participants. Each year, the government strives to award 3 percent of prime contracting dollars to HUBZone firms. Three percent is big business—around $15 billion annually. To reach its goal, the government sets aside many procurements exclusively for competition among HUBZone small businesses, and even awards some smaller contracts on a sole source basis; in other words, without any competition at all. Even on unrestricted procurements, HUBZone companies may be entitled to a price evaluation preference, making their proposals more attractive to procuring agencies.

Participating in the HUBZone Program can help your small business gain a competitive "leg up," but as is the case for all government contracting programs, you must understand and carefully follow the rules. In the HUBZone Program, scrupulous compliance is especially important, because, in the wake of a 2008 GAO report criticizing the SBA's oversight of the program, the SBA stepped up its enforcement, revoking many companies' HUBZone certifications and, in a number of cases, proposing that noncompliant companies be suspended or debarred from all government contracting. In at least one case, a contractor ended up paying thousands in False Claims Act penalties as a result of HUBZone Program violations.[1] This chapter will help you enjoy the benefits of HUBZone participation while avoiding such harsh sanctions.

Certification as a HUBZone Small Business

You cannot self-certify as a HUBZone small business. Before submitting an offer on a HUBZone set-aside contract or holding your company out as a HUBZone firm, you must obtain a certification from the SBA confirming your HUBZone status.

You can apply for HUBZone certification online, using the SBA's web portal at www.eweb1sp.sba.gov/hubzone/internet/. You will be asked to provide a great deal of documentation, including copies of your lease, rental agreement, or deed for your principal office; payroll records; your articles of incorporation or bylaws; and information (such as copies of drivers' licenses) verifying where your employees live. Carefully review your documents and check them against the eligibility criteria we will discuss in the next section before you hit "submit."

How Long May My Small Business Participate in the HUBZone Program?

Your small business may participate in the HUBZone Program indefinitely, as long as it continues to meet the eligibility requirements. However, your initial HUBZone certification lasts only three years. In order to maintain your certification, you must formally recertify to the SBA that your small business remains eligible. If you fail to file the certification within 30 days after the third anniversary of your admission to the program, the SBA will decertify your small business. You must continue to recertify every three years in order to remain in the program.

What About Joint Ventures?

Unlike for the VA's SDVO Program, a joint venture need not be certified as a HUBZone participant in order to bid on a HUBZone set-aside contract. But as we will discuss later in this chapter, both joint venture partners must be HUBZone-certified.

Can a Competitor Challenge My HUBZone Status?

HUBZone certification is not a magic shield, protecting your small business from allegations that it is ineligible to win a HUBZone contract. After you are certified, a competitor may still challenge your eligibility to receive a HUBZone set-aside contract by filing an eligibility protest. The protest could result in an adverse eligibility decision if the SBA discovers that it overlooked something when it processed the application or—more likely—that something changed after you were certified.

> QuickDri receives its HUBZone certification in June 2012. The following month, QuickDri opens a second office, which is not located in a HUBZone. Business grows at the new location, and by

July 2012, QuickDri has more employees at the new office than at its original office. In August 2013, QuickDri wins a HUBZone set-aside contract and a competitor files an eligibility protest.

Result: The SBA sustains the eligibility protest, because QuickDri's principal office is not located in a HUBZone. QuickDri loses the contract (and will probably lose its HUBZone certification, too).

The bottom line is that even after you receive your HUBZone certification, you must continue to ensure that you meet all of the program's requirements, or you could end up in hot water. In the next section, we'll discuss those requirements—including the "principal office" rule that QuickDri violated.

Eligibility for the HUBZone Program

Your small business qualifies for the HUBZone Program if:

- It is at least 51 percent unconditionally and directly owned and controlled by U.S. citizens.
- It is a small business, both within its primary industry and the size standard for any HUBZone set-aside procurements it bids on.
- Its principal office is located within a HUBZone.
- At least 35 percent of its employees reside in a HUBZone.

This basic definition is a good starting point, but if you intend to participate in the HUBZone Program, you should understand how the SBA interprets it. For instance, the SBA considers your "principal office" to be the office where more employees work than at any other location—even if you call another office your headquarters.

Note that Indian tribes may own HUBZone companies, and that the eligibility rules for tribally owned companies are a little different. We will discuss those special rules in Chapter 15.

Does My Company Meet the HUBZone Program's Control Requirement?

To be eligible for the HUBZone Program, your small business must be unconditionally and directly controlled by one or more U.S. citizens. "Control" means that U.S. citizens must be in charge of both the day-to-day management and long-term decision making. You can avoid any "control" problems by ensuring that all of the company's owners are U.S. citizens. If this is not the case, you should carefully review your company's bylaws, operating agreement, and other governing documents to ensure U.S. citizens have the absolute right to control the company.

Unlike the 8(a) Program and the VA's SDVO program, the HUBZone Program does not specifically require that a U.S. citizen serve as the company's highest officer or be the highest-compensated employee. Nevertheless, it may be difficult to convince the SBA that a U.S. citizen "unconditionally" controls the company if a non-citizen is the company's top officer or top earner.

Does My Company Meet the HUBZone Program's Size Requirements?

To qualify for admission to the HUBZone Program, your company must be small under the size standard corresponding to your *primary industry*, typically, the NAICS code in which your company earned the most revenues in the preceding year. Once you are admitted to the program, you must also qualify as small under the NAICS code designated for any HUBZone set-aside procurement you wish to bid on.

Mean Clean, Inc., a dry cleaning company priding itself on its brusque but efficient service, earns most of its revenues under NAICS code 812310, which carries a $7 million size standard. Gene, the president of Mean Clean, wants to bid on an upcoming series of HUBZone set-aside procurements designated with

NAICS code 812320, which carries a $5 million size standard, and decides to apply for the HUBZone Program. Mean Clean's three-year average annual receipts are $6 million.

Result: Because Mean Clean is a small business under its primary NAICS code, it qualifies as small for purposes of admission to the HUBZone Program. However, even after it is admitted to the program, it cannot bid on the upcoming procurements, because its average annual receipts exceed the $5 million size standard.

For a thorough discussion of how to calculate your size (including the sizes of any affiliates), see Chapters 1 through 3.

Does My Company Meet the HUBZone Program's Ownership Requirement?

To qualify as a HUBZone small business, your company must be at least 51 percent "unconditionally and directly" owned by U.S. citizens. Unfortunately, unlike the SDVO Program, the SBA does not publish written "case law" decisions interpreting the rules, making it unclear how strictly the SBA applies the "unconditional" requirement. But based on the SBA's strict interpretation of a similar requirement in the SDVO Program, you would be wise to assume that any right of first refusal provisions or other restrictions giving non-U.S. citizens "veto power" over the ability of the company's U.S. citizen owners to sell their interests in the company are likely invalid.

Richard, a U.S. citizen, owns 75 percent of Hello Electronics, Inc. Pierre, a French citizen, owns the remaining 25 percent. Hello Electronics' bylaws state that if either owner wishes to sell his ownership interest, he must first offer it to the other owner, and can only sell it on the open market if the other owner declines to purchase it.

> **Result:** The right of first refusal provision prohibits Richard, the U.S. citizen, from doing whatever he wants with his ownership interest, because he cannot sell it to someone other than Pierre without Pierre's permission. The provision means that a U.S. citizen does not unconditionally control Hello Electronics and will likely cause the SBA to deny the company's application.

"Unconditional" ownership also likely means that there cannot be any other strings, like options to purchase majority interests in the company, attached to the U.S. citizens' ownership rights. Of course, if your company is owned exclusively by U.S. citizens, you need not worry about right of first refusal provisions and options.

Can an American Company Own a HUBZone Firm? A HUBZone company must be at least 51 percent owned by *natural persons*—that is, flesh and blood human beings—who are U.S. citizens. With the exception of the special tribal rules we will discuss in Chapter 15, a company (even an American company) cannot own a majority share in a HUBZone firm.

What Net Worth and Income Restrictions Apply? Unlike the 8(a) Program, you need not meet any net worth or income restrictions to qualify for the HUBZone Program. If you are a billionaire, you can own a HUBZone company, so long as you are a U.S. citizen (though, if you have a few billion in the bank, you probably have more exciting hobbies than government contracting).

Does My Company Meet the HUBZone Program's Principal Office Requirement?

In order to be eligible for the HUBZone Program, your company's principal office must be located in a HUBZone. Your *principal office* is the office where the largest number of your employees work—even if another office is your headquarters. Put another way, your principal office is the office where more of your employees work than in any other office.

> Mean Clean, Inc., has three offices in Kansas. Its headquarters, where Gene and the other top officers work, is located in Overland Park. Ten employees work at headquarters. Twenty employees work out of Mean Clean's office in Atchison, and another 15 in its Topeka office.
>
> **Result:** Because it has the largest number of the company's employees, Mean Clean's Atchison office is its principal office for HUBZone purposes, even though Gene considers the Overland Park office to be the company's headquarters.

You need not have a majority of your total employees working in a particular office in order for it to qualify as your principal office. In the example, Mean Clean's Atchison office is its principal office even though only 20 of the company's 45 employees (approximately 44 percent) work there.

The "Jobsite Employee" Exception. If your primary industry is service or construction, you should exclude from your "principal office" calculation any employees who perform the majority of their work at customers' jobsites.

> North Border Builders, Inc., a construction firm, has 15 employees at an office in Pembina, North Dakota, and another five in an office in Grand Forks, North Dakota. At the time it applies to the HUBZone program, North Border Builders has 80 employees working at a federal jobsite at Minot Air Force Base, North Dakota and 60 at a commercial jobsite in Minneapolis.

Result: Because the majority of its employees perform their work in Pembina, it is considered North Border Builders' principal office, even though a far greater share of the company's employees work at the Minot and Minneapolis jobsites.

Is My Company's Principal Office in a HUBZone? Once you have figured out which office is your "principal" office, the next step is to determine whether that office is in a HUBZone. To do so, visit the SBA's HUBZone website at http://map.sba.gov/hubzone/init.asp#address. By inputting your principal office's address into the SBA's web form, you can determine in seconds if your office is in a HUBZone.

If your principal office isn't in a HUBZone, you don't necessarily have to give up on joining the HUBZone program. If you have multiple offices, one of them may be located in a HUBZone. By shifting enough employees to your HUBZone office, you will transform it into your principal office.

Even if none of your offices are located in a HUBZone, there may be a HUBZone just a few miles (or blocks) away. Take a look at the SBA's HUBZone website to see where the nearest HUBZones are located, and consider whether you can move your office from its current location into a HUBZone. There's nothing sneaky or wrong about moving your principal office just to obtain a HUBZone certification—in fact, attracting businesses to HUBZones is one of the underlying goals of the program.

Does My Company Meet the HUBZone Program's Employee Residency Requirement?

To qualify for the HUBZone program, at least 35 percent of your employees must reside in HUBZones. Any HUBZone counts—your employees need not all live in the same HUBZone or in the HUBZone where your principal office is located.

It sounds simple enough, but think about it for a minute. How do you prove that your employees live in HUBZones? What if your employees move or quit? Questions like these make the 35 percent residency requirement the trickiest component of HUBZone eligibility. Ensuring compliance will take some thought and information gathering before you apply to the program (and ongoing monitoring after you are admitted).

Who Is an "Employee"? An "employee," for HUBZone purposes, is anyone who works at least 40 hours per month for your company. Employees obtained from temporary employee agencies or employee leasing companies count, as long as they work the 40-hour monthly minimum.

> CALCulators, Inc., a small accounting firm, has four employees: Cal (its owner), Casey, Sharon, and Felipe. Cal and Sharon each work 40 hours per week. Felipe and Casey are both graduate students at a local university, working as paid interns. Felipe works 15 hours per week, and Casey works five.
>
> **Result:** Cal, Sharon, and Felipe all count as employees for HUBZone purposes because they work more than 40 hours per month. Casey, who works approximately 20 hours per month, does not count as an employee.

Note that Felipe is a *paid* intern. Unpaid volunteers, including unpaid interns, do not usually count as employees for HUBZone purposes. However, if Cal elected not to take a salary (something small business owners sometimes do during the start-up phase), he would nevertheless count as an employee. A company's owner counts as an employee, even if he or she chooses to forgo a salary, unless he or she does not work at least 40 hours per month for the company.

Do My Employees Reside in HUBZones? After you figure out who your "employees" are for HUBZone purposes, the next step is to figure out whether those employees "reside" in HUBZones. A person resides in a HUBZone if:

1. His or her primary residence is in the HUBZone.
2. He or she intends to live there indefinitely.
3. The person has lived in the HUBZone for 180 days, or has lived there fewer than 180 days, but has registered to vote in that location.

CALCulators has three employees for HUBZone purposes: Cal, Sharon, and Felipe. (As noted in the example above, Casey, its fourth employee, works only five hours per week and therefore doesn't count.) Cal has lived in a HUBZone for seven years and has no plans to move. Sharon lives in a HUBZone, but recently signed a contract to purchase a new home that is not located in a HUBZone. Felipe has lived in a HUBZone for three months, but has not registered to vote.

Result: For HUBZone eligibility purposes, Cal resides in a HUBZone because he has lived in one for more than 180 days and plans to stay indefinitely. Sharon does not reside in a HUBZone because, although she has lived in one for more than 180 days, she plans to move. Felipe does not reside in a HUBZone because he has lived in one for less than 180 days and has not registered to vote.

How Do I Apply the 35 Percent Requirement to My Employees? To figure out whether you meet the HUBZone 35 percent requirement, simply multiply the total number of employees by 35 percent to determine how many employees must reside in HUBZones, then compare the result to your number of HUBZone employees

> Ace Contractors, Inc., has 81 employees. Twenty-eight of those employees live in HUBZones.
>
> **Result:** Horace, Ace's owner, multiplies 81 by 0.35, and discovers that Ace must have 29 employees residing in HUBZones to qualify for the HUBZone Program. Comparing the result to the number of Ace's employees residing in HUBZones, Horace discovers that Ace does not meet the HUBZone program's 35 percent requirement.

If you are a mental math whiz, you may be saying "wait a second—35 percent of 81 is 28.35, not 29." Horace can't hire a fraction of an employee, can he? Shouldn't he have been able to round the 28.35 figure down to 28?

No. When it comes to your HUBZone employee count, forget what your third grade teacher told you, because you can never round down. If your HUBZone calculation results in a fraction (which is often the case), round up to determine how many HUBZone employees you must have.

Can I Exclude "Jobsite Employees" from the 35 Percent Calculation? The "jobsite employee" exception only applies to determining your principal office. When it comes to meeting the 35 percent residency requirement, you must count all paid employees who work at least 40 hours monthly, regardless of whether they work in one of your offices or at a customer's jobsite.

> North Border Builders has 15 employees at an office in Pembina, North Dakota, and another five in an office in Grand Forks, North Dakota. At the time it applies to the HUBZone Program, North Border Builders has 80 employees working at a federal jobsite at Minot Air Force Base, North Dakota, and 60 at a commercial jobsite in Minneapolis. With the exception of supervisory personnel, the employees at the Minot and Minneapolis jobsites are tempo-

rary workers and are not expected to stay with the company after completion of the projects.

Result: North Border Builders' compliance with the 35 percent residency requirement is determined using all 160 of its employees—including the 140 employees who work at jobsites. The fact that many of these employees are temporary does not affect the calculation.

If your company works in the construction industry or another industry with high employee turnover, complying with the 35 percent residency requirement can be a real headache. Not only must you continually ensure that enough of your employees reside in HUBZones, but you must collect proof of residency—such as photocopies of drivers' licenses or utility bills—which can be particularly burdensome if, for example, many of your employees are transient or live in temporary housing. Nevertheless, the rules are the rules, and there are no jobsite or temporary employee exceptions from the 35 percent requirement. You will need to show the SBA that you meet the requirement, no matter what your industry.

Maintaining HUBZone Eligibility

Applying to the HUBZone Program can be an intensive process as you gather and submit all the necessary documentation. But once you are admitted, don't let down your guard. With the exception of a little wiggle room in the 35 percent residency requirement, which we will discuss below, you must continue to meet all of the initial eligibility requirements we discussed above throughout your tenure in the program.

The "Attempt to Maintain" Exception

The SBA understands that the normal comings and goings of employees may cause your firm to temporarily dip below the 35 percent residency requirement. For that reason, the SBA likely will not decertify your small business if it briefly fails to meet the requirement, as long as you are actively *attempting* to regain compliance.

To demonstrate that you are attempting to regain compliance, you should be able to show the SBA that you are taking concrete steps to address the problem. For instance, you might post employment advertisements targeting individuals who live in HUBZones, or offer bonuses to current employees who choose to move to HUBZones. If you are not taking any good faith, specific steps to regain compliance, but simply crossing your fingers and hoping that your ordinary hiring processes will bring you some new HUBZone employees, the SBA might decide that you are not doing enough and remove your small business from the program.

Importantly, while you can continue performing existing HUBZone contracts while attempting to regain compliance with the 35 percent residency requirement, you cannot bid on any new HUBZone set-aside contracts, or self-certify as a HUBZone small business for any other government contract, until you actually regain compliance.

CALCulators has three employees for HUBZone purposes: Cal, Sharon, and Felipe. Felipe registers to vote in his HUBZone location. Together with Cal, who also lives in a HUBZone, CALCulators meets the 35 percent residency requirement and is admitted to the HUBZone Program. However, six months later, Felipe quits. To replace him, Cal hires Chrissie, who does not live in a HUBZone. Shortly thereafter, Cal spots a HUBZone set-aside opportunity and would like to submit a bid.

Result: As a result of Felipe's departure and Chrissie's hiring, only one of CALCulators' three employees reside in HUBZones, which puts CALCulators beneath the 35 percent requirement. Provided CALCulators is actively trying to address the problem, the SBA will probably not decertify it from the HUBZone Program, but

> CALCulators cannot bid on the new HUBZone set-aside procurement—or any other HUBZone set-aside procurement—until it regains compliance.

Small businesses sometimes unintentionally violate this requirement, believing that as long as they are attempting to meet the 35 percent residency requirement, they may bid on new HUBZone work. Not so. Be sure that you meet the requirement before submitting any new offer as a HUBZone firm.

Note that the "attempting to comply" exception applies only to the 35 percent requirement, not other components of HUBZone eligibility. Attempting to comply with the ownership, control, principal office, or size requirements won't cut it, even if you do not bid on new HUBZone work.

How Do I Ensure Ongoing Compliance with the 35 Percent Residency Requirement?

If your small business is like most HUBZone companies, remaining in compliance with the 35 percent residency requirement will be the most difficult part of your ongoing eligibility obligations. However, with some advance planning—and the help of your employees—you can minimize the hassles of maintaining compliance. To help ensure ongoing compliance, you should consider the following actions:

- Educate your employees about the HUBZone Program and employees' importance in helping you maintain compliance, using seminars, handouts, and so on.

- Require your employees to disclose how long they have lived at their primary residences and whether they are registered to vote at their primary residences.

- Include, as part of your employment contracts, or in your employee handbook, a requirement that each employee notify you some reasonable time in advance (say, 30 or 60 days) of any intended change in primary residence.

- Require your employees, upon request, to provide you with current proof of residency (such as photocopies of drivers' licenses, voter registration cards, or current utility bills).

- In your hiring practices, target employees who reside in HUBZones. Consider checking the address listed on each prospective employee's resume against the HUBZone map before making a hire.

- Consider bonuses or other incentives to encourage employees to move to (or remain in) HUBZones.

What If My Small Business Falls Out of Compliance?

If your company falls out of compliance with the 35 percent requirement, or any other HUBZone Program requirement, you must immediately inform the SBA in writing. Do not postpone the notice, even if you believe that you will quickly regain your eligibility. In recent years, the SBA has decertified firms that waited a month or two to notify it of a loss of eligibility, and in a few cases, has even proposed suspending or debarring companies from all government contracting for failing to promptly provide the required notice.

In your written notice, explain to the SBA how you intend to fix the problem. For instance, if you no longer meet the 35 percent eligibility requirement, describe the efforts you are taking to regain compliance. If you cannot fix the problem—say, for instance, your company has outgrown the size standard in its primary NAICS code—you should voluntarily withdraw from the HUBZone Program rather than merely notifying the SBA that you have a permanent eligibility issue.

If you notify the SBA of an eligibility problem, whether short term or long term, immediately stop representing your small business as a

HUBZone participant in any public forum until you regain eligibility. In conjunction with your SBA notice, update your website, CCR profile, and other public databases to remove any references to your company's HUBZone certification until you regain compliance.

Subcontracting on HUBZone Procurements

Like ordinary small business set-aside procurements, your small business can only subcontract so much of a HUBZone contract—unless you subcontract to another HUBZone small business. If you subcontract to a non-HUBZone business, the subcontracting limitations for services contracts are the same as for small business set-aside contracts. See Chapter 4 for a full discussion.

Subcontracting to Other HUBZone Small Businesses

For services contracts, a special rule applies if you subcontract to one or more other HUBZone small businesses: you may subcontract in excess of the ordinary 50 percent limit as long as the work performed by your small business, plus its HUBZone subcontractors, meets the 50 percent requirement.

After regaining its HUBZone eligibility, CALCulators bids on a HUBZone set-aside procurement for accounting services. CALCulators plans to spend 30 percent of the cost of the contract incurred for personnel on its own employees, subcontract an additional 25 percent to another HUBZone company, and subcontract the remaining 45 percent to a non-HUBZone company.

Result: CALCulators' subcontracting plan is compliant because, together, CALCulators and its HUBZone small business subcontractor will incur 55 percent of the cost of the contract incurred for personnel on their own employees.

As the example demonstrates, you have a little more flexibility to satisfy the subcontracting limits on HUBZone set-aside services procurements than on ordinary small business set-aside procurements because you can count HUBZone subcontractors' work toward the requirement. But be careful: This special rule only applies to HUBZone procurements. Had the procurement been a small business set-aside, rather than HUBZone set-aside, CALCulators would have violated the subcontracting limits.

In addition, keep in mind that satisfying the subcontracting limits does not necessarily mean that you will avoid ostensible subcontractor affiliation. If your small business will perform very little of the contract work itself, the SBA may be more likely to deem you affiliated with your subcontractors. For a thorough discussion of ostensible subcontractor affiliation, see Chapter 3.

Special Construction Subcontracting Requirements

Meeting your subcontracting limits on services contracts may be easier on HUBZone set-aside procurements, but for general construction and specialty trade construction contracts, it can be more difficult. Not only must your HUBZone small business meet the 15 percent or 25 percent performance requirements with its own employees, but you must also ensure that at least 50 percent of the cost of the contract incurred for personnel be spent on employees of HUBZone companies—either your small business or HUBZone subcontractors.

XPert Constructors obtains its HUBZone certification and submits a bid on a HUBZone set-aside procurement for general construction. XPert intends to perform 20 percent of the contract with its own employees and subcontract the remaining 80 percent to a non-HUBZone company.

Result: Because the subcontractor will perform 80 percent of the cost of the contract, it is likely that more than 50 percent of the cost of the contract incurred for personnel will be spent on the subcontractor's employees (see Chapter 4 for a discussion of "cost of the contract" and "cost of the contract incurred for personnel," in the section discussing the subcontracting limitations on small business set-aside contracts. If this is the case, the subcontracting plan is non-compliant.

In XPert's case, its subcontracting plan would have been compliant had the contract been set-aside for small businesses. But because it was a HUBZone set-aside, XPert was tripped up by the special 50 percent rule. If you are a HUBZone construction contractor, reach out to potential HUBZone subcontractors early in the procurement process to ensure that you meet the 50 percent requirement (unless you plan to perform at least 50 percent of the cost of the contract incurred for personnel on your own employees).

The procuring agency may waive the 50 percent requirement if it determines that it is not reasonable to believe that it can be met on a particular procurement. This might be the case, for instance, if the project is located in a rural area and yours is the only HUBZone construction company for miles around. If you believe that a waiver is appropriate, approach the contracting officer and make your case. But even if the agency grants your request, you still must meet the baseline 15 percent or 25 percent requirements we discussed in Chapter 4.

What about Joint Ventures?

If your HUBZone small business forms a joint venture with another company, the subcontracting limits apply to the joint venture, not your small business individually. Unlike in the 8(a) Program, there is no requirement that your small business perform 40 percent (or any other defined percent) of the joint venture's work. However, as we will discuss in the next section, joint venturing is not as popular an option for HUBZone procurements as for other government procurements because you are limited in your choice of a joint venture partner.

Joint Venturing on HUBZone Procurements

You may form a joint venture with another company to submit a proposal for a HUBZone set-aside procurement, but only if both joint venture partners are certified HUBZone participants. You cannot joint venture with a non-HUBZone company, large or small, for a HUBZone set-aside procurement. For this reason, many small businesses forgo joint ventures on HUBZone procurements in favor of prime/subcontractor arrangements, for which there are no similar restrictions.

Size Requirements for HUBZone Joint Ventures

If you do joint venture with another HUBZone company, the joint venture must meet certain size requirements to qualify for the procurement. As a general matter, you must add your company's size to your joint venture partner's size to determine whether your joint venture qualifies as small for a HUBZone set-aside procurement. But for some competitive procurements, your joint venture will qualify as small so long as each joint venture member, individually, is small under the NAICS code assigned to the contract. The special "individual size treatment" rule applies when:

- For a procurement with a revenue-based size standard, the procurement exceeds half the size standard corresponding to the NAICS code.

- For a procurement having an employee-based size standard, the procurement exceeds $10 million.

Note that, unlike in the SDVO Program, your HUBZone company need not be less than half the size standard corresponding to the NAICS code in order to take advantage of the "individual size treatment" rule. Rather, application of the rule turns solely on the size of the procurement. If the procurement is not large enough, the SBA will aggregate the sizes of your company and its joint venture partner.

Are There Any Mandatory Joint Venture Provisions?

Unlike in the 8(a) and SDVO Programs, your HUBZone joint venture agreement need not contain any mandatory terms. This makes sense: The SBA is not concerned about ensuring that a HUBZone firm controls the joint venture, since both joint venture partners must be HUBZone participants.

Even though you need not include any mandatory provisions, your joint venture agreement is a binding contractual document, establishing the framework of your working relationship with your teammate. You should prepare a comprehensive agreement, including provisions on how profits and losses will be distributed, how disputes between the teammates will be resolved, how the joint venture will be managed, and other matters that may arise as you and your partner compete together for federal contracts.

The Primary Rules: Where to Find Them

Here's where to find the primary rules discussed in this chapter:

- 13 C.F.R. § 126.300 through 13 C.F.R. § 126.309 (certification)
- 13 C.F.R. § 126.502 (indefinite participation)
- 13 C.F.R. § 126.500 (recertification)

- 13 C.F.R. § 126.800 through 13 C.F.R. § 126.805 (HUBZone protests)
- 13 C.F.R. § 126.201 (ownership)
- 13 C.F.R. § 126.202 (control)
- 13 C.F.R. § 126.203 (size)
- 13 C.F.R. § 126.103 and 13 C.F.R. § 126.200 (principal office)
- 13 C.F.R. § 126.103 and 13 C.F.R. § 126.200 (35 percent residency requirement)
- 13 C.F.R. § 126.200 ("attempt to maintain" exception)
- 13 C.F.R. § 126.501 (reporting eligibility changes to the SBA)
- 13 C.F.R. § 125.6 and 13 C.F.R. § 126.700 (subcontracting)
- 13 C.F.R. § 126.616 (joint venturing)

Compliance at a Glance: The HUBZone Program

☐ Before bidding on any HUBZone set-aside contracts or holding your small business out as a HUBZone firm, apply for and receive a HUBZone certification from the SBA.

☐ Renew your HUBZone certification every three years.

☐ To qualify for the HUBZone Program, ensure that your company is at least 51 percent unconditionally and directly owned by U.S. citizens who are natural persons (not companies or other entities).

☐ If non-U.S. citizens own a portion of your small business, carefully review your bylaws, operating agreement, shareholders' agreements, and other governing documents and amend them to eliminate right of first refusal provisions or similar provisions restricting the U.S. citizens' ability to sell their interests in the company to anyone at any time.

☐ To qualify for the HUBZone Program, ensure that your company is at least 51 percent unconditionally and directly controlled by U.S. citizens who are natural persons (not companies or other entities).

☐ Ensure that your company's highest officer is a U.S. citizen and that the highest paid employee is a U.S. citizen (recommended).

☐ To qualify for the HUBZone Program, confirm that your company is a small business within the size standard corresponding to its primary industry, typically, the NAICS code in which your company earned the most revenues in the preceding year.

☐ To qualify for the HUBZone Program, ensure that your company's principal office—defined as the office where there largest number of your employees work (excluding so-called "jobsite employees")—is located in a HUBZone.

☐ To qualify for the HUBZone Program, ensure that at least 35 percent of your employees reside in a HUBZone.

☐ Once your small business is admitted to the HUBZone Program, maintain compliance with all of the initial eligibility criteria.

☐ If your small business briefly falls out of compliance with the 35 percent residency requirement, "attempt to maintain" compliance by posting employee advertisements targeted at HUBZones, offering employees incentives to move to HUBZones, and so on.

☐ Do not bid on any new HUBZone set-aside contracts or self-certify as a HUBZone participant for any other contract unless your company currently meets all HUBZone eligibility criteria, including the 35 percent residency requirement.

☐ If your small business falls out of compliance with any HUBZone eligibility requirement, immediately inform the SBA in writing.

☐ Do not subcontract work in excess of the HUBZone Program's subcontracting limitations, which are stricter for construction contracts than the ordinary small business subcontracting limitations.

❑ If you form a joint venture for a HUBZone set-aside procurement, ensure that your joint venture partner is a certified HUBZone participant and that your joint venture will qualify as a small business for the procurement.

CHAPTER 14

THE WOMEN-OWNED SMALL BUSINESS PROGRAM

IT TOOK TEN YEARS and countless revisions, but in 2010, the SBA enacted a program designed to "give 'em five," that is, ensure that at least 5 percent of federal prime contracting dollars flow to women-owned businesses. Although women are not a minority in American society, the 5 percent goal demonstrates just how underrepresented women-owned businesses are in the federal marketplace. At the time the SBA adopted the final rule, women-owned businesses received less than 3.5 percent of federal prime contracts.

The Women-Owned Small Business (WOSB) Program (or as it is occasionally called, the 8(m) Program) provides special contracting preferences to businesses owned and controlled by women. The WOSB program is similar in many respects to the SBA's other small business programs. However, the program includes several unique aspects, including a special subprogram designed for so-called Economically Disadvantaged Women-Owned Small Businesses, or EDWOSBs.

The WOSB Program also differs from the 8(a), SDVO, and HUB-Zone Programs in two not-so-great respects. First, not all government contracts can be set-aside for WOSBs. The program only authorizes set-aside procurements in industries where women-owned businesses have been found to be underrepresented. Before obtaining your certification, you may want to double-check that the SBA allows WOSB set-asides in your primary industry. A list of applicable NAICS codes is available on the SBA's website at sba.gov/content/contracting-opportunities-women-owned-small-businesses. Second, contracts cannot be awarded to WOSBs on a sole source (or "no competition") basis. All WOSB set-asides must be competed.

That said, the WOSB Program can still provide tremendous benefits to your small business if you are in the right line of work. Because the program is in its infancy, it is not yet clear how strictly the SBA will enforce the program's regulations. The smart money, though, says that the SBA, which has sometimes been criticized for its oversight of its other small business programs, will see the WOSB program as an opportunity to "get it right" from the start by stringently ensuring that only eligible businesses participate and that the program's rules are followed to the letter.

With that in mind, it's important for women-owned small businesses to get it right from the start, too. This chapter explains the WOSB Program's eligibility and compliance requirements.

Certification as a Women-Owned Small Business

For small business set-aside contracts, you may self-certify your eligibility. For some of the special small business contracting programs, like the 8(a) and HUBZone Programs, you must be formally certified in order to participate. When it created the women-owned small business program, the SBA decided to "split the baby." For WOSB set-aside procurements, you have two choices: self-certify by submitting a number of documents to a special database or obtain a WOSB certification in advance, which allows you to skip most of the self-certification process.

Self-Certification

To self-certify as a WOSB for a particular procurement, you must first register your company as a WOSB in the CCR and ORCA databases. See Chapter 10 for a discussion of these databases and how to register in them. But be careful not to identify yourself as a WOSB in the databases until you are sure that you qualify. Thoroughly read the section on eligibility below before updating your online profiles.

Registration in these databases is not the end of the process. When it comes to WOSB self-certification, the SBA has adopted Ronald Reagan's old maxim: "trust, but verify." The SBA does not wait until a competitor files a size protest to ask you to submit documents establishing your eligibility; you must submit them in advance. At the time you submit an offer on a WOSB set-aside contract, you must submit the following documents to the WOSB Repository, a secure online database designed to collect WOSB eligibility information:

- Birth certificates, naturalization papers, or unexpired passports for the women owners, demonstrating U.S. citizenship
- Corporate governance documents, including articles of organization and operating agreements (for limited liability companies), articles of incorporation and bylaws (for corporations), or the partnership agreement (for partnerships)
- For corporations, all issued stock certificates—including the front and back, and signed in accordance with the bylaws—and the stock ledger
- A signed copy of the official Women-Owned Small Business Program Certification—WOSBs or EDWOSBs, as applicable (available at sba.gov/content/women-owned-small-business-wosb-program-certification)
- If applicable, a copy of the joint venture agreement
- If applicable, an assumed/fictitious name certificate

In addition, if you are self-certifying as a EDWOSB, you must submit a completed SBA Form 413 for each woman claiming economic disadvantage, as well as an SBA Form 413 for each economically disadvantaged woman's spouse (if any). SBA Form 413 is available at sba.gov/content/personal-financial-statement.

The WOSB Repository is available through the SBA's General Login System at eweb.sba.gov/gls. If the WOSB Repository is off-line or unavailable, you must submit the required documents directly to the contracting officer. Once you self-certify on a WOSB procurement, you must retain all documents demonstrating your eligibility for that procurement for at least six years following self-certification. These documents must be retained even if they are later amended or superseded.

Formal Certification

In lieu of providing many of the documents required for the self-certification process, your small business may obtain a formal certification of its WOSB status from a third party, like the U.S. Women's Chamber of Commerce, approved by the SBA to provide WOSB certifications. For a list of approved providers and links to their websites, visit sba.gov/content/contracting-opportunities-women-owned-small-businesses.

Obtaining a formal WOSB certification requires you to submit the same documentation described above to the third-party provider, which (assuming everything checks out) will certify you as a WOSB. Once you are certified, you no longer need submit most of the documents to the WOSB Repository in connection with your offers on WOSB set-aside procurements. Instead, submit your formal certification, plus any joint venture agreement (if applicable) and the signed certification available on the SBA's website. If you plan to bid on a lot of WOSB set-aside contracts, it makes sense to obtain a formal certification, since it will cut down on the hassle of repeatedly updating your WOSB Repository documents. And, from a public relations standpoint, being able to say that your company is a "certified women-owned small business" can't hurt.

Can a Competitor Challenge My WOSB Status?

Does formal WOSB certification etch your WOSB status in stone? No. Regardless of whether you self-certify or have obtained a formal certification from a third-party certifier, a competitor may still challenge your eligibility to receive a WOSB set-aside procurement by way of an eligibility protest filed with the SBA. Lose the eligibility protest, and you will lose your WOSB set-aside contract—and your WOSB status, too.

After CompuTrain, Inc., a computer training company, receives its formal WOSB certification, its owner, Rachel, sells the company to Luke. CompuTrain subsequently bids on and wins a WOSB set-aside procurement, and a competitor files an eligibility protest.

Result: CompuTrain is no longer owned and controlled by a woman, so it is ineligible to receive a WOSB set-aside procurement, despite its formal certification.

Whether you self-certify or obtain a formal certification, your status as a WOSB is always subject to challenge. Carefully review the remainder of this chapter and ensure that your small business remains in strict compliance with the WOSB Program's requirements. Of course, your competitors don't have a monopoly on WOSB status protests. If you believe that an ineligible competitor has won a WOSB set-aside contract, you can file a protest yourself.

How Long May I Remain in the WOSB Program?

Unlike the 8(a) Program, which carries a nine-year program term, your small business may remain in the WOSB Program as long as it complies with all of the eligibility requirements. You must update your

CCR and ORCA profiles no less than once a year to ensure that your status remains up-to-date.

Eligibility for the WOSB Program

Your small business qualifies for the WOSB Program if it is:

1. A small business under the NAICS code assigned to a particular procurement

2. At least 51 percent unconditionally owned by one or more women who are United States citizens

3. Unconditionally controlled by one or more women who are U.S. citizens

To qualify as an EDWOSB, your small business must meet all three WOSB criteria and the women who own and control the business must be considered economically disadvantaged. In addition, to qualify as an EDWOSB, your business must qualify as small for its primary NAICS code (typically, the NAICS code in which you earned the most revenues in the previous year), as well as for the NAICS code assigned to a particular procurement.

This basic definition is a good starting point, but complying with the eligibility requirements necessitates going a little further. For instance, as we will learn, the SBA does not believe that a woman controls a small business if a man serves as the business's highest officer—even if the woman owns 100 percent of the company. Understanding nuances like this are critical to ensuring that your company is a compliant WOSB.

Is My Company Small Enough for WOSB Program Purposes?

Your company qualifies as a WOSB so long as it is small under the NAICS code assigned to a particular procurement. For a discussion on how to calculate your company's size, see Chapters 1 through 3.

Unlike in the 8(a) and HUBZone Programs, your company need not be small in its primary industry to participate in the WOSB Program, though it must be to qualify as an EDWOSB.

> Amanda's company, Texas Treatments, Inc., provides waste treatment and disposal services in Texas and the surrounding areas. At $10 million in three-year average annual receipts, Texas Treatments has outgrown the $7 million size standard in its primary NAICS code, 562991. However, Amanda would like to bid on WOSB set-aside contracts under NAICS code 562111, which carries a $12.5 million size standard.
>
> **Result:** Texas Treatments qualifies as a small business under NAICS code 562111. Provided it meets the other WOSB eligibility criteria, it can qualify for WOSB set-aside contracts in that NAICS code, even though it is not a small business in its primary NAICS code.

The bottom line? Even if your business is not "small" for much of its work, it may qualify as a WOSB in secondary lines of work. If so, WOSB status may help your company develop its business in those areas.

Does My Company Meet the "Unconditional Ownership" Requirement?

To qualify for the WOSB Program, your company must be at least 51 percent unconditionally and directly owned by one or more women who are United States citizens. If ownership is split 50–50 between a woman and her husband (a relatively common occurrence), or if men otherwise own more than 49 percent, your company will not qualify.

In addition, if ownership is subject to conditions or options that would potentially enable men to control the company, the SBA will treat the options as exercised and your company will not qualify.

> Amanda owns 51 percent of Texas Treatments. Her brother, Bobby, owns the remaining 49 percent. Bobby also holds an option to purchase 2 percent of Amanda's interest, but has not exercised the option.
>
> **Result:** Amanda does not unconditionally control Texas Treatments because Bobby can assume majority ownership at any time. Texas Treatments does not qualify for the WOSB Program.

There is one exception to the unconditional ownership rule: As a woman owner, you may pledge your stock or ownership interest as collateral, and maintain your "unconditional" ownership, as long as the pledge is made pursuant to ordinary commercial practices and as long as you will maintain control unless you violate the agreement. If you intend to pledge your stock or ownership interest as collateral, carefully review the agreement to ensure it complies.

Ownership by women must be "direct," that is, it cannot flow through other entities, such as a parent company, trust, or employee stock ownership plan, even if a woman ultimately controls the other entity.

> Staff Solutions, LLC, a small staffing company, is a wholly owned subsidiary of Dry Dry Again, which is owned by Jane. Staff Solutions would like to qualify for the WOSB Program based on Jane's ownership.
>
> **Result:** Staff Solutions is not directly owned by women, because Jane owns the company indirectly through Dry Dry Again. Staff Solutions is ineligible for participation in the WOSB program (and may have size problems, as well, given its affiliation with a large company).

Although the SBA has not yet issued decisions interpreting the unconditional ownership rule, its treatment of the same term in the

SDVO Program suggests that it will likely find that right of first refusal provisions and similar restrictions on ownership transfers may interfere with "unconditional" control. Before applying for the WOSB Program or self-certifying as a WOSB, give your corporate documents a thorough review, paying close attention to any restrictions on ownership transfers.

What Net Worth and Income Restrictions Apply? Unlike in the 8(a) Program, you need not meet any net worth or income restrictions to qualify for the WOSB Program. If you happen to be a billionaire, and also own a qualifying small business, you can participate. As we will discuss later in this chapter, you must meet certain net worth and income restrictions in order for your company to qualify as an EDWOSB.

Does My Company Meet the "Unconditional Control" Requirement?

The term "women-owned small business" is misleading because it suggests that a company may qualify for the WOSB Program solely on the basis of its ownership. In fact, the program would be more accurately described as the "Women Owned *and Controlled* Small Business Program," because even if your small business is 51 percent owned by women, it will not qualify for the program unless it is also unconditionally controlled by women.

If you read the previous chapters on the 8(a) Program and SDVO Programs, the control requirements may seem familiar, because the SBA borrowed heavily from these programs in establishing the WOSB control guidelines. As in the 8(a) and SDVO Programs, in general, "control" means that both the long-term decision making and the day-to-day management and administration of business operations must be conducted by women.

Let's look at two examples of how this requirement can affect your company's WOSB eligibility.

Stephanie owns 100 percent of Spiky Hairdressers, Inc., a company specializing in giving "buzz cuts" to new military recruits. Stephanie, an avid gardener, spends most of her time in her greenhouse, while her son, Karl, manages Spiky Hairdressers' day-to-day affairs. Karl's employment agreement with Spiky Hairdressers allows Stephanie to fire him at any time if she wishes to assume day-to-day management of the company herself.

Result: Spiky Hairdressers is ineligible for the WOSB Program because its day-to-day operations are not managed by a woman.

As the example indicates, even 100 percent ownership does not equate to "control" for WOSB purposes if the women owners are not actively involved in the day-to-day management of the company. It makes no difference that, theoretically, Stephanie could fire Karl at any time and assume day-to-day management herself.

Karrie owns 51 percent of Big Dog Vets, LLC, a provider of veterinary services to the armed forces. Her cousin, Hamlet, owns the remaining 49 percent. The company's bylaws require unanimous consent of the owners to enter into contracts, take out loans, or make capital expenditures of $5,000 or more.

Result: Karrie does not control Big Dog Vets because she cannot make a number of business decisions without Hamlet's consent. The unanimity provisions prevent Big Dog Vets from being eligible for the WOSB Program.

As the above example suggests, when the SBA evaluates control, the first place it will look is your company's corporate documents—such as articles of incorporation or organization, bylaws, and operating agreements. You should ensure that your corporate documents reflect that the company is owned and controlled by women.

The documents should indicate that a woman holds the highest officer position, has final authority over big picture and day-to-day decision making, and cannot be overruled by men or outside interests. Although men may participate in management, you must be especially careful to avoid "unanimous consent" or "supermajority" provisions in your bylaws or operating agreements. A provision that gives a man or other entity the ability to veto the company's business decisions may cause the SBA to hold that women do not control the firm.

Beyond the general requirement that women control the company's decisions, the SBA will also examine a number of subfactors, including whether a woman holds the highest officer position, and possesses sufficient experience to effectively run the company.

Managerial Position. To qualify as a WOSB, a woman must hold your company's highest officer position (usually president or CEO). There are no ifs, ands, or buts to this rule: If a man holds the firm's highest position (even if the women owners can fire him at any time), the firm does not qualify.

To make sure that you do not get tripped up on the "highest officer" requirement, ensure that your small business's governing documents clearly indicate which position is the company's highest officer position and clearly indicate that a woman holds that position.

Degree of Relevant Experience. The SBA will not consider your small business to be controlled by a woman unless the woman who holds the highest officer position has managerial experience of the extent and complexity needed to run the business. The intent is to avoid "figurehead" arrangements, in which a company meets the WOSB ownership and highest officer requirements, but an inexperienced woman, in practice, relies upon men to actually run the company.

After ten years spent as a Vegas lounge singer, Mary forms MaryIT, a technology contractor focusing on providing computer programming services to the government. Mary has never worked in the IT industry before. MaryIT's vice president, Carlos, who met Mary in her lounge, has been a computer programmer for 20 years. Mary submits an offer on a WOSB set-aside procurement and a competitor files an eligibility protest.

Result: Because Mary lacks any experience in the industry, the SBA is likely to conclude that Mary lacks the requisite experience to effectively manage the company without leaning too heavily on Carlos, and that as a result MaryIT does not qualify as a WOSB.

The experience requirement does not mean that a woman must be the most experienced person in the company. It is perfectly acceptable for a viable WOSB to hire men who have greater levels of experience than the women owners. The focus is on whether the women have enough experience to understand the industry and direct the company's employees.

Unfortunately, the regulations are vague as to what constitutes "enough" experience to qualify. Use your best judgment. If a reasonable person might question whether you have sufficient knowledge and experience to effectively direct your company's operations, you may wish to forgo bidding on WOSB contracts until you gain additional experience.

Full-Time Employment. In order for your small business to qualify as a WOSB, the woman who holds the company's highest officer position must manage it on a full-time basis, and must work for the company full-time during the normal working hours of firms in the same or similar lines of work. She cannot take on outside employment that prevents her from devoting sufficient time and attention to the company's daily business affairs. Accordingly, if you must work a second job, be sure to devote at least 40 hours per week to the WOSB—and document your work so that you can show you are devoting full-time efforts to your company.

Special EDWOSB Requirements

Qualifying as an EDWOSB can allow your firm to access additional contracting opportunities: Procurements in some NAICS codes may be set aside for EDWOSBs, but not "ordinary" WOSBs. Remember that an EDWOSB is a subcategory of a WOSB. To qualify as an EDWOSB, your small business must meet the size, ownership, and control requirements described above, plus the women who own and control it must fall beneath certain net worth and ownership requirements.

Fortunately, as is the case in the 8(a) Program, meeting the EDWOSB's economic disadvantage requirements do not mean that you must be living in a "van down by the river," as memorably put by Matt Foley, the character played by Chris Farley on *Saturday Night Live*. In fact, the requirements are quite fair—perhaps even generous.

Net Worth. To be considered economically disadvantaged for purposes of the EDWOSB program, your net worth must be less than $750,000, excluding:

- Ownership interest in your business
- Equity interest in your primary personal residence
- If your EDWOSB is an S corporation, LLC or partnership, "pass-through" income received from the EDWOSB, as long as you can provide documentary evidence demonstrating that the income was reinvested in the business or used solely to pay business taxes (pass-through losses, however, do not reduce net worth)
- Funds invested in an Individual Retirement Account (IRA) or other official retirement account, as long as the funds are unavailable until retirement age without significant penalties

To calculate your net worth, you must include all funds in checking accounts; savings accounts; and stocks, bonds, and investment accounts (except excluded retirement accounts). You must also count the value of personal property, including automobiles, electronics, jewelry, and the like, as well as the value of any real estate that is not your primary residence. The SBA does not expect you to obtain a formal appraisal of your personal property, but it does expect you to provide a good faith estimate. If you tell the SBA that you only have $500 in personal property, the SBA is likely to be quite skeptical.

The SBA requires EDWOSB owners to submit Form 413, which is used to calculate an individual's personal net worth. The form is available on the SBA's website at www.sba.gov/sbaforms/sba413.pdf. If you are uncertain if your net worth exceeds the $750,000 threshold, complete Form 413 early in the process, and see how the numbers come out. But don't forget to exclude the IRA/Retirement Account line item on Form 413 from the net worth calculation. Although the SBA wants you to disclose the information, IRAs and qualified retirement accounts don't count toward your net worth for purposes of the EDWOSB program.

Finally, you should be aware that although the value of your primary residence and your ownership interest in your small business are ordinarily not considered in the SBA's calculation, you are not economically disadvantaged for EDWOSB purposes if the fair market value of your assets, *including* your home equity and business interest, exceed $6 million. IRA and qualified retirement assets are excluded from this $6 million calculation.

Personal Income. If your adjusted gross yearly income, averaged over the three preceding years, exceeds $350,000, the SBA will presume that you are not economically disadvantaged. You have the right to attempt to rebut the presumption, such as by showing that you experienced significant financial losses commensurate with your earnings. Keep in mind that the SBA employees evaluating EDWOSB status do not make anything close to $350,000 annually, and may be hesitant to find you economically disadvantaged based on a rebuttal of the presumption unless you have a very strong case.

In calculating your adjusted gross income, the SBA will deduct "pass-through" income from an LLC, S corporation, or partnership, as long you have documentary evidence that the income was reinvested in the EDWOSB or used to pay the EDWOSB's business taxes. Pass-through losses, however, do not reduce your personal income for EDWOSB purposes.

Other Factors. Although net worth and personal income are the primary components of the SBA's economic disadvantage analysis, it may look at other factors as well. Perhaps most importantly, it may examine the financial situation of your spouse, particularly if your spouse is employed by the business or has provided any financial support to the business. Understandably, the SBA wants to avoid labeling a woman as "disadvantaged" if her own net worth and income fall beneath the thresholds, but her spouse is featured in *Forbes* magazine's annual list of the world's wealthiest people.

Joint Venturing on WOSB Procurements

You may form a joint venture with another company to submit a proposal for a procurement set-aside for WOSBs or EDWOSBs. Your joint venture partner need not be another WOSB (unlike in the HUBZone Program, where both partners must be HUBZone-certified). However, the joint venture must meet certain size requirements and adopt a joint venture agreement containing a number of mandatory provisions.

Size Requirements for WOSB Joint Ventures

As a general matter, you must add your company's size to your joint venture partner's size to determine whether your joint venture qualifies as small for a WOSB set-aside procurement. For some competitive procurements, your joint venture will qualify as small as long as each joint venture member, individually, is small under the NAICS code assigned to the contract. The special "individual size treatment" rule applies when:

- For a procurement with a revenue-based size standard, the dollar value of the procurement, including options, exceeds half the size standard corresponding to the NAICS code.
- For a procurement having an employee-based size standard, the dollar value of the procurement, including options, exceeds $10 million.

Unlike in the 8(a) and SDVO Programs, your WOSB company need not be less than half the size standard in order for the individual size treatment rule to apply. The rule is based solely on the size of the procurement.

Mandatory WOSB Joint Venture Provisions

In order to submit a bid as a joint venture on a WOSB or EDWOSB set-aside procurement, your company and its joint venture partner must execute a written joint venture agreement containing a number of mandatory terms. The terms are very similar to those required in the SDVO Program. For a full list of the required terms, see 13 C.F.R. § 127.506(c).

You do not need to obtain the SBA's prior approval of your joint venture agreement. But it won't take the government long to catch on if your joint venture agreement does not comply, because you must submit a copy of the joint venture agreement to the WOSB Repository and the procuring agency's contracting officer, who will examine it before awarding the contract.

Subcontracting on WOSB Procurements

We know your time is valuable, so we will cut to the chase: The subcontracting limits for WOSB set-aside procurements are the same as those for ordinary small business set-aside contracts. See Chapter 4 for a detailed discussion of the limits and an explanation of how to determine whether you comply.

Unlike in the SDVO Programs, you cannot meet your own performance requirements by subcontracting to other WOSBs. Fortunately for construction contractors, the special 50 percent rule under the HUBZone Program does not apply to the WOSB Program, either.

The Primary Rules: Where to Find Them

Here's where to find the primary rules discussed in this chapter:

- 13 C.F.R. § 127.300 and 13 C.F.R. § 127.301 (self-certification)
- 13 C.F.R. § 127.300, 13 C.F.R. § 127.302, and 13 C.F.R. § 127.304 (formal certification)
- 13 C.F.R. § 127.600 (eligibility protests)
- 13 C.F.R. § 127.200 (size)
- 13 C.F.R. § 127.200 and 13 C.F.R. § 127.201 (ownership)
- 13 C.F.R. § 127.200 and 13 C.F.R. § 127.202 (control)
- 13 C.F.R. § 127.200 and 13 C.F.R. § 127.203 (special EDWOSB requirements)
- 13 C.F.R. § 127.506 (joint ventures)
- 13 C.F.R. § 125.6 (subcontracting)

Compliance at a Glance: The Women-Owned Small Business Program

❑ To self-certify as a WOSB, register your company as a WOSB in the CCR and ORCA databases.

- ☐ To self-certify as a WOSB for a WOSB set-aside procurement, submit all required documents to the WOSB Repository.

- ☐ To self-certify as an EDWOSB, submit a completed SBA Form 413 for each woman claiming economic disadvantage, as well as an SBA Form 413 for each economically disadvantaged woman's spouse (if any).

- ☐ To obtain a formal WOSB certification, contact an SBA-approved certification provider.

- ☐ Ensure that your company is small under the NAICS code assigned to a particular WOSB set-aside procurement.

- ☐ Ensure that your company is at least 51 percent unconditionally and directly owned by one or more women who are United States citizens.

- ☐ Review your bylaws, operating agreement, shareholders' agreements, and other governing documents and amend them to eliminate right of first refusal provisions or similar provisions restricting the women owners' ability to sell their interest in the company to anyone at any time.

- ☐ Ensure that women control both the long-term decision making and day-to-day management and administration of your company's business operations.

- ☐ Review your bylaws, operating agreement, shareholders' agreements, and other governing documents and amend them to eliminate unanimity provisions or any other provisions preventing women from exercising absolute control over the company.

- ☐ Ensure that a woman holds your company's highest officer position (usually president or CEO).

- ☐ Ensure that the woman who holds the company's highest officer position has managerial experience of the extent and complexity needed to effectively run the business.

- ☐ Ensure that the woman who holds the company's highest officer position manages the company on a full time basis and works for the company full-time during the normal working hours of firms in the same or similar lines of work.

❑ To qualify as an EDWOSB, ensure that your net worth is less than $750,000, excluding ownership interest in the EDWOSB, equity interest in your primary personal residence, certain "pass-through" income, and qualified retirement account funds.

❑ To qualify as an EDWOSB, ensure that the fair market value of your assets, including your home equity and interest in the business, but excluding qualified retirement assets, is less than $6 million.

❑ To qualify as an EDWOSB, ensure that your adjusted gross income, averaged over the preceding three years, falls beneath $350,000.

❑ To form a joint venture for a WOSB set-aside procurement, enter into a joint venture agreement containing the mandatory provisions in 13 C.F.R. § 127.506(c).

❑ Do not subcontract WOSB set-aside contract work in excess of the subcontracting limitations, which are the same as for small business set-aside contracts.

CHAPTER 15

SPECIAL RULES FOR TRIBES, ANCS, AND NHOS

IF YOU READ the *Washington Post*, you may be familiar with recent debate surrounding one of the special contracting preferences for Alaska Native Corporations, or ANCs. In 2010, the *Post* published a four-part series investigating the special preferences afforded ANCs in the 8(a) Program—preferences which some members of Congress have proposed curtailing.[1] The *Post* series turned a very public spotlight on the participation of Indian tribes, ANCs, and Native Hawaiian Organizations (NHOs) in the nation's federal small business contracting programs, but the debate over the unique contracting rules governing these organizations has been percolating for some time both on Capitol Hill and across the country.

In this chapter, we will discuss the special rules governing tribes, ANCs, and NHOs in four areas: affiliation, the 8(a) Program, the HUBZone Program, and subcontracting. We understand that some of the special rules—particularly the 8(a) rules—are controversial. Keep in mind that this book is a compliance guide. We describe the rules, but do not take sides. Regardless of your position, it pays to understand exactly what the rules are and how they work.

If your small business is not owned by a tribe, ANC, or NHO, finishing that detective novel you bought at the airport may seem a little more enticing than boning up on contracting rules that don't directly apply to your company. But don't skip this chapter. Understanding what your competitors can and cannot do may help your company come out on top. For instance, you may have heard that one tribally owned company cannot be affiliated with another company owned by the same tribe, and decide that it is no use filing a size protest. However, as we will see, tribally owned firms do enjoy an exception from affiliation, but it is not absolute—there may still be reason to file a size protest.

Affiliation

We titled Chapter 2 "The Affiliation Problem" because affiliation is such an important hurdle for many small government contractors. But for companies owned and controlled by Indian tribes, ANCs, and NHOs, affiliation is less of a problem, because two exceptions exist: one absolute, the other narrower.

The first exception is that a company owned and controlled by a tribe, ANC, or NHO is not considered an affiliate of its majority owner for size purposes.

> Bering Strait Holdings, Inc., an ANC, has three-year average annual receipts of $50 million. Bering Strait Holdings owns 100 percent of BS Conventioneers, LLC, a convention and trade show organizing company, which has three-year average annual receipts of $3 million. BS Conventioneers submits an offer on a small business set-aside contract designated with NAICS code 561920, which carries a $7 million size standard.
>
> **Result:** Because of the special exception from affiliation, BS Conventioneers is not affiliated with Bering Strait Holdings. Unless BS Conventioneers has other affiliates with combined annual average receipts of more than $4 million, it qualifies as a small business for purposes of the procurement.

A company owned and controlled by a tribe, ANC, or NHO is never affiliated with that organization, even if the parent is much larger than the size standard, as Bering Strait Holdings was in our example. Of course, this doesn't mean that the company itself is free to exceed the size standards. If BS Conventioneers had three-year average annual receipts over $7 million in its own right, it could not have validly submitted an offer.

The second exception from affiliation is a little narrower, and applies to sister companies owned by the same organization. Under that rule, one company is not affiliated with another company owned by the same tribe, ANC, or NHO based on common ownership or common management, nor will affiliation be found on the basis of common administrative services, such as bookkeeping and payroll, as long as the company makes adequate payment for those services. However, affiliation can be found for other reasons.

> Bering Strait Holdings forms a second small company, BS Labs, LLC, which provides medical laboratory testing services. Bering Strait Holdings owns 100 percent of BS Labs. The same three individuals sit on the boards of directors of BS Labs and BS Conventioneers. There are no other ties between the two companies, which operate in different lines of work.
>
> **Result:** Due to the special exception from affiliation, BS Labs and BS Conventioneers cannot be found affiliated on the basis of common ownership or management. Because there are no other ties between the companies, they are not affiliated.

The fact that there are no other ties between BS Labs and BS Conventioneers is important, because the exemption from affiliation does not extend beyond ownership and control.

BS Labs proves successful and quickly outgrows the size standard in its primary industry. In an effort to continue winning small business set-aside contracts, Bering Strait Holdings forms a new company, Bering Medical, in the same line of work as BS Labs. Bering Medical submits an offer on a set-aside procurement and proposes BS Labs as its subcontractor. Because Bering Medical has no experience of its own, the proposal states that BS Labs will provide the contract's management team and will perform 75 percent of the work.

Result: The exception from affiliation for ANC "sister" companies does not extend to violations of the ostensible subcontractor rule (for a complete discussion of the rule, see Chapter 3. Because BS Labs will perform such a large percent of the contract and will provide the management team, the SBA will almost certainly find the companies affiliated for purposes of this procurement.

As seen in these examples, when it comes to tribal, ANC, and sister companies, the exception from affiliation is powerful, but not absolute. You still must avoid ostensible subcontractor affiliation and other indicia of affiliation covered in Chapter 2, such as economic dependence, that do not fall within the exception.

The 8(a) Program

Tribes, ANCs, and NHOs may own 8(a) companies. If you read Chapter 11, where we discussed the 8(a) Program in detail, you know that's an unusual exception in itself, because ordinarily 8(a) companies must be owned by socially and economically disadvantaged individuals—flesh-and-blood human beings—not companies or other entities. Although most of the 8(a) Program's regulations apply to companies owned by tribes, ANCs, and NHOs, there are a number of differences when it comes to program eligibility. Below, we discuss some of the most important.

Tribal Economic Disadvantage

An Indian tribe is automatically considered socially disadvantaged, but before it can own an 8(a) company, it must also establish that it is economically disadvantaged. In evaluating whether this is the case, the SBA will examine the unemployment rate of tribal members, the per capita income of tribal members, the poverty rate among members, and the tribe's total assets, as well as any other evidence the tribe may present to demonstrate its disadvantaged status.

The good news is that the economic disadvantage requirement must only be satisfied once. After a tribe establishes that it is economically disadvantaged, it need not do so in connection with future 8(a) applications for other companies owned by the tribe.

A similar economic disadvantage requirement applies to NHOs, but not to ANCs, which are automatically considered economically disadvantaged.

8(a) Program Eligibility

After economic disadvantage is established, a company owned by a tribe or ANC is eligible to participate in the 8(a) Program provided it meets certain organizational, size, ownership, and management requirements, which are not the same as those for "regular" 8(a) companies. (The rules for NHOs are slightly different. We will discuss them at the end of this section.)

Organizational Requirements. An 8(a) company owned by a tribe or ANC must be a legal entity organized for profit (tribes and ANCs may also form non-profit entities, but these entities cannot gain admission to the 8(a) Program).

In addition, a tribally owned company must include in its articles of incorporation or articles of organization a clause expressly waiving sovereign immunity or a "sue and be sued" clause designating the U.S. federal courts as courts of competent jurisdiction for all matters related to the SBA's programs. It is not enough to include this language in corporate bylaws or a limited liability company's operating agreement; it must be contained in the actual articles filed with the organizing governmental authority. Companies owned by ANCs need not include these provisions in their governing documents.

Size Requirements. Like all other 8(a) companies, a business owned by a tribe or ANC must be small under the size standard corresponding to its primary industry classification—typically, the NAICS code in which it did the most business in the prior fiscal year. However, in determining size for 8(a) Program eligibility purposes, the SBA will not count the sizes of affiliated parent or sister companies, except in unusual circumstances.

After your tribally owned or ANC-owned company gains admission to the 8(a) Program and begins bidding on contracts, it must be small both within its primary NAICS code and the NAICS code assigned to each 8(a) set-aside solicitation. The affiliation exceptions we described above apply to your company's size for 8(a) set-aside procurements.

Ownership Requirements. To qualify for the 8(a) Program, the company must be at least 51 percent unconditionally owned by the tribe or ANC. Outside individuals or entities may own a minority interest in the company (subject to the "overlapping ownership" restrictions we discussed in Chapter 11), but cannot hold options to obtain a majority interest in the company.

The Snake River Tribe owns 51 percent of Snakeskin, Inc., an engineering company. Big Time Construction, Inc., which is not a tribally owned company, owns the remaining 49 percent. In exchange for additional capital contributions, the tribe grants Big Time Construction an option to purchase an additional 10 percent of the company for a nominal sum.

Result: Because Big Time Construction can purchase a controlling interest in the company at any time, Snakeskin is not at least 51 percent "unconditionally" owned by the Snake River Tribe. The company does not qualify for the 8(a) Program.

Tribal "Overlapping Ownership" Restrictions. Tribes and ANCs are not subject to the ordinary "overlapping ownership" restrictions discussed in Chapter 11. In fact, unlike most 8(a) owners, a tribe or ANC may own more than one 8(a) company at a time. They may not, however, own more than 51 percent of a second 8(a) firm that, at any time within the previous two years, has been operating in the 8(a) Program under the same primary NAICS code as another 8(a) firm owned by the same tribe or ANC.

To address Snakeskin, Inc.'s eligibility problem, the Snake River Tribe purchases Big Time Construction's interest in the company and becomes Snakeskin's 100 percent owner. The tribe then submits an 8(a) application to the SBA on Snakeskin's behalf. Snakeskin's primary NAICS code is 541330 (Engineering Services). The Snake River Tribe also owns River Engineers, LLC, a current 8(a) participant operating primarily in the same NAICS code.

Result: Snakeskin is not eligible for the 8(a) Program because the Snake River Tribe currently owns another 8(a) company operating in the same line of work.

The restrictions only apply if the companies share a primary NAICS code. If Snakeskin worked primarily in another NAICS code, but performed some work under NAICS code 541330, the overlapping ownership rule would not have prevented it from gaining admission to the 8(a) Program.

Management Requirements. A special statute called the Alaska Native Claims Settlement Act, or ANCSA, provides that if a company is majority owned by an ANC, it is automatically deemed controlled by the Alaska natives. As long as the ownership requirement is met, it need not take additional steps to demonstrate that an 8(a) company it owns is controlled by Alaska Natives.

ANCSA does not apply to tribes. In order for a tribally owned company to be eligible for the 8(a) Program, the tribe must control the company's management and daily business operations. This can be accomplished in three ways.

First, and simplest, the tribe can directly control the company through one or more tribal members who have sufficient experience and knowledge to effectively run the company. Second, the tribe can manage the company through a board of directors or similar committee that is itself controlled by tribal members.

River Engineers, LLC, is managed by a board of directors comprised of three individuals. Two of the individuals are members of the Snake River Tribe, but the third is not. The company's operating agreement states that two votes are necessary for the board of directors to take any action.

Result: River Engineers' management system complies with the 8(a) Program's rules because the two tribal members, with their votes, can control the board of directors.

If your tribally owned company intends to have tribal members control the company through a board of directors or a similar committee, carefully review your bylaws or operating agreement to ensure that non-tribal members do not have the power to unilaterally make decisions or to veto the decisions made by tribal members (typically, through unanimity or supermajority provisions).

As a third option, a tribally owned company may be managed on a day-to-day basis by one or more non-tribal members, but only if three criteria are met:

1. The tribe has the ability to hire and fire the managers.
2. The tribe retains for itself the "big picture" powers typically reserved for boards of directors, including strategic planning, budget approval, and the compensation of officers.
3. The tribe adopts a written business development plan explaining how the non-tribal managers will train tribal members so that the company (or similar companies owned by the tribe in the future) can be managed by tribal members.

If your tribe plans to hire non-native managers for its 8(a) company, be sure to carefully review the company's governing documents to ensure that the tribe retains control over "big picture" matters and develop a comprehensive business development plan explaining how the arrangement will help tribal members learn the management skills necessary to manage the company in the future.

The "Two Years in Business" Requirement

As we learned in Chapter 11, a company usually must be in business for at least two years before it can gain admission to the 8(a) Program. Not so for companies owned by tribes and ANCs. Even if a tribally owned or ANC-owned company is brand-new, it can be admitted to the 8(a) Program as long as the tribe or ANC pledges, in writing, to financially support the new company's operations, and has the resources to do so.

What about NHOs?

Like companies owned by tribes and ANCs, a business owned by an NHO must be small under the size standard corresponding to its primary industry classification. It must also be small under the size standard corresponding to any 8(a) set-aside procurement the company bids upon. Similar ownership, overlapping ownership, and two-years-in-business rules also apply. However, there are a few important differences between how businesses owned by tribes and ANCs qualify for the 8(a) Program and the rules applicable to companies owned by NHOs.

Perhaps most important, an NHO must establish that it is economically disadvantaged, but the SBA does not evaluate economic disadvantage in the same manner as for tribes. Instead, the NHO must demonstrate that a majority of the NHO's members qualify as economically disadvantaged under the net worth and income rules applicable to ordinary 8(a) companies. See Chapter 11 for a full discussion of those rules.

NHOs must also demonstrate that Native Hawaiians will benefit from the company's admission to the 8(a) Program. In your 8(a) application, describe the activities, if any, the NHO has previously done to benefit Native Hawaiians. You must also include statements in the NHO's bylaws or operating agreements identifying the benefits that Native Hawaiians will receive, as well as a detailed plan demonstrating how the NHO's revenues will principally benefit Native Hawaiians.

As is the case for companies owned by tribes, a company owned by an NHO must also be controlled by the NHO in order for it to be eligible for the 8(a) Program. However, NHOs have fewer options than tribes when it comes to demonstrating control. There are no provisions for direct management by Native Hawaiians or management by non-natives. Instead, the NHO must control the company's board of directors.

So, Where's the Controversy?

If you haven't read the *Post* or followed the debate over the role of tribes, ANCs, and NHOs in the 8(a) Program, you might be wondering—where's the controversy? Sure, the fact that tribes and ANCs can own multiple 8(a) companies could seem unfair, but what's wrong about the rest of the rules discussed above?

The controversy stems primarily from a rule we did not discuss, because it's not a compliance rule: the so-called "sole source exception." Unlike typical 8(a) companies, which can only receive sole source (or "no competition") awards up to a few million dollars, 8(a) firms owned by tribes and ANCs can receive sole source awards at any dollar amount. NHOs, too, can receive unlimited sole source awards, but only for procurements issued by the Department of Defense.

The ability of companies owned by tribes, ANCs, and NHOs to receive large contracts without competition has rubbed some competitors the wrong way, and it remains a matter of intense debate. At least as of this writing, though, the ongoing debate had not led to any curtailment of the sole source authority or other significant changes in policy.

The HUBZone Program

Although the role of tribes and ANCs in the 8(a) Program has drawn the most attention, tribes and ANCs (but not NHOs) may also own companies participating in the HUBZone Program. Most of the same rules discussed in Chapter 13 apply to HUBZone companies owned by tribes and ANCs, but there are two key differences in terms of ownership and the principal office/35 percent residency requirements.

Tribal Ownership Requirements

Generally, as we learned in Chapter 13, a company must be at least 51 percent unconditionally owned by U.S. citizens to participate in the HUBZone Program. Tribes and ANCs have a little more leeway when it comes to meeting the ownership requirements. A tribally owned company (but not an ANC-owned company) satisfies the HUBZone ownership requirements if one of four criteria is met:

1. The tribe directly owns 100 percent of the small business.

2. The tribe directly owns 100 percent of another company, which in turn owns 100 percent of the small business.

3. The tribe owns part of the small business and the remainder is owned by U.S. citizens.

4. The tribe directly owns 100 percent of another company, which in turn owns part of the small business and the remainder is owned by U.S. citizens.

The Snake River Tribe owns 75 percent of Coastal Yardworks, Inc., a landscaping company. The remainder is owned by Melody, a U.S. citizen. Coastal Yardworks, in turn, owns 100 percent of Yardworks Junior, LLC, a small landscaping company. The Snake River Tribe would like to obtain a HUBZone certification for Yardworks Junior.

Result: Yardworks Junior does not qualify for the HUBZone program because its owner, Coastal Yardworks, is not wholly owned by the tribe. However, if Coastal Yardworks meets the other HUBZone eligibility criteria, it may be able to gain admission to the program, because it need not be 100 percent owned by the tribe to qualify.

As the above example shows, a tribe need not own 100 percent of a small business in order for the small business to qualify for the HUBZone Program. But if a small business wants to qualify on the strength of its parent company's tribal ownership, the parent company must be wholly owned by the tribe in order for its subsidiary to qualify for the program.

ANC Ownership Requirements

A company qualifies for the HUBZone Program if it is an ANC itself, or if it is a subsidiary, joint venture, or partnership majority owned by an ANC.

Bering Strait Holdings, an ANC, owns 51 percent of BS Talk, Inc., a satellite communications company. Voices Carry, Inc., a large telecommunications company, owns the remaining 49 percent.

Result: BS Talk is eligible for the HUBZone Program because it is a subsidiary of an ANC. However, the company needs to be careful to ensure that it does not become affiliated with Voices Carry, its minority owner, or it could miss out on the HUBZone Program due to size problems.

Principal Office/35 Percent Ownership Requirements

If you read Chapter 13, you know that the principal office and 35 percent employee residency requirements can be the most difficult components of HUBZone eligibility to acquire and maintain. A company owned by an Indian tribe—though not one owned by an ANC—has a unique option to satisfy these requirements: The company can simply certify, as part of its initial HUBZone application, that when it performs a HUBZone contract, at least 35 percent of its employees performing work on the contract will reside within an Indian reservation governed by the tribal owner or in any HUBZone adjoining an Indian reservation governed by the tribal owner.

Snakeskin, Inc.'s principal office is located in Seattle, Washington, and is not in a HUBZone. Only 20 percent of Snakeskin's employees live in HUBZones. Snakeskin applies to the HUBZone Program, certifying that if it wins a HUBZone contract, at least 35 percent of the employees working on the contract will be residents of the Snake River Indian Reservation or adjoining HUBZones.

Result: Snakeskin is eligible for the HUBZone Program even though it does not meet either of the ordinary principal office and 35 percent residency requirements because the Snake River Tribe has elected to qualify the firm using the special 35 percent "performance of work" rule.

The special rule Snakeskin used to qualify replaces *both* the principal office and 35 percent residency requirements, meaning you need not concern yourself with either if you elect to qualify for the HUBZone Program in this way. But before you rush to use this rule to join the HUBZone Program, think it through: Does your company perform most of its work locally or will it bid on HUBZone requirements in other areas?

The special rule is merely a second option for tribal companies, not a requirement. Your company can also elect to qualify under the "ordinary" rules we discussed in Chapter 13. If your company qualifies for the HUBZone Program under the special rule, you may be stuck performing contracts very close to home—or paying the expenses to temporarily relocate enough of your employees to ensure that you meet the 35 percent performance of work requirement on HUBZone contracts in other areas. If your business operates nationally, or even within a large regional area, you may wish to qualify under the ordinary principal office and 35 percent residency requirements.

Subcontracting

Remember the subcontracting plans we briefly discussed in Chapter 4? We didn't delve too deeply, because small businesses usually are not required to submit subcontracting plans to the government. But there is an important rule to know about if your company wants to serve as a subcontractor to a large company: Prime contractors may count subcontract awards to companies owned by tribes and ANCs toward their small business and small disadvantaged business subcontracting goals, even if the subcontractors are not actually small businesses.

Big Time Construction, Inc., a large construction contractor, wins an unrestricted procurement. Big Time's subcontracting plan calls for 25 percent of its subcontract awards to be made to small businesses and 10 percent to small disadvantaged businesses. Big Time would like to subcontract certain design work to Tribal Concepts, LLC, a tribally owned architecture firm. However, Tribal Concepts exceeds the size standard under NAICS code 541310 (Architecture Services).

Result: Big Time can take credit toward its small business and small disadvantaged business goals for a subcontract award to Tribal Concepts, even though Tribal Concepts is not a small business.

If your small business is in Tribal Concepts' position, be sure to let prospective prime contractors know that they can take small business and small disadvantaged business credit for awarding you subcontracts. You would be surprised at how often large prime contractors with experienced legal departments and contracting staffs simply don't realize this and overlook tribally owned and ANC-owned companies because they believe they are too large to qualify for their subcontracting goals.

The Primary Rules: Where to Find Them

Here's where to find the primary rules discussed in this chapter:

- 13 C.F.R. § 121.103 (affiliation)
- 13 C.F.R. § 124.109 (tribal and ANC 8(a) rules)
- 13 C.F.R. § 124.110 (NHO 8(a) rules)
- 13 C.F.R. § 126.200 (tribal and ANC HUBZone rules)
- FAR 19.703 (subcontracting credit)

Compliance at a Glance: Special Rules for Tribes, ANCs, and NHOs

❑ To prevent affiliation, avoid significant ties between "sister companies" owned by the same tribe, ANC, or NHO except common management, ownership, and administrative services.

❑ To obtain 8(a) certification for a tribally owned company, demonstrate to the SBA that the tribe itself is economically disadvantaged. Consider meeting with the SBA before submitting an 8(a) application to understand how the SBA will evaluate economic disadvantage in your case.

❑ Ensure any prospective 8(a) company owned by a tribe or ANC is a for-profit entity.

❑ For any prospective 8(a) company owned by a tribe, include, in the articles of incorporation or articles of organization, a clause expressly waiving sovereign immunity or a "sue and be sued" clause designating the U.S. federal courts as courts of competent jurisdiction for all matters related to the SBA's programs.

❑ Ensure that any prospective 8(a) company owned by a tribe, ANC, or NHO is small under its primary NAICS code and the NAICS code for any 8(a) set-aside contract it bids upon.

❑ Ensure that the tribe, ANC, or NHO unconditionally owns at least 51 percent of the company.

❑ For tribally owned companies, ensure that the tribe controls the company (1) directly through tribal members, (2) through a board of directors or similar committee that is itself controlled by tribal members, or (3) through non-tribal members, but only if the tribe can hire and fire those managers, retains "big picture" control, and adopts a written business development plan explaining how the non-native managers will train tribal members so that the company (or similar companies owned by the tribe in the future) can be managed by tribal members

❏ For a NHO to qualify as economically disadvantaged, ensure that a majority of the members of the NHO qualify as economically disadvantaged under the 8(a) Program's net worth and income rules (see Chapter 11).

❏ Include in the bylaws or operating agreement of the NHO a statement of the benefits that Native Hawaiians receive from the NHO and a detailed plan showing how revenues will principally benefit Native Hawaiians.

❏ Ensure that the NHO controls the board of directors of any 8(a) company or 8(a) applicant owned by the NHO.

❏ For a tribally owned company to participate in the HUBZone Program, ensure that one of four ownership structures exists: (1) the tribe directly owns 100 percent of the small business; (2) the tribe directly owns 100 percent of another company, which in turn owns 100 percent of the small business; (3) the tribe owns part of the small business and the remainder is owned by U.S. citizens; or (4) the tribe directly owns 100 percent of another company, which in turn owns part of the small business and the remainder is owned by U.S. citizens.

❏ For a company owned by an ANC to participate in the HUBZone Program, ensure that it is majority owned by the ANC.

❏ For a tribally owned company to gain admission to the HUBZone Program, consider whether to abide by the "ordinary" principal office and 35 percent employee residency requirements (see Chapter 13) or certify that at least 35 percent of employees performing a HUBZone contract will reside within an Indian reservation governed by the tribal owner or in any HUBZone adjoining an Indian reservation governed by the tribal owner.

❏ Remind prime contractors that they may take small business and small disadvantaged business credit for subcontract awards to a company owned by a tribe or ANC, even if the company exceeds the applicable size standard.

NOTES

Chapter 1

1. As this book was being written, the SBA was upwardly revising the size standards applicable to many NAICS codes. As you read this book, keep in mind that the size standards referenced in the examples may have increased. Up-to-date size standard information is available on the SBA's website, http://www.sba.gov/category/navigation-structure/contracting/contracting-officials/eligibility-size-standards.

2. *Size Appeal of J.M. Waller Assocs., Inc.,* SBA No. SIZ-5108 (2010).

3. 13 C.F.R. § 121.106(a).

Chapter 2

1. In October 2010, the SBA suspended GTSI Corporation, a top-100 federal contractor in terms of revenues, from all government contracting. The suspension notice alleged that GTSI, as a subcontractor, had, in essence, violated the ostensible subcontractor rule in various ways. The SBA eventually allowed GTSI to resume contracting with the government, but only after GTSI agreed to tough settlement terms, including the resignations of several top employees, a ban on participation in small business set-aside contracts, and paying for an on-site SBA compliance monitor.

2. For ease of reference, this chapter uses the term *share* to refer both to shares in a corporation and similar forms of ownership interests in other organizations (such as membership interests in a limited liability company).

3. See *Size Appeal of The H.L. Turner Group, Inc.,* SBA No. SIZ-4896 (2008).

4. See *Size Appeal of Simsum, Inc.,* SBA No. 3159 (1989).

Chapter 3

1. See *Morris-Griffin Corp. v. C&L Serv. Corp.*, 731 F.Supp.2d 488 (E.D.Va. 2010).

2. See *Size Appeal of Alutiiq Educ. & Training, LLC*, SBA No. SIZ-5192 (2011).

3. See, e.g., *Size Appeals of CWU, Inc. & U.S. Dept' of Homeland Security*, SBA No. SIZ-5118 (2010).

4. *Size Appeal of Four Winds Servs., Inc.*, SBA No. SIZ-5260 (2011).

Chapter 4

1. In some cases, a so-called "non-manufacturer" may qualify as a small business on a supply contract set-aside for small businesses, even though the company did not manufacture the products itself. For more information on the non-manufacturer rule, visit the SBA's website at *http://www.sba.gov/content/non-manufacturer-waivers*.

2. See *United States ex rel. D.L.I. Inc. v. Allegheny Jefferson Millwork, LLC*, 540 F.Supp. 165 (D.D.C. 2008).

3. FAR 52.203–11(c).

Chapter 8

1. See *Morse Diesel Int'l, Inc. v. United States*, 66 Fed. Cl. 788 (2005).

Chapter 11

1. For Asian Americans, the presumption applies to individuals with origins from the following countries and territories: Burma, Thailand, Malaysia, Indonesia, Singapore, Brunei, Japan, China, Taiwan, Laos, Cambodia, Vietnam, Korea, the Philippines, Palau, Marshall Islands, Micronesia, Northern Mariana Islands, Guam, Samoa, Macao, Fiji, Tonga, Kiribati, Tuvalu, Nauru, India, Pakistan, Bangladesh, Sri Lanka, Bhutan, the Maldives Islands, and Nepal.

2. *Tony Vacca Constr., Inc.*, SBA No. BDP-321 (2009).

3. *Posche Promotions*, SBA No. SDBA-162 (2004).

Chapter 12

1. *Veterans Constr. Servs.*, SBA No. VET-167 (2009).

2. See *Construction Eng'g Servs., LLC*, SBA No. VET-213 (2011). Full disclosure: The author represented Construction Engineering Services, LLC, the joint venture seeking to overturn OHA's prior rule.

Chapter 13

1. See "Alabama Defense Contractor and Its President to Pay $200,000 to Resolve False Claims Act Allegations," available at *http://www.justice.gov/opa/pr/2011/September/11-civ-1230.html.*

Chapter 15

1. See "Two Worlds: A *Washington Post* Investigation," available at *http://www.washingtonpost.com/wp-srv/special/nation/alaska-native/.*

INDEX